Under the Floorboards

Under the Floorboards

John Kiss

Note To The Reader

Dear Reader,

I grew up with the Holocaust. It was a constant presence in my home, unspoken, like a shadow.

The Second World War left its mark on the body of my grandfather. Three scars of the bullets penetrating his body when he fled the Nazis.

As a child, I remember he showed me the scars; his arm, his thigh, and his foot. I remember touching the scars. The skin felt hard around the stitches yet soft and wrinkly past them.

My grandmother, at the age of 18, fled from the Nazis deep into Russia, carrying her mother along. Soon her mother died of hunger, and my grandmother had to bury her with her own bare hands in the frozen ground.

Her elderly grandfather—who stayed behind in Kishinev—was hung by the Nazis. All my family who remained were killed, including a cousin, his wife and a little girl. After the war, when a few Jews returned, the locals pointed at mounds that covered the corpses. The little girl's dress and red shoes were found in the remains.

My grandmother was haunted by what she saw during the Holocaust. In her later years, she refused to leave her apartment in Haifa, afraid of the dangers lurking outside. I remember as a child trying to convince her to go to the playground with me, begging her. During the last fifteen years of her life, she never once stepped outside.

In 1974, my parents moved from Kishinev to Israel, where I was born. The Holocaust was forever present- yet unspoken of. It was a subject not to be brought up, a sadness as deep as the sea, reflecting in my grandparents' eyes. My four grandparents had buried stories of a cousin killed by the Nazis a few days before liberation. Of an aunt who took the train fleeing from the Nazis only to be killed as the train was bombed leaving Kishinev. Stories of fleeing refugees, of robberies by locals, of my grandfather seeing two men shot next to him, before his eyes.

Had my grandparents not escaped Kishinev, I would have never been born to tell their stories. Yet they did not want to talk about them. It was easier for them to speak of other nations' plights than our own.

After all of my grandparents passed away, my father began wanting to share stories with us. Over a decade ago, he introduced me to a story not of our own family, but of the late Dr. Felix Zandman. It was easier for my father to speak about family trauma through *another* family's story.

That story touched me in ways I could not foresee. I contacted the Zandman family. I interviewed the wife of the late Dr. Zandman, Ruta, and was encouraged by her to tell her husband's survival story.

The book you are holding is my gift to Ruta for continuing her husband's legacy. It is a gift to my father, for trying to speak, amidst long heavy pauses, about the stories he heard from his parents. It is a gift to my mother, who read the drafts of this novel and cried along with me as I wrote it.

Although I shed many tears while writing, *Under The Floorboards* is a novel about love. It is a story of Christians who saved their Jewish neighbors at the risk of their own lives. I am proud to tell this story after a decade of research, and I hope it will inspire you as much as it inspired me.

John Kiss, August 2024

Dedicated to the Zandman and Puchalsky families

Felix Zandman, age 17, at the end of WWII, 1945

Based on a true story

Prologue

Danzig, 1945

The war was over. The young man was going to fulfill his lifelong dream of going to Paris. The war had sculpted him into a man, chiseling away the innocence of childhood. At seventeen, his gaze was haunted, the eyes of one who had seen too much horror.

He approached the ticket booth at the almost empty train station. "One ticket, please," he said, exchanging coins for a single passage from Danzig all the way to Paris, the City of Light. His trembling voice was tinged with sadness, but also the hope of a thousand unspoken dreams.

As he waited upon the platform clutching his valise, he had to remind himself that he was safe. He no longer had to hide.

He stared at the horizon, willing the train to come. *Did he hear something?* Was it a rumble of a train approaching, or was it just his imagination?

He did not want to remain in Grodno, the city of his childhood, or anywhere in Poland. Now, after the war, Poland felt like a giant graveyard.

During the last few months, he went to the train station every day, waiting for his family to return. He had scrutinized every face he passed, searching for the many relatives he had lost.

Now, with soul-crushing finality, he faced the cruel truth: his family was gone, never to return.

All he had left was inside the valise he held tightly against his body: two tattered photographs—a family portrait and a photo of him with his uncle, a brown envelope containing his grandfather's yarmulke cap, and a piece of a shattered window. They were all items he had recovered from a visit to his grandparents' destroyed home in Grodno.

The valise also contained a small notebook, enough zloty bills to last for a few weeks in Paris, some clothes, and a newspaper clipping announcing the end of the war that he wanted to keep forever.

His thoughts were interrupted by a sound in the distance. He tilted his head and heard the thrum of approaching iron wheels growing louder. The train emerged, then slowed down, the wheels making a screeching noise against the tracks.

He took his valise and climbed on the train, determined to leave the past behind, to forget his desperate escape from the ghetto—to forget it all.

The train emitted a high-pitched whistle.

Two years earlier, the trains took his kin, his whole family, to one destination: Auschwitz.

He suddenly stood up. A powerful urge seized him to feel the winds of freedom, to be one with it. He rose from his seat as he felt the train wagon swaying beneath his feet. He unlatched the narrow window, cracking it open.

A rush of cold wind blew into the passenger car.

He slid his hand through the narrow window. The cold air whispered secrets against his skin, stirring his soul as it danced through his outstretched fingers. He closed his eyes and thanked his good fortune. He was alive. *He was alive!*

An hour later, he made it to the border, the edge of Poland, the country that he no longer called home.

The train slowed to a stop and the border police officers climbed on the train, their footsteps thumping loudly, in rhythm with the young man's anxious heartbeat.

Will he be able to continue his journey?

"Passport," the border police officer shouted at him.

The young man handed over his Polish passport.

"Where to?"

"France," the young man choked out. "Paris."

The young man expected he might be arrested. Instead, he saw the officer's eyes flicker with jealousy as he examined the passport.

After a long moment, the border officer handed the passport back and walked to another passenger car.

Relieved, the young man let out a sigh. The train began moving forward, carrying him into Czechoslovakia. Mountains shone in the darkness, a grand lake spreading below. The shimmering waters of the lake mirrored the moon above.

The young man was relieved when the train arrived in Switzerland four hours later. One last country before France. Border control officers again asked for his papers. He showed his passport, his breath steady this time, amazed at the ease of travel from place to place without needing to hide, without searching for a hidden pit to bury himself in.

As the train sped through Switzerland, the young man, face glued to the window, wondered what it would be like *there*. In Paris.

Paris—a distant dream soon to be within reach. The train journey had carried him farther than he had ever ventured. He had never traveled so far away from home.

Paris, with its iconic Eiffel Tower, beckoned to him like a lighthouse.

When the train crossed into France in the early morning, he showed the border officer not only his new Polish passport, but also his visa. He hoped he would be allowed to enter.

The officer returned the documents to the young man. "Bienvenu en France."

Welcome. To. France.

The young man recited those three words as if they were a prayer. In two hours, he would arrive in Paris.

The train sped up. He recited the words again: "Bienvenue en France." Though the language was foreign to his ears, he vowed to make it his own.

The young man sat by the window, his face pressed against the cool glass, eyes wide with wonder. He looked at the bright sky. Back home, the light was soft, almost timid—peeking shyly through the clouds, casting muted shadows on the worn cobblestone streets. It was a light that never fully revealed itself, always retreating behind a veil of mist.

But here, as the train sped further, everything seemed to change.

He was leaving behind a world of shadows, stepping into a realm where the light embraced him. An adventure, a new beginning.

He was almost in Paris. He pronounced the name as the French did. *Pari. Pari! Pari.* He savored the word on his tongue, rolling it like a fine wine. *Pari*—the city of dreams.

The sun rose, and his pilgrimage neared its end. Paris.

The rhythmic hum of the train wagon gradually diminished as it eased into the bustling station. The young man cast an eager glance out of the window. He saw many people on the platform excitedly waiting to greet their loved ones.

No one was waiting for him.

The train came to a halt, and the doors sighed open.

With his valise clutched tightly in his hand, he stepped out of the train onto the platform.

Excitement filled the air as families and friends awaited reunions with their loved ones. With each step, he was determined to leave the past behind, to forget his desperate escape from the ghetto and begging for shelter. He wanted to forget it all. To forget running through the forest two years earlier, gunshots whistling behind him.

Chapter 1: Darkness

Poland, 1943

Age 15

I

Running as fast as he could through the dark forest, the boy looked over his shoulder. His heart raced. His lungs burned. Had he escaped the soldiers?

The snow crunched beneath his feet. In the distance, he heard the sharp echoes of gunshots. They came from the city he had just left behind, far away—yet not far enough. He kept running. He had to.

Exhausted, he criss-crossed between the trees as he ascended the hill. He could barely breathe. Four long years of war and hunger had left his body weak.

More gunshots. He thought of his cousin. She, too, tried to escape the ghetto, but was shot right before his eyes, her body dropping to the ground with a thud, a halo of blood emerging around her.

She was only fourteen.

He was going to share her fate unless he could outrun the soldiers. Unless he could reach it. The cabin at the top of the hill was his only refuge—*if* he would be let inside.

At last, panting, his limbs burning with exhaustion, he saw the trail covered in snow. He hid behind a large tree and peered. He could see the cabin. The small wooden house had been a sanctuary in his childhood.

Would they let him in?

A light went on in the kitchen window.

Though he wanted to run to the cabin, he decided to wait. The maid would be inside, but so would her husband and five children. He knew the family. The maid was his grandparents' maid before the war.

Soon the maid's husband would leave for work and her three eldest daughters would go to school. Then he would knock.

He waited. The sky began to lighten. Never had the boy despised the ascending sun more, its glow threatening to reveal him to the soldiers. In times of war, darkness had been his ally. The SS were combing the woods with their attack dogs, looking for anyone who somehow escaped the ghetto.

More snow fell. He trembled in the biting cold, trying to stay out of sight, ready to run again if he was discovered.

Suddenly, he saw the cabin door swing open.

Standing in the woods, the boy saw the cabin door swing open.

The boy recognized the mustached man who emerged from the cabin. He was the maid's husband.

Where was the maid?

Behind the husband, the three daughters soon followed. The boy's eyes were instantly drawn to the maid's eldest daughter. They had played catch together in bygone summers, before the war.

The girls and their father headed down the trail toward the village. A chilling wind whispered through the branches.

The boy watched the family disappear into the horizon. He stared at the door across the trail.

He knew he had to take this chance. If he hesitated now, the regret would be unbearable. He had to live for his family.

Casting furtive glances in every direction, he fled the woods toward the cabin, his heart pounding with a silent terror.

He knocked on the door. He glanced over his shoulder. He knocked again. The window caught his eyes, the curtain shifting ever so slightly.

The boy heard tentative footsteps echoing inside the cabin. He wondered if the maid would dare to open the door for him. If he were in her position, he thought, he would not. He knew all too well the consequences for harboring Jews.

The sound of the latch lifting, followed by the creaking door, revealed the wide-eyed maid peering through the crack. "Oh, dear God!" she gasped and flung the door open the rest of the way.

Embracing the boy tightly, the maid ushered him into the small cabin. With practiced vigilance, she scanned the trail and the encroaching woods to ensure their surroundings were devoid of prying eyes. She cautiously closed the door behind her, the click of the lock resonating in the quiet cabin.

Warmth! The boy was relieved to be inside. The heat from the hearth prickled his frozen fingertips.

The maid took his icy hands in hers, her expression full of concern. "My goodness," she exclaimed, "you're freezing."

"Th-Thank you for l-letting me in," he stuttered.

"Oh, forget it!" the maid proclaimed, "This is *your* home."

It *had* been his home. His family had once possessed wealth. Now, it was all lost.

Placing a kettle on the stove, the maid insisted, "We must get you warm."

The cabin was quiet, save for the soft breathing of the children in their room. The boy wandered from the entrance and peered into once-familiar doorways. Furnishings old and new to him in redecorated rooms in a way that confused his heart and mind. It was like he was exploring a dream. The maid's toddler son and her baby girl slept peacefully, unaware of what was happening outside.

The boy shuddered at the thought of the peril that awaited the family if he was caught standing in their living room.

Approaching the window, he shut the curtains. "I promise, I'll only stay here today. Once night falls, I'll be on my way."

"Are you out of your mind?" the maid questioned. "You are

family!" She opened the pantry, took out a piece of bread and handed it to the boy.

He devoured the bread; he had not eaten in days. He then shook his head, a mix of gratitude and concern in his eyes. He wondered if she was aware of the danger she was putting her family in. He said, "If the soldiers find out that you are hiding me—they'll kill you—you and your whole family!"

She looked at him adamantly, a fierce determination in her eyes. "Whatever happens to you," she affirmed, "will happen to us." The whistle of the kettle pierced the air. She poured a cup of tea for the boy and one for herself and placed them on the table. "Now sit down."

As the maid poured tea for them both, the boy could not shake the feeling of dread that hung over them like a dark cloud. "Thank you," he said as he slumped in the chair. He wrapped his hands around the warm cup.

The maid sat down. "Now, tell me about your grandmother, how is she faring?"

The boy stared at the maid, his eyes filled first with disbelief, then with desperation. "They took her—them…everyone," he whispered, voice barely audible, "to the trains."

A quiet breath escaped her throat in shock. Not knowing what to say, she hung her head low and uttered, "May God protect them all."

The boy remained silent, his mind consumed by thoughts of the loved ones he had lost and the uncertain future that lay ahead.

"Your grandmother," the maid clapped her hands together, "what an angel. Many years ago, when I was pregnant with my second daughter, she was…" her voice trailed off. She looked over at the children's room and lowered her voice. "You see, my husband, he's a good man…"

The boy nodded, noticing how the maid struggled to find the right words.

She continued, "But sometimes, he drinks too much."

The boy did not know what to say.

"I was nearly due…and he…drank…" she faltered. "He threw

me out in the street. I didn't have anywhere to go. Then I thought of your grandmother. She was always so kind to me."

The boy's thoughts were consumed by the impending danger. By now the trains had already left with the last remaining people. The soldiers would likely search the outskirts of the city hunting for more Jews. Every forest would be searched, every house scoured.

The maid's voice trembled. "It was midnight, I knocked on your grandparents' door. And your grandmother… 'Come in,' she said, 'It is good you came here.' She hosted me until I gave birth. What a special woman. My husband was so apologetic afterwards, and I returned home. But I never forgot the kindness of your grandmother."

The boy sipped the hot tea, savoring the warmth spreading through him. He knew he needed to warm up before the maid reconsidered her decision and asked him to leave. Or worse, before the inevitable loud rapping of the soldiers.

The boy's thoughts scattered as fear gripped him. "Please," he whispered, "I am afraid you don't understand what you are doing…Do you want me to go away now?"

"Nonsense!" the maid said, her voice tinged with defiance. "I told you. You are here to stay."

The boy could not fathom the maid's naivety. He looked around the kitchen. What would happen if someone came? Where would he hide?

He turned away from the kitchen, his gaze drifting to the maid's small bedroom with its lone bed and wardrobe. Then, his eyes moved towards the children's room, with its four beds and a crib, where the toddler boy and the baby girl were sleeping peacefully.

He was so fixated on finding somewhere in the small cabin to hide from danger that he did not hear the main cabin door swinging open.

Chapter 2: Light

Paris, 1945

Age 17

I

At the Paris train station, no one was waiting for the young man. He tried pushing away the memories of the war. Yet the absence of his entire family pressed down on him, like a heavy cloak of loneliness that nothing could lift.

He forced a smile, determined not to let his isolation dim the brightness of his dreams. With his shoulders pulled back and head tilted up, he gripped the valise as he walked down the crowded platform, determined to carve out a place for himself in this new world.

Each step was a silent vow to honor those he had lost, by living bravely in the city he had dreamed of.

There was one thing he wanted to see, one structure that had held his attention during the years of darkness—the famous tower, a symbol of hope and resilience, a dream now within reach: the Eiffel Tower.

II

Outside the train station, the young man was greeted by a warm sensation of newfound liberation. The radiant morning sun cast a golden glow over the street.

Where was the Eiffel Tower? He was certain that the tower

could be seen from everywhere. He strained his neck as he looked all around.

He saw a couple on a bench, sharing a tender kiss, and he blushed, looking quickly away. *They were kissing! Out in the open!*

The unfamiliarity of this place dawned on him—it was a strange contrast to the modesty he had known at home.

He liked it already. He felt like a resurrected mian, coming out of the grave.

As the young man stepped onto the cobblestoned street, the city unfolded before him like a vibrant tapestry of life reclaiming its vigor after a long Nazi occupation.

Elegant buildings stood tall, adorned with wrought iron balconies and ornate facades. Cafés lined the boulevard and tables spilled onto the sidewalk, draped in checkered tablecloths. Frenchmen sipped espressos, indulging in animated conversations.

The young man salivated at the smell of croissants, a gleaming bakery storefront displaying an array of pastries behind glass windows.

He was amazed. *How could the people forget that a war just ended? A war that spanned six years!*

Nonetheless, people walked, talked, sat on benches and laughed; mothers with their children, sisters with their brothers, grandparents, and families. *He had no one left.*

No—he shook his head—*he must not think of that.*

He looked around. Where was that elusive tower? He was disappointed not to see it. The sight of the tower would be his confirmation, the tangible proof that he wasn't trapped in a dream, but truly free.

Finally, he mustered the courage to ask an old man for directions, but the old man did not understand him.

The young man exclaimed, "Eiffel! Eiffel!"

"Ah," the old man smiled, "Tour Eiffel!" and pointed in the opposite direction.

Running, the young man headed in the new direction,

memories of reading about the tower flooding him. He remembered how Mr. Eiffel had designed the tower so that the wind would be able to flow through it freely.

At the end of the boulevard, there was a bridge over a narrow river. Just as the young man began crossing it, he turned his head—there: he saw it in the distance, brilliant in the morning sun.

Chapter 3: Darkness

Poland, 1943

Age 15

The maid swung the door of the cabin wide open, completely exposing the boy to any prying eyes that might be waiting outside.

She hurried outside, grabbing the ladder. With firm hands, she shook and thumped the ladder, dislodging the clinging snow.

"Now-now, do not worry, dear!" she said, lugging the hefty ladder inside. She shut the door behind her and secured the latch, but she found no sign of the boy in the kitchen. *Where did he go?*

She peered into her small bedroom, but finding no trace of the boy, she turned her attention to the children's room. She started to inspect the room and eventually found the boy hiding under an empty bed. The maid knelt down. "It is alright. Come, come!" She pointed up to the kitchen ceiling. "The attic!"

"Attic?" the boy asked. He crawled from under the bed and cautiously followed walking out to the kitchen, noticing the small door in the ceiling. The maid propped up the ladder and climbed it, opening the narrow entrance.

She came down, and the boy hurried up the slippery ladder. What space the attic could afford was only enough for one person to lie in. *This would do, at least for the time being.*

He carefully came back down, still afraid to embrace hope. *How long would they let him be here? A day? Two? How long before the soldiers would find him, before their 'butcher' tracks him down?*

He looked at the maid. "But, your husband…?"

She motioned to the chair next to the kitchen table. "He will do as I tell him, and besides, he will be *glad* to see you! Now, back to your grandmother…"

The boy reluctantly sat down.

Once again, he tried to focus on the maid's story, but his mind was preoccupied. The boy looked up at the kitchen attic. *Wouldn't the soldiers search the attic right away?*

The maid sighed. "Well, my husband regretted drinking so much, and he convinced me to come back home, and I did but"—she raised her finger in the air—"I never forgot your grandmother's goodness. And then, a few years ago, your grandmother needed someone to take care of the summer cabins, and she asked me—Such a special lady—"

A sudden knock on the door startled them both. The boy had seen it coming. *He was discovered.*

The sound of approaching footsteps outside sent a shiver down his spine.

A voice from outside shouted, "Open up!"

Chapter 4: Light

Paris, 1945

Age 17

The young man stood frozen, gripping his valise, his eyes wide with disbelief as the Eiffel Tower glistened in the radiant spring sun.

His feet propelled him towards the tower, running through bustling streets, past vibrant markets, into narrow alleys, and across expansive gardens. With each flying step, the iconic tower grew in stature before him, rising in all its splendor.

As he neared the base of the tower, he could not help but feel dizzy. He craned his neck, attempting to absorb the sheer magnificence of the structure. The grand steel latticework of iron beams perfectly supporting one another awed him.

Yet, in the midst of his admiration, he felt a pang of loneliness. The vastness of the tower left him feeling small and insignificant.

He was alone. So utterly alone. A tidal wave of isolation threatened to drown him.

There he stood, finally face to face with the enthralling tower that had sustained his imagination during captivity. Yet he had no one to share this moment with.

The immense weight of guilt for having survived pressed upon him. He survived in place of his sister, who was never to return; he survived while his parents likely lay lifeless in some cold forest, without a grave, victims of an unspeakable end.

He knew a true brother would have stood by his sister; a dutiful son would have remained by his parents; a proud grandson would have protected his elderly grandparents. He should have been there with them, saving them, honoring them, sharing their fate— exactly as his father had stood by his *own* parents.

What right did the young man have to be there among the carefree visitors? Amidst life, he was an intruder. He belonged with the dead.

The feeling of loneliness that he had evaded while running from danger finally clutched his soul with its merciless long fingers.

He was alone in the entire world. Of his family tree, he was the only branch left.

Who was to mother him and kiss him on the forehead? Who was to father him and look at him with an approving nod? Who was there to taunt him, tickle him and fight with him—who would be his sister, to whom he never said: "I love you?"

He felt the air leaving his body. Who would fill this gulf, this ever-expanding void in him? Who would be his mentor like his wise grandfather with his witticisms and his old village lore? Who would replace his kind grandmother, her warm hand holding his as they crossed the Grodno street?

Who?

How he would have done things differently! He would not dare to tease his sister, nor upset his father, nor allow his mother to wash the dishes on her own…

Never again would he see them.

He sank to his knees in the midst of the lively crowd, and wept.

The Eiffel Tower stood tall, a silent witness to his insurmountable mountain of sorrow. Engulfed in longing for what would never return.

Suddenly hands grabbed him

Chapter 5: Darkness

Poland, 1943

Age 15

The maid approached the door, feigning a cheerful tone. "Who is it?"

An old woman's voice yelled, "Open up already! It's me, you stupid hag!"

The maid turned to whisper to the boy to go to the attic, but he had already hurried up the ladder, closing the attic door from the inside.

There was no room for sitting in the dark attic. He laid down, his hand gripping the door lest it swing open. The air hung heavy with dust, and a rotten scent enveloped the confined space.

The silence that followed the voice from outside was unsettling. Anxiety gripped him, tightening its hold with every passing second. He heard a thump in the kitchen below. Had the maid fallen? Did she need help? Why was it quiet?

The oppressive darkness of the attic pressed in from all sides and trapped him. He wasn't sure if he should have come to the cabin. *But where else could he have gone? The soldiers with their dogs were everywhere.*

Meanwhile, in the kitchen below, the maid had set the ladder aside and opened the door.

The old neighbor's eyes darted around the small cabin. "Are you alone?" she questioned, suspicion lining her gaze.

"Why, of course!" the maid said.

The old neighbor pushed past her. "Let me see!" She scanned the small cabin thoroughly with her sharp eyes, walking into the bedrooms.

The boy held his breath. He heard the old woman's voice below. He thought of the prizes offered by the army for turning his kin in. The old neighbor could earn rice, flour, and sugar. Those were high commodities now at the height of war. These things would not have made a person betray another a few years ago. But now the war had left everyone hungry, distressed, and wanting to terminate all of his people.

The old neighbor looked into both rooms and then returned to the kitchen. "But I heard voices."

"I was talking…to the children!" the maid said, pointing at the children's room, her voice too high-pitched.

The old neighbor peered again at the room where the toddler boy and the baby girl were sleeping. She gave the maid a long, piercing stare. "Don't do anything silly, dear."

"What do you mean?" The maid blushed as beads of perspiration formed on her temple.

"The soldiers sent all of *them* away." The old neighbor looked around as she spoke.

The boy heard the way the old neighbor said the word 'them.' It was clear who she was speaking about. He shut his eyes tightly. The old neighbor was looking for *him*.

"Really?" the maid asked.

"Yes! Yesterday, there was a large transport. They cleared out the segregated enclosure. The city is now purified of all those parasites. Yet," she continued, her eyes fixed on the maid, "some fled. The soldiers are looking for those cockroaches…"

The maid did not dare say a word. She looked down at her feet, partly trying to conceal the anxiety etched on her face, partly avoiding looking at the attic door.

The old neighbor sat down with a sigh near the small table. "Aren't you going to offer me some tea?"

"Of course," the maid said with a forced smile and turned to boil a fresh pot. She breathed heavily.

The attic pressed in around the boy, its walls seeming to close on him.

The old neighbor said, "The occupying army is very strong. They are advancing east… You are young and stupid. But don't do anything you might regret, you hear?"

"What do you mean?" the maid murmured, her voice wavering.

"I mean that you shouldn't do anything that will get you and your family into trouble." The old neighbor took one last glance around the kitchen. She pointed at the ladder. "What is that ladder doing inside?"

Chapter 6: Light

Paris, 1945

Age 17

I

The young man was weeping under the Eiffel tower when he suddenly felt hands grabbing him.

The young man, anticipating hostility, hurried to protect his face with his elbow, bracing for a potential beating. Yet, to his astonishment, two men helped him stand up, their expressions filled with genuine concern. They spoke in French to him.

"Qu'est-ce qui s'est passé?"

The young man did not understand them, but he saw their eyes were concerned, not hateful. Surprised, he mumbled something incoherent and dusted off his knees. One of the men placed his hand on the young man's shoulder, offering a firm look that seemed to convey, 'You will be okay.'

He knew that look. It was given to him countless times. Yet now he felt a strange peace — an inkling of hope.

Then, as swiftly as the two men appeared, they were gone.

All that time, from afar, a woman observed the scene unfold near one of the tower's great pillars. Without a word, she walked over to the young man and, not asking for permission, she reached out her hands and enveloped him in an embrace.

He stood there, frozen and shocked, feeling her arms around him.

The woman squeezed him tightly, her warmth a contrast to everything he had grown used to. She then stared at him, her fingers clutching his coat, her eyes assuring him without words.

She suddenly reached for her pocket and pulled out a small paper bag and handed it to him.

Then she, too, left.

The young man felt rattled, unhinged by what had just transpired. He unfolded the paper bag and saw that it was a chocolate ball—a truffle? He crammed the whole thing in his mouth in amazement. *Chocolate!*

He took his valise in hand, wondering who these people were. At home, in his war-torn world, if someone fell on the street, on his knees, people would walk away in fear, as if this state of despair was contagious.

But here, in the shadow of the Eiffel Tower, not just one person had reached out to help him, but three.

More tears came, but these were tears of gratitude. He bit his lip, swallowing the chocolate, determined not to cry again.

He began walking through the park nearby. He walked slowly, as if in a dream, entering the neighboring streets.

His back straightened, shoulders pulled back, chin raised. At home, his people—his kin—were never allowed to walk this way; *it attracted trouble.*

And yet here, in the heart of Paris, he *could.* He could. . . And he did. He held his head up high, each step a declaration of newfound freedom in a city that embraced him.

As he wandered through narrow cobblestone streets, the air became imbued with the irresistible aroma of freshly baked bread, aromatic cheeses, and fragrant flowers. Vendors proudly displayed their wares, from baskets of ripe, sun-kissed fruits and vegetables to neatly arranged displays of artisanal food, charcuterie, and fish. Hunger gnawed at him.

A symphony of voices spoke in rapid-fire French, punctuated by laughter and animated boisterous conversation.

As he admired the market, he was also searching for someone with whom he could exchange his money. Unfortunately, the language barrier proved challenging, leaving him in a sea of unintelligible responses.

Undeterred, the young man pulled out a zloty bill and exclaimed, "Change! Change!"

His persistence paid off when a kind, old lady understood his plea and gestured for him to follow. He navigated through the market until they reached its far end. The old lady exchanged a few words with a chubby, short man with a hawkish nose and dark eyes who stood with a weathered valise. Judging from his blackboard with signs and numbers signaling different currencies, he was a moneychanger.

The young man wanted to thank her, but she had already left.

Turning his attention to the moneychanger, the young man was taken aback by the man's appearance—a tubby figure in his forties.

The moneychanger spoke in French, so the young man could not grasp the meaning. Instead, the young man waved his bill and produced a few more from his valise, hoping that the universal language of currency would bridge the gap.

The moneychanger froze. He studied the bills and then looked at the young man, a bewildered, thoughtful expression crossing his face. "Zloty?" His gaze shifted from the currency to the young man — taking in his clothes facial features, and valise, as if trying to decipher a riddle.

Suddenly, the moneychanger's eyes glistened. He leaned in and whispered, "I presume you and I are from the same opera."

At the Parisian market, the moneychanger's eyes glistened with emotion. He leaned closer to the young man and whispered, "I presume you and I are from the same opera."

The young man did not understand.

The moneychanger did not lose hope. "I," he said, and gestured at himself, "and you," he pointed at the young man, "same opera!"

The young man shook his head, helpless, not understanding the moneychanger's words.

Finally, the moneychanger tried to remember what he knew of Yiddish. He exclaimed in Yiddish. "You, I," he joined his two fingers together, "brothers."

The young man was startled to hear the old Yiddish, his grandparents' tongue, being spoken so far away from home by a total stranger.

The moneychanger reached over and tried to hug him. "Brother, you-me-brother!"

The young man mumbled, pointing at the bills, "But, the change…"

"Forget the change!" the moneychanger exclaimed in French. He tried again, in Yiddish, which he barely spoke. "You must-hungry-be, no?"

The young man was hungry, but he said nothing.

"Of course you are!" the moneychanger said.

He began closing up his small shop. First, the moneychanger brought down the shutters and fetched a small lock and key from his pocket. Then he locked the shutters in place.

The moneychanger then put the money in his coat pockets. One pocket was reserved for each currency. Francs were in the left upper pocket. Pounds were in the lower left. American dollars went into the upper right one.

The moneychanger turned to his neighbor in the stalls, another man in his forties who sold pastries. "*À demain,*" he said, clapping the neighbor on his shoulder.

He turned to the young man.

He spoke in French. The young man did not understand. The moneychanger gestured to his mouth. He pressed his fingertips to one another and kissed them in a chef's kiss full of excitement.

The moneychanger led the confused young man out of the market onto a quiet side street. He looked at the young man's valise, and offered to carry it for him, thinking to himself that the young man was so thin and gaunt looking.

The young man resisted the gesture, tightly gripping his valise, pulling it away from the stubborn moneychanger.

"Of course," said the moneychanger. He realized the young man was scared, and he hurried to place his hands on his chest in apology. "Of course, pardon…"

Feeling the weight of the young man's apprehension, the moneychanger's heart softened with empathy. He observed the young man's pronounced cheekbones and haunted eyes, silently noting the unmistakable air of vulnerability that surrounded him. He was but a boy, yet he seemed afflicted, exposed, like a rattled bird fallen out of a nest.

They finally made it to another narrow alley, where no people were. The moneychanger turned into another passage between two buildings.

The hairs on the young man's arms rose, his body warning him of an imminent danger. He realized that he had followed a total stranger into an alley, completely alone. *How could he have been so foolish? What would his parents say?*

The moneychanger pleaded with him in Yiddish, "Come, follow me, come!"

But the young man knew very well what was going to happen. He had money in his valise. The moneychanger knew that, of course. He had isolated him from the crowd, and now he was about to steal his money—that was the best-case scenario. The worst-case scenario… The young man knew what that could be. *He had not made it all the way here, surviving all that he had, only to be fooled now.*

He began walking away.

"No!" the moneychanger exclaimed and grabbed the young man by the sleeve. "Please!"

The young man was startled, pulling away.

The moneychanger gestured with his adamant hands, his palms open, "Wait here!"

Seeing the moneychanger walking down the passage, the young man was apprehensive. *Should he wait? Was this a trap to rob him?*

He looked down the narrow passage. At any moment, the man could come back with his gang… *Should the young man run now, while he still had a chance?*

He hesitated. *Wasn't there something good in the moneychanger's eyes?* If the war had taught him anything, it was to not trust anyone. Suddenly, he heard footsteps from behind the alley.

Chapter 7: Darkness

Poland, 1943

Age 15

The old neighbor's finger remained pointed at the ladder. "What is that doing there?"

The boy stiffened as he heard her question. He tried not to gasp, not to breathe.

"I…was…" The maid hesitated. She gritted her jaw. "I was fetching some potatoes."

"From the attic?" the old neighbor pointed at the attic. The old neighbor's eyes narrowed. "Potatoes in the attic?"

"So I don't have to go outside," the maid hurried to say.

The old neighbor stared at the maid, incredulous. "Why would you bother lifting potatoes to the attic, when you can store them in the kitchen cabinets?"

"Oh, the cabinets were infested with mice," the maid said, entangling herself deeper in lies.

In the hushed solitude of the attic, the boy grappled with the gravity of the situation. Breathless, he knew this could be his end.

The old neighbor squinted and leaned forward. She pointed at the maid.

The maid stood with her back to the unwanted visitor. The maid struggled to maintain her composure.

Usually, the maid was talkative, making friendly gossip. But now she was silent, almost trembling. She faced the stove.

Suddenly the old neighbor said, "Wait, don't you have a potato cellar outside?"

Chapter 8: Light

Paris, 1945

Age 17

In the Parisian alley, the young man heard footsteps rapidly approaching him. The moneychanger appeared from around the building, carrying a plate and a bowl heaped with food.

Food? The young man thought. The young man's stomach urged him to stay put and allow the large man to approach him.

The moneychanger came closer and handed him two dishes to hold. The young man tried to maintain eye contact with the moneychanger, but he could not help but divert his gaze to the plates.

What he noticed amazed him.

The young man gazed at the familiar mixture of dill, carrots, and balls of beautiful round dough floating in a hot broth. He tentatively leaned in and deeply inhaled the hot steam.

His eyes flicked back up to the moneychanger. He recognized there a familial pity and a relief at the young man's recognition of the food. He remembered his uncle, his father, and his grandfather, sitting around a table and sharing this very same food.

He averted his gaze to examine the plate in the moneychanger's other hand. There, upon an old and ornately decorated plate, he identified the shredded potato flats, shiny with the oil that his grandmother would deep fry them in. He remembered her stories about the oil that saved his people from the dark.

The young man's gaze flickered between the plates and the moneychanger.

On the plates was *his* food. His kin's food. His grandmother's cooking. The slow-cooked vegetables, including his favorite, the earthy beet. The dollop of tangy cream and the delicate sprinkle of fresh dill brought on a new wave of hunger.

The moneychanger noticed the young man staring at all the food and laughed out loud, "See? Come on now!"

The young man trailed behind the moneychanger, his steps weighed down by the burden of memories that flooded his mind.

Could it truly be? Here, in the bustling streets of Paris, a taste of home?

He could almost hear his grandmother's gentle voice, her thick accent resonating with warmth and love. "This is a family recipe from Vishay," she would say. "My own grandmother used to make it…"

A bittersweet smile tugged at the corners of his lips. The young man's chest tightened painfully with a pang of homesickness, as he remembered that home was no more. His family was gone, taken from him.

As they rounded the corner of the building, the young man's eyes fell upon a quaint restaurant nestled at the rear. With a sense of quiet anticipation, he trailed closely behind the moneychanger as the dim lighting cast gentle shadows across the room, enveloping it in an atmosphere that whispered of bygone days and cherished memories.

As his gaze swept across the interior, a wave of nostalgia washed over the young man, evoked by the sight of weathered dark wood and framed, faded photographs adorning the walls.

In this quiet haven, time seemed to stand still, offering a sanctuary from the bustle of the outside world and a refuge for weary souls in search of solace.

For the young man, the sight of the restaurant's interior stirred, once again, this strange homesickness that tugged at his heartstrings.

There were a few tables scattered across the room, each

adorned with tablecloths. The scent of home-cooked meals, infused with spices and memories, wafted through the air.

He snapped back into reality when the moneychanger placed the two plates on the table, offering the young man a seat.

The young man sat and soon scarfed down everything on the plate.

When he was done, the moneychanger walked to the restaurant's kitchen and asked the chef to bring the young man another plate.

The young man wasted no time, his hunger voracious as he swiftly devoured every morsel upon his plate. With a satisfied sigh, he leaned back, contentment spreading across his features like a gentle dawn.

Observing the young man's empty plate, the moneychanger rose from his seat and paid the chef.

The moneychanger returned to the table and asked in Yiddish, "You, family—Paris?"

The young man shook his head.

The moneychanger smiled eagerly. "I, you, family!"

The young man wanted to trust him, but he felt hesitant. There was something almost too eager, too kind, too self-interested in his mannerisms.

The young man was happy to eat the food, but he did not forget that this could very well be a sign that the moneychanger *wanted* something from him. The young man had to remind himself to keep his guard up.

"I can pay," he said, and pulled his money from his jacket pocket.

"Nonsense!" The moneychanger said. "Come!"

They left the little restaurant.

The young man followed the moneychanger. The moneychanger led the young man down a few other alleys.

Where was the moneychanger taking him? Should he turn back and run away? Why were they not heading back towards the market?

"Where are we going?" he asked.

"Trust me," said the moneychanger.

The young man's brow furrowed as he tried to memorize the route. "Wait, why are we going this way?" he ventured, his voice betraying a hint of uncertainty.

A smile played across the lips of the moneychanger as he glanced back at the young man. "Trust me," he murmured.

Suddenly, with a swift and unexpected movement, the moneychanger's left hand shot forward, grabbing the young man's valise.

Chapter 9: Darkness

Poland, 1943

Age 15

In the confined attic, the boy tried desperately to stay still. He lay motionless, his breath suspended in the stifling air. His life depended on it.

The shriek of the whistling kettle cut through the tension, providing a welcome task for the maid to undertake while she quickly thought of a response.

The maid tried to speak calmly while she grabbed the kettle with her towel. "Some mice were infesting the potatoes in the cellar, so I moved some to the attic," the maid explained. "Also, I hate to go outside in this terrible snow."

The old neighbor narrowed her eyes. She could have sworn she heard another voice behind the door before she knocked.

The maid looked around nervously as she tried her hardest to make polite conversation despite her personal feelings toward the old neighbor. "And how is your niece faring? You told me she was sick?"

The old neighbor did not answer.

Sitting in the attic, the boy knew that the reason for the lack of conversation was him.

The maid poured the tea for the old neighbor and sat down by the table, he trying to seem casual. "Is your niece well?"

The old neighbor was silent. She studied the table, her hand lingering near the steaming teacup before her, then glanced at the maid's teacup. To her surprise, there was a *third* teacup.

The maid, seeing the old neighbor's prying eyes, followed her gaze. The old neighbor's eyes fixated on the teacup that seemed out of place. "My husband…" the maid stammered, "he did not finish his tea this morning."

The old neighbor was still. Her internal clock reminded her that the husband always left early with his daughters. In fact, she watched them pass by her house over an hour ago. If this story was true, that teacup must be cold. She reached her hand towards it.

Chapter 10: Light

PARIS, 1945

AGE 17

The money changer grabbed the young man's valise.

The young man resisted, forcefully pulling the valise back and shouting violently like an animal. "No!"

"Help!" shouted the moneychanger, "I—you—help! Brother!" he grabbed the valise.

"No!" Shouted the young man. "Mine!" He pulled the valise forcefully from the money changer. The impact was so strong that he fell back and the valise fell on the ground, away from him.

The young man gasped, looking at the standing moneychanger and then at the valise on the alley's cobblestone ground—this was the opportunity for the moneychanger to grab the valise and run away.

Instead, the moneychanger leaned forward, apologetic for his rude behavior. "Pardon, pardon!" The money changer offered his hand to the young man and said with a sense of urgency and helplessness, "I brother, I brother."

The young man stood up, ignoring the moneychanger's hand. He was rattled. Everything that the war had taught him screamed inside his head for him to run away, for him to leave this man who certainly wanted something from him. People were not kind for no reason.

"I brother!" The moneychanger exclaimed again with misty

eyes.

Should he follow the moneychanger? He reasoned that if the man wanted to rob him, he could have done it by now. And the money changer was so kind to pay for such a generous meal.

Could he trust him? His eyes fixed on the moneychanger while he slowly reached for his valise. Hesitantly holding the luggage in both hands, the young man followed him.

The moneychanger spoke in French, exuberantly. The young man did not understand.

The moneychanger pointed at a bakery and then pointed at his round belly saying, "*Magnifique! Magnifique!*"

They kept walking. "Paris! Paris!" he said with pride as if he himself was the owner of the garden or the mayor of the city.

As the young man followed the moneychanger through the Garden of Luxembourg, he was captivated by the enchanting beauty surrounding him. The air was filled with the scent of blooming flowers, and the gentle melody of birdsongs danced through the trees. Sunlight filtered through the lush foliage, casting dappled shadows on the winding paths.

As they walked, the moneychanger gestured towards one of the grand fountains, its waters dancing gracefully in the basin. "*Extraordinaire!*" he exclaimed with a wide smile, his eyes reflecting the joy of the moment. The young man could not help but marvel at the sight, feeling a sense of wonder wash over him in the presence of such beauty.

Together, they continued their stroll through the verdant pathways, the vibrant colors and serene atmosphere of the garden enveloping them.

The young man tried not to be swept away by the beauty of the lush foliage and grand fountains.. He kept alert as to where they were headed. He tried to remember the way they walked.

They arrived at a four-story building and the moneychanger looked up.

Suddenly, the young man saw the moneychanger becoming too eager, and signaled to someone up in the building that they were coming.

The moneychanger opened the door to the building and invited the young man to walk in.

The young man held his valise tightly.

Hesitantly, he stepped past the grinning moneychanger and through the open door.

The young man cautiously entered the imposing Parisian building. This was a wealthy building, even displaying a black telephone on the right, hooked to the wall above an ornate wooden console.

To his left, a narrow steep staircase spiraled upward. To the right, an open arched door led to a small inner cobblestone courtyard nestled between the buildings.

The moneychanger went first, climbing up the steep, winding staircase, holding onto the railing and panting.

The young man followed him up slowly, constantly looking back down at the building door, ensuring that if something went wrong he could charge downstairs and away from the danger.

After a tiring climb, they reached the fourth floor. The moneychanger banged on the door, looking eagerly at the young man.

The young man suddenly regretted having followed the moneychanger. *This must be a trap.* There was something wholly strange about the moneychanger taking the young man to this building, climbing to this very last floor. This must be the attic. The young man was terrified of attics.

As he stood on the stairs, anxiety began to overwhelm him again. The echoes of the war rang in his ears. Even though the war was technically over, the young man knew very well that hatred towards his kin was far from over.

He heard the subtle slide of a peephole. The moneychanger stuck his face closer to it. He then turned and looked nervously at the young man and knocked on the door again, louder this time.

The young man hesitated, taking a step back, his hands tightly gripping the railing. His instincts told him to flee. An invisible force held him in place.

A subtle noise echoed through the corridor—the distinct click of a door latch being turned. Another click reverberated through the corridor. Then another one. *How many locks were there?*

The young man's heart pounded in his chest. He looked down at the winding staircase, feeling suddenly dizzy. *I am trapped,* he thought. The young man took a step back, gripping the railing, ready to run as quickly as he could.

The door opened slightly, but a rusty chain was still latched.

CHAPTER 11: DARKNESS

POLAND, 1943

AGE 15

The old neighbor reached her hand toward the third teacup. The maid abruptly snatched the teacup, spilling tea on the table. Her face flushed with embarrassment as she hurried to the small sink.

"I'm not feeling well!" she said, her voice shaky. "I better… lie down… before the young ones awake!"

The old neighbor reluctantly stood up, her eyes casting a warning glance as she scrutinized the cabin one last time. She glanced back at the attic. "Don't forget what they did to the tanner's family, after they found out they hid that Jew. Their bodies rotted for weeks on the gallows." She glared. "I'll be back."

The maid's eyes followed her neighbor as she walked down the road. As the old neighbor vanished from her view, the maid closed the door in a hurry. She leaned her body against it and sighed in relief.

What was she doing, risking the life of her entire family?

The boy stayed in the attic all day, the walls echoing with the sounds from inside the cabin. He listened intently to the toddler crying and the maid humming as she completed her household chores.

When the children napped in the afternoon, the maid brought him a hot potato and a glass of water, her movements cautious. She did not say a word, and from reading her face, the boy knew that he would not be able to stay much longer.

The maid did not dare invite the boy to come down, and he dared not request it. Ever since the old neighbor left, he knew his hours were numbered.

In the evening, he heard the entire family's voices fill the cabin with laughter. His thoughts turned to his own family. His father, always wearing his spectacles, his eyes piercing the boy's heart. His mother, with her soft, ever-warm hands. He thought of his uncle, the engineer who always encouraged him to keep learning. He thought of his grandfather whom he always tried to appease. He thought of his grandmother and her never-ending kindness. What had happened to all of them? Were they still alive?

He found solace in the relative warmth of the attic, shielded from the soldiers outside. He knew that his time was limited. Soon the maid and her husband would cut ties with him for good. Or the old neighbor would turn him in to the soldiers in exchange for a bag of flour.

Late at night, when the five children went to sleep, the boy heard the maid and her husband arguing in the small bedroom, behind a closed door. Their voices were muffled, but he could decipher their words.

"We cannot hide him here!" the husband protested.

"It is not a question!" the maid retorted, unwavering determination in every word.

The husband whispered, "Do you have any idea what they will do to us? You are endangering all of us! Think of the family!"

"He and his family are like family to me, to us!"

The husband groaned. "I will not allow it. They will *kill all of us*," he insisted, hissing through his teeth at her.

The boy knew very well that the maid would not convince her husband. He would be sent out into the snow again. He shivered at the thought.

He felt like an animal trapped in the tiny attic waiting to be handed over for slaughter. The attic would be the first place they would inspect, especially because the neighbor might have reported him hiding there.

An abrupt knock on the main door startled the boy and caused him to hit his head on the roof of the attic, making a loud noise.

The conversation halted in the bedroom.

Fearful, the maid and her husband moved towards the locked door in silence. Another knock followed, louder this time.

The husband asked, "Who is that at this time of night?"

Chapter 12: Light

Paris, 1945

Age 17

At the Parisian building, on the fourth floor, the young man saw the heavy door creak open. The moneychanger stepped back.

A small, ancient-looking woman peeked from behind the crack. A pale blue floral head scarf framed her face, with two shining silver teeth. Her eyes, though weathered, were an intense shade of blue. It was as if she were able to read the young man's mind.

The young man had not expected to see an elderly lady open the door. Her headscarf and demeanor reminded him of his own grandmother, before the war began and before she became melancholy with sorrow after her husband was taken.

The old mama squinted suspiciously at the young man. Then she turned to the moneychanger. "What are you doing home so early? And who is this young man?"

"Mama, open up already!"

The old mama slowly shut the door and, a moment later, released the chain and opened it again.

She was wearing an apron and her face was frightening, staring at the young man as if he were the accused in a futile trial in which he could never win.

Standing on the top stair, he held his valise tightly, wondering if he should apologize and excuse himself from the situation, leaving the odd couple.

The moneychanger, seeing the hesitation of the young man, said, "Come!"

The young man stood there, breathing heavily. They were strangers. He wanted to trust them, but how could he be so naive after everything he went through?

The moneychanger spoke to the old mama in French, "He's one of us, Mama! From *there!*"

The old mama seemed doubtful. Examining the young man she asked in the old tongue, her pronunciation guttural and cough-like: "Amcha—Your-People?"

The young man smiled. "Amcha—Your-People!" he said back, using his grandparents' distinct guttural pronunciation. For his kin, it was a cypher—a way to recognize if another person was one of you.It was loaded with the weight of a haunted people who, for generations, had not known who to trust and who to fear.

The young man repeated it again, as if hearing the voice of his own grandparents speaking through him. "Amcha—Your-People! Amcha!"

The old mama's demeanor changed at once, hearing the very language so beautifully pronounced in the old Yiddish, assisting lost souls in recognizing their brethren. She stepped forward and fell onto the young man, grabbing his face with her wrinkled hands and kissing him violently several times on each cheek.

He was stunned.

The moneychanger laughed. "Mama! You are attacking him!"

"You shut up!" the old mama said and pushed the young man inside the home, happily closing the door behind him. "He must be hungry!" she said as she latched the five locks, her two silver teeth shining as she grinned.

The moneychanger laughed. "Mama, I just fed him, twice!"

"Nonsense," the old mama muttered and announced, "He shall eat!" She then said to the young man in a loud voice, as if he were deaf, "You, shall, eat!"

The young man smiled. He looked around at the antique, enchanting apartment.

The moneychanger put his hand on the young man's shoulder. The young man drew back only a little.

The moneychanger exclaimed, "I-go. You-Mama. I-work. Go evening-I home."

The young man did not know what to say. "Thank you," he muttered.

The moneychanger left.

The old mama made a huge racket rattling pans and pots down the hall.

Peering around the parlor, the young man noticed there were countless photographs on the narrow hallway walls. Seeing all these family pictures brought tears to his eyes. With most of his family gone, those photos felt too overwhelming for him. He closed his eyes and squeezed them tightly shut. He would not cry. *All is well*, he told himself, *all is well*.

The air was filled with a comforting mix of aged wood and the scent of old books. He noticed the walls were adorned with intricate flowery wallpaper. A little velvet chair was tucked in the corner.

Embroidered cushions were left scattered across the divan.

In a bid to distract himself from crying, the young man focused his attention on a bookcase along the wall.

He turned to look at the books — classics by Hugo, Dumas, and Molière. His grandmother had read some of them to him, years before, in Polish.

He then saw large-scale thick books, one of which carried the name "Le Louvre Musée," and the young man felt tingling in his fingers. He had always wanted to visit the famous Louvre museum.

Time passed, and the old mama remained in the kitchen. Hesitantly, he pulled the book out and began looking at reproductions of artworks. While he could not read the French, he could still enjoy the pictures.

The old French mama carried a tray with several small plates. Her hands shook. The young man took the tray from her in gratitude. At first she resisted, but then she seemed pleased with his gesture, her natural and silver teeth gleaming in happiness. He placed it on the lounge.

The old mama looked at him and saw that he had not taken off his coat. She walked over to the young man and forcefully grabbed his shoulders. "Off!" she demanded, twitching in irritation at the shy young man moving slowly.

The young man was hesitant to let the old mama take his coat. He wasn't planning on staying long.

The old mama took his coat and hung it up in a mahogany wardrobe.

The aroma of freshly baked bread filled the air. As the young man took the first bite of the freshly baked bread, he was enveloped in a cloud of warmth and comfort. The crust crackled softly beneath his fingers, giving way to a pillowy interior that was light and airy with a subtle hint of sweetness.

The young man's senses came alive as he explored the intricacies of each dish, savoring the nuances of flavor and texture with childlike delight. He had not enjoyed food in years, and he vowed to never take a proper meal for granted again.

The old mama watched him attentively, glad to see him eating. She also ate, the silver replacements shining with each bite.

He moaned with delight.

She clapped her hands, pleased.

As he finished his last bite, the old mama reached for the tray.

The young man shook his head.

The old mama looked at him incredulously. "What are you doing? Give me the tray!"

"I can take it to the kitchen," the young man quietly replied.

"No, tu imbécile," defied the old mama. "I can do it myself." With no other words, she whisked the tray away from the young man and took it into the kitchen. Yet, the young man could not stop looking at her silver teeth as she spoke.

The old mama bustled about. With practiced hands, she set about preparing the divan for the young man's much-needed rest, her movements methodical and precise.

She went to the wardrobe, opened it, and signaled for the young man to pull out a heavy quilt.

He pulled it out.

She took out a sheet, remnants of a time long past, and with care and diligence, she draped it over the divan, smoothing out the wrinkles with a tender touch.

Finally, she completed the setup with a pillow from her own bed.

"Now you rest," she said firmly.

He thought of his own grandmother. She would do the same for him whenever he used to come visit his grandparents.

He could not believe that he had just arrived in Paris a few hours earlier, was fed for the third time, and was offered a bed for free.

He brought his valise closer to his chest. It contained his only possessions. He felt safe with the old mama, but he was still hesitant about trusting a stranger. He did not feel comfortable going to sleep there, although he realized he was very tired after completing the overnight journey to France and needed to sleep. He had not slept since he was in Poland.

He placed the valise between his legs and slouched against the big comfortable pillow. The security that he felt lying on the bed was something that he had not felt in a long time. Yet somehow his thoughts always turned back to the war.

Chapter 13: Darkness

Poland, 1943

Age 15

The husband asked again, his voice betraying his fear. "Who is it?"

Alone in the stifling confines of the attic, the boy remained as quiet as he possibly could. His heartbeat thumped loudly. At that moment, he forgot that he was hungry; he forgot that he longed to be released from the attic; he forgot he had to relieve himself for hours. He forgot about it all, his survival instincts forcing him to be still, to be invisible, to disappear.

Muffled footsteps resonated from below. *Were the soldiers there?*

He knew that the soldiers would be noisy—with their boots thumping loudly against floorboards and their habit of haphazardly grabbing and throwing objects against the walls. He tried not to think of the moment they stormed into his family's apartment, splinters of wood flying through the air as a soldier smashed the boy's violin against the wall. He could still hear the screeching sound it had made as it cracked.

Why did they have to be so destructive?

Who was it down there?

The conversation down below was getting louder and clearer, the faint murmurs now merging with the tension in the air.

He tried to use his fingers to hold the door of the attic closed from the inside, but there was no latch, no handle, no lock. There was nothing to protect him. He forced his two middle fingers into a narrow crack in between the doorframe, his fingers throbbing. He must not let the door open.

The boy strained to catch a familiar cadence, a phrase, anything that might confirm their identity.

He heard the shuffling of the ladder moving towards the attic entrance. His heart skipped a beat. *This was it. It had to be.* He heard a thump and the creak of the ladder steps. Someone was climbing the ladder.

Chapter 14: Light

Paris, 1945

Age 17

The young man sprinted through the woods. He kept looking back to see if the soldiers with their dogs had caught up to him. Then, he saw the butcher.

The butcher's face was malevolent, twisted with cruelty and his eyes bored into his soul. His uniform was tattered and soaked in blood. The young man tried escaping him, but the butcher was running, catching up, almost able to touch the young man, his rifle in his hand, laughing. The young man could hear the crunch of every twig and leaf beneath his feet, his small body ducking and weaving through trees and branches, running with pure terror. The steady pounding of the butcher's boots was behind him. He felt the butcher approaching, and his skeletal fingers caught his shoulders. The young man tried to escape, but the butcher had already loaded the rifle. The metallic sound of the bullet releasing the chamber echoed, the butcher pointing it directly at the young man's back. "No!" the young man screamed, as the butcher pressed the trigger. A deafening blast shattered the silence, and the young man's body jolted.

His eyes snapped open, and he sat up, awakening from the dream, his body drenched in a cold sweat.

Where was he? Was he at his grandmother's home? The young man turned his head, relieved to see his valise, but he suddenly gasped as he saw the old mama's face looking at him from the narrow hallway.

He had known it was a mistake to fall asleep—not because of possibly losing his valise—but due to his embarrassment now that the old mama had witnessed his distress.

The old mama stood there, watching the young man have a bad dream, not knowing what to say or do. Should she have woken him up? She mumbled with pity. "Poor boy," she murmured, "*Pauvre type…*"

The young man, realizing where he was, tried to gain his composure. "Sorry," he mumbled, "sorry…"

The old mama wanted to walk over to him and hug him, to tell him that it was all going to be alright. But the young man seemed as if he would not welcome it.

Carefully, she sat down beside him on the edge of the divan-turned-bed.

She did not look at him. Although she knew he would not understand, she spoke in French, as if to herself. "No need for apologies, child," she let out a long sigh, full of memories and sorrow. "We've all got our own demons to wrestle with."

Although he did not know the words, at that moment, there was a deeper understanding between them. He felt a lump forming in his throat. He looked down, embarrassed again. He felt that he had to leave, that he was overstaying his welcome.

Suddenly, the old mama clapped her hands loudly. "You must be hungry!" she exclaimed in Yiddish, smiling largely, revealing her two silver teeth. She got up and walked to the kitchen.

Within a minute, she walked back to him slowly, her hands rattling a silver tray with three small plates.

It was late afternoon. As the young man ate the lavish meal the old mama had prepared for him, he thought he'd better leave soon. He had to find a hotel, and—indeed—to change money; the moneychanger had refused to take his zloty, but the young man still needed the local currency.

The old mama was in the kitchen. He probably had bothered her enough.

The young man finished eating, quietly stacked the small plates one on top of the other on the tray, and got up. He folded the blanket as neatly as he could, opened the moth-ball smelling wardrobe, and placed the blanket and the pillow on the top shelf before quietly closing the mahogany wardrobe door.

He took his coat from the hanger and was relieved to find all the bills there. He counted the money. He made sure to leave enough money on the small table, thinking that surely her son could change it for her. This was the polite thing to do. After all, she had fed him twice and gave him shelter for the day. Surely the old mama would appreciate compensation for the ingredients, if not for her terrific cooking.

He began walking toward the kitchen through the small narrow hallway but then froze. He wanted to say goodbye, but he felt that he was already too much of a burden. He had already stayed too long—what was he thinking, taking her time and allowing himself to barge in on her privacy? The polite thing to do was to simply disappear.

He turned around and, with heavy steps, headed to the door. He did not really want to leave. Paris was promising outside, but it was already early evening. And he did not know where to go. He reassured himself that he would be able to find a hotel. He pulled back his shoulders. He was a big boy. He could take care of himself now.

He unlocked the five locks on the door with a heavy heart, not wanting to leave the warmth of the home, of this house with the old photographs, the old wood, and the smell.

He was just starting to open the door when he heard a voice behind him.

Chapter 15: Darkness

Poland, 1943

Age 15

The door of the attic rattled. *No!* The boy clung with his fingertips to the edge of the door, pulling as hard as he could to stop the entrance from revealing his hiding place, but alas, his awkward grip was not strong enough.

The attic door flew open.

He shielded his face with his hands, squeezing his eyes shut and expecting the barking of the soldiers' voices, expecting a forceful grip yanking him down, expecting the swift, lethal sting of a bullet.

Instead, he heard a gasp. Then a familiar voice. "You got out!"

He looked down and saw a familiar face, sharp, dark eyes framed by bushy eyebrows and a wearied grin—his uncle!

His uncle stood there, tall. Behind him stood the maid, smiling, and her husband, frowning underneath his mustache.

"You made it here!" The uncle exclaimed and skipped the steps of the ladder, climbing up and taking the boy's thin face in his hands.

His uncle's hands brought comfort to the boy, who had been hiding the entire day.

"Uncle," he whispered, his voice breaking. He reached out his own shaking hands to his uncle. The uncle helped him down. His uncle's grip was strong and sturdy. Familiar.

The boy suddenly thought that maybe—since his uncle was

here—maybe his parents and sister also escaped? "Uncle, did… mama? Papa?"

His uncle's eyes darkened as he looked away. "I don't know," he said.

The maid clasped her hand, sensing the tension. "Now-now, you two must be hungry. I'll heat up some soup."

The boy glanced at the maid's husband, seeing his astonishment at his wife's behavior. The boy knew the maid's husband wanted the two unwanted guests out.

Suddenly the uncle looked at the maid and at her husband. "I'm afraid I did not come alone."

Chapter 16: Light

Paris 1945

Age 17

I

In the narrow hallway of the Paris apartment, the old mama looked confused, wiping her wet hands on her apron, and threw the kitchen towel over her shoulder as she looked at the young man at the door.

She saw the young man, his coat on, by the door, and—on the low lounge table—did she see correctly? She peered into the parlor. Yes, she was right! On the table, the young man had left *money*.

"Stupid!" she exclaimed, and—as if she had never had a bad hip—she leaped towards the young man, hitting him with the kitchen towel. *"Merde! Imbecile!"* she uttered a string of curses in French, which the young man was fortunate enough not to understand.

Baffled, the young man tried to apologize, but the old mama would have none of it. "Stupid!" she yelled, "stupid, brainless, foolish, mindless, idiotic boy!"

She remembered he did not understand her, so she switched to Yiddish, carefully picking the juiciest curses she could recall. "You imbecile! Go jump in the lake and drown! May pimples grow on your tongue! May all your teeth fall out—except one that will make you suffer! May your luck be as bright as a new moon!"

She pushed him from the corridor into the living room. "May

God give you the best of Pharaoh's plagues! No—may he sprinkle Job's scabies on top! May salt be thrown in your eyes! And pepper in your nose!"

She grabbed the money from the lounge table and threw it at the young man's stunned face. "Shove it up your tush! No—may you have to spend it all on doctors!"

She grabbed at the hem of the frightened young man's coat. "May leeches drink you dry! May the jailers free a madman, and lock you up instead!"

Then she served up the greatest of curses, one that the young man knew from his own grandfather. Her eyes widened and she uttered slowly, "May you have a large store, and whatever people want to buy—you will *not* have! And everything you do have— may people never want to buy!"

The young man tried to move away from the crazy old woman, but she pulled him back into the apartment. "Where do you think you're going? How dare you behave in this way to an old lady!"

The young man was reminded of the old mama's strength and found himself thrown onto the divan. Her eyes were burning with rage.

He swallowed nervously. *What had he done?* All he had wanted was to be cordial, to be polite. He was afraid she'd pull out a revolver.

She shook her head and said, "Get up and help me!"

He did as she instructed. She hit the divan and gestured for the young man to push it away from the wall. Puzzled, he pulled it. She nodded, pleased.

There, behind the divan, on the floor, the old lady tapped with her foot on the tiles signaling to the young man that there was one loose tile. "Out!"

The young man, unsure, knelt down and did as she instructed. He poked the tile. He wondered what he would find there. *Money? A gun?* He managed to get the tile out by squeezing his fingers together and pressing it upwards.

He saw a wooden box, and he was about to take it out, when the old mama pushed him aside. "Me only!"

She knelt down, sighing as she did so. Bowed like a mountain, she bent, her face sinking towards her knees. The young man observed as her weary hand stretched toward the floor, grasping the wooden box.

She touched the treasure with her wrinkled fingers. Her fingers shook, lovingly stroking the engraving on the surface of the box. She let out a sigh. Then she lifted it out and slowly made her way upright, leaning on the young man's shoulder. She tapped the divan's back, gesturing for him to push it back against the wall.

He did as she instructed.

She sat down on the divan, sighing, placing the box on her knees. She pointed her finger to the seat next to her on the divan. "Sit!"

The young man dutifully sat down.

The old mama shook her head and mumbled to herself. It seemed as if she were saying a prayer. She looked at the young man's eyes. He looked down.

"This," she murmured, "is the most precious thing in this whole household."

She opened the top of the engraved wooden box.

The wooden box contained a yarmulke cap. It was white, with golden embroidery.

The young man looked at it.

The old mama pointed to a large golden-framed picture hanging in the narrow hallway. "Go bring that! Yes, that one."

The young man quickly lifted the golden-framed black-and-white picture off its nail. As he brought it back to the divan, he tried not to step on the bills on the floor. He sat down, displaying the picture before her.

The old mama pointed at an old bearded man wearing a yarmulke cap. "This," the old mama said, still pointing at the old bearded man wearing a yarmulke cap, "was my grandfather. A great man. An important man… He died in the Great War. The first war," she added.

The young man gestured in agreement.

"And this," she pointed at an old lady, "is my grandmama. In her household, everyone was welcomed. People from all over came to enjoy her food, her hospitality. we had a big house, not like this," she said and spat on the floor.

The young man smiled as a wave of memories washed over him. The spitting reminded him so much of his own late grandmother. He felt a lump forming in his throat.

The old mama then turned her attention back to the young man. "Now, you fool," the old mama said, "What do you think my grandmama would say, were she to see *you*," she said, stabbing his shoulder with her finger, "giving *this* to me?!" She kicked her foot at the money bills on the floor.

"I'm sorry," the young man mumbled, embarrassed at having hurt this kind old lady, disrespecting her kind-hearted hospitality and disgracing her family. He whispered, his voice barely audible, "I didn't—I didn't—I was—" He felt tears forming. *No!* He caught himself. *No!* He had promised himself he would not cry. No!

I must not cry, he told himself, reminding himself that he was no longer a child. He swallowed his tears, pulled his shoulders back, and raised his chin up.

The old mama shook her head, observing his struggle to remain composed. "You fool..." she said, and suddenly wrapped her arm around him, forcefully bringing his head onto her lap. "You fool! Schmuck!"

She began crying, and adjusted her headscarf. "You fool... you fool... what a poor fool..."

The young man tried not to cry. He did not understand what had made her now become so... *kind...*

"Now, fool," she whispered, "where is your family?"

The young man bit his quivering lips.

He said nothing.

The old mama sighed, searching his eyes. "Family?"

The young man remained silent.

"Anyone? Not one?"

"One, my mother's brother," the young man whispered.

"Do you have a father?"

The young man shook his head.

"Your mother?"

The young man gazed at the floor as if he did not hear her.

The old mama grabbed the young man's hand firmly. She closed her eyes. "Now you are my son, you hear me?"

The young man did not want to cry. *He did not want to cry!*

"You are now my son. *Do you hear me?*"

He squeezed her hand, as if to say yes, trying to hold back the tears that began streaming down his face.

The old mama squeezed back. "Son of mine," she said, rocking back and forth, "son of mine…"

II

The young man was worried about the moneychanger returning. Had he overstayed his welcome?

He thought of leaving but was too scared to offend the old mama again. She, at the same time, seemed so happy and sanguine, walking around the house and singing to herself in a low voice.

He enjoyed looking at the many books in her library and the beautiful apartment. It reminded him of his grandparents' home.

Pain gripped his heart as he remembered going to his grandparents' home when the war ended and seeing that the house was desolate, ravaged by looters. Everything was stolen except a forgotten yarmulke cap and a few photographs.

Yet, in stark contrast to his grandparents' apartment, the young man found himself in this time capsule of an apartment. It was as if there was never a war — a house that had china, tapestry, and furniture from the turn of the previous century. In this museum-like apartment, the boy felt somehow secure.

He cherished the afternoon at the old mama's house, and for the first time in years, he felt a sense of belonging.

The young man found himself irresistibly drawn to the old mama's large book collection. Excitement bubbled within him as he explored the collection. The language barrier did not diminish the magic that radiated from the shelves. Books! *Books*! How long had it been since he had been in the vicinity of books?

He had spent years trapped in the suffocating depths of war, confined to that desolate pit cloaked in almost complete darkness.

In a household where the value of books held little significance, unlike the reverence they were afforded by his father and grandparents, the young man found himself in a world where literacy was not held in the same esteem by the maid and her husband.

Books were sacred. Books were more important than food. And here he was again in the proximity of worlds of knowledge encapsulated within books.

The young man's fingers traced the spines of the books that

lined the old mama's shelves, each one a silent invitation to a world of secrets and desires.

The weight and smell of hardcovers in his hands sent a shiver through him. As a boy, he had never appreciated them. But now he understood they were the remnants of culture.

It was no wonder that the occupiers' army searched for forbidden volumes and set them on fire. Books were reason; books were hope; books were the bridge from one soul to another. And now he was amazed to see so many of them!

As he navigated through the pages, the young man's heart swelled with awe, although all the books were in French and he could not understand any of them.

Each one held a promise, a possibility, and the young man, like a seaman who had experienced a shipwreck, eagerly embraced the refuge that the old mama's collection provided.

His eyes were specifically drawn yet again to the large book with a gold engraving: *Le Musée du Louvre*.

He had heard about the museum while he was still in school but had never dedicated a second thought to it. But now this book was calling him.

He was pleased to find monochrome photograph reproductions neatly glued into the pages. The young man could not read any of the books, but for now, he could just appreciate the photographs and not worry about a language he did not know.

He flipped through the pages and then stopped on a page that halted his breath. In front of him was the most famous painting he had ever heard of or seen. He had seen reproductions of it. The lady looked straight at him with a gentle and inviting smile.

The young man did not know that the Louvre housed *that* painting. He was excited to recognize at least one painting.

The war had stopped his schooling and his hobbies. He used to play sports and paint with watercolors. The war had taken all his family, all his friends. Who was left? An uncle in Poland? A friend of his parents in Palestine? Who?

Yet here, in this book, was a painting that he recognized from before the war. In one of the last lessons before the war, when he was still nine years old, the teacher showed them this very painting. And this painting still existed, did it not?

Any bridge to life before the war was welcome in his mind, cherished, framed, secured and brought close to his heart. He stared at the lady in the painting with fascination.

"Ah *La Joconde,* the Mona Lisa!" said the old mama. The young man was so engrossed in the reproduction of the painting that he did not notice she was standing above him. "The great seducer!"

The young man mumbled, "This is in the museum, right? Still?"

"Oh, yes. And from what I hear, the museum reopened. Those damn Nazis could not steal her!"

"Can I visit this place?" The young man was very excited about the notion of meeting face to face with an iconic symbol of human achievement.

"Of course!" said the old mama. "You should go tomorrow!"

The young man suddenly sat up with a renewed sense of purpose. He owed it to his family—to all of them—to go and experience this. Soon he would have to find work in Paris, settle down, but maybe tomorrow he would go and see the Mona Lisa.

The old mama said, "My son will be coming soon. I will go make dinner; if there is no food for him, he cries like a baby!" Her face changed in a comic series of expressions, winking at him, her two silver teeth shining.

The young man put the heavy book on the lounge table and began standing up. "I can help in the kitchen!"

"You sit, sit and read!" she said, pleased, and made her way to the kitchen.

The young man remained in the parlor. He saw several photographs of a 20-year-old man, sometimes posing with the old mama and the moneychanger.

The old mama saw him looking.

"Who is that?" the young man asked.

The old mama froze for a long moment. She shook her head and tut-tutted, disappearing into the kitchen.

The young man walked back to the parlor and looked at the many shelves of books. He spotted a dictionary. Polish-French. He pulled it out. All the words were here, all the meanings.

He began gulping the words, trying to pronounce those long, unpronounceable multi-syllable words, tasting them, contemplating the meaning of them, happy to notice some words were actually the same as in the old tongue. Radio was radio. Wine was Vin. Telegraph was Télégraphe. Theater was Théâtre. Coffee was Café. He was pleased with every word he recognized.

The young man heard shuffling. He jumped, startled by the sudden sound of someone moving on the other side of the door. Was it the moneychanger? Or was someone coming for him?

Chapter 17: Darkness

POLAND, 1943

AGE 15

"I'm afraid I did not come alone," the uncle said gravely. The boy felt the tension in the room rise. The uncle briefly glanced at the shocked couple before he opened the door and disappeared into the night.

The husband muttered curses. He turned to his wife with raised eyebrows, raising one burly arm in gesture to the events unfolding in their family's kitchen. The maid kept a steady gaze upon the door. The boy looked there too, growing more uncertain about the safety of his hiding place by the minute.

The uncle returned along with two strangers, a short, stout man and a gaunt woman.

In the kitchen, the silence thickened as the maid's husband glared at the unwanted visitors. He smoothed his mustache with agitation.

"Please meet my friends," the uncle said. He put his hand on the stout man's shoulder. "A lawyer, well-known in Grodno before the war. And his wife."

"A seamstress," the lawyer's wife hurried to say, moving forward to shake the maid's hand. "Madam," she said and then turned to the maid's husband. "Sir," she slouched humbly before them, "Thank you for hiding us for the night! I am a seamstress… A-a very good one if I may say, I had a workshop on Kopernika street. Had twelve girls working for me…"

"Ma'am—" The maid's husband started, his stern tone attempting to silence the frantic woman.

"If you need clothes mended…Or-or new ones sewn, I could… Just tell me! I will get started right aw—"

"Ma'am!" The husband shouted, and then whispered, "you are making too much noise."

The boy sensed what was to come. The husband did not approve of them staying.

"Now-now," the maid said and walked to the sink and added water to the already-diluted soup, "You," she said to the uncle, "How is your mother?" she smiled nervously.

The uncle did not respond. The silence was palpable.

The maid stirred the pot on the stove, shaking her head in amazement. It was unimaginable to her how this once wealthy family had become so desperate in the insane climate of the war.

She glanced at her husband, standing there, shaking his head slowly.

Her husband looked back at her, gravity in his every movement. He turned to look at the room where the children were sleeping, then at the four fugitives. He looked at the ladder and at the tiny attic above that could barely fit one person. He went to the stove and turned the fire out from under the soup. "I'm sorry," he said to the uncle. "We cannot."

CHAPTER 18: LIGHT

PARIS 1945

AGE 17

I

The young man heard shuffling behind the door. Then he heard someone knocking on the door loudly.

"Mama! Mama! Let me in!"

The old mama walked hurriedly to the door, her hands shaking with excitement. She winked at the young man as she unlocked the five locks.

The old mama embraced her son, kissed him five times on the cheeks and said, "You've sent me an angel!"

His face lit up as he glanced at the young man. He was happy his mother had company, finally. He saw the young man reading a book. "What are you reading?" Then, seeing the confused look on the young man's face, he switched to his limited knowledge of Yiddish. "What—read?"

The young man showed the moneychanger the book cover.

The moneychanger chuckled. "The dictionary? You're reading the dictionary!"

The young man shrugged his shoulders, and said, in French, "Slowly learning, slowly smarting!"

The moneychanger burst into laughter and patted the young man on the shoulder. Then he sat down heavily and shouted to the old mama, "Where is my dinner?"

"Here, here, here!" the old mama said as she came out of the kitchen into the narrow hallway, bringing a tray for him. The young man still could not help looking at the silver teeth gleaming whenever the old mama smiled and spoke out loud. But of course, he would not dare ask her about them, even though he wanted to.

The food the old mama served was a cabbage roll filled with ground beef. The young man was grateful for the simple yet delicious food that filled the apartment and smelled superb.

The young man kept rereading the dictionary, feeling a little awkward. *Was he really invited to stay here? Should he leave?* The thought of how he had tried to leave a few hours before was etched in his mind. He shook his head as he recalled the old mama's profanities; that old lady had quite the talent for cursing. He could not bear to hear the old lady firing curses at him like one of those rapid-firing machine guns again.

The old mama sat in the living room and said something in French to her son. He looked surprised. "Where?" he asked in French.

"Here," she said and pointed at the divan. "He doesn't have any family in France. We shall be his family."

The moneychanger looked at her. He knew his mother very well; she was the most suspicious of people—she *had* to be. She had learned much about people and their nature.

During the war, she had survived on her own without relying on anyone. The moneychanger had left her to escape underground and was afraid she would not be found alive when he returned. Her other son had been taken by the trains. But she somehow survived, stayed home for five years, never left the apartment, and lived on potatoes and leeks that kind neighbors in the building had shared with her. Not one person in the building betrayed her.

She had witnessed horrid things from behind that kitchen curtain, seeing many of her kin dragged out of their homes, rounded up, marching the streets, taken to the Vélodrome d'Hiver, only to be sent to the trains. Many of them were betrayed by their very friends—their own neighbors.

She knew that to trust was to lay your life in the hands of another person. And here she was allowing a total stranger into her home. To sleep. The moneychanger sighed. "As you wish,

Mama, but—"

"Sans but," she said.

The young man stared at them, sensing something was wrong.

The old mama smiled a large smile at him, her two silver teeth shining. She then turned to her son and said, "Tomorrow, you will take him to see some *culture*, some museums…"

"Mama! I have to work!"

"Work!" the old mama shouted, "You are married to your work!"

The moneychanger wondered whether this could get her out of the house. "*You* go with him!" he said.

"With my hip?"

The moneychanger smiled. "We'll both carry you down the stairs."

She laughed. "You will fall, and he," she looked at the thin young man, "he'll snap in two!"

The old mama and her son burst into laughter.

The young man did not understand the conversation.

The old mama looked at the young man. She hit him playfully with her kitchen towel, forcing an awkward smile from him. "Laugh!" She said, "Humor is good for health!"

The young man buried himself in the dictionary, determined to learn the language as fast as he could.

The old mama sighed. She looked satisfied watching her son eat. When he was done, she said in French, "Look at this fallen bird; he *needs* to go to the museums, see the greatness of France, the art, the culture…"

"He's a big boy, Mama!" her son groaned. He pushed the tray aside and began pulling out envelopes for counting money.

The young man avoided looking directly at the money, but out of the corner of his eye, he saw the different currencies and the moneychanger painstakingly writing the sums of each bill for each currency, adding them up in long rows.

The young man quickly calculated the sums of each currency.

The old mama took the tray and came back with a tray for the young man.

He thanked her and put the dictionary back on the shelf, not wanting to put it away; it was a bridge to the new language, to the new world.

The old mama sat in the armchair and smiled at the young man as he ate the cabbage rolls. "Tomorrow," she said excitedly, "you'll visit the Louvre! And the Jeu de Paume as well."

He nodded.

"I cannot go," she sighed, making a dramatic sweep with her hand in a French actor's fashion, her face fallen in a sulky pout, "I can't handle the stairs…"

The young man was baffled. *But she lived on the fourth floor!*

"…and my son," the old mama continued in Yiddish and pointed at her son counting his money, "he is a lazy putz."

"Mama, what are you saying? What's that word?"

"Shush!" said the old mama. "But you," she pointed at the young man with a shaky finger, "You will do as I tell you." Her eyebrows rose. "And after the Louvre you'll go to the Jeu de Paume to see some avant-garde art!"

She got up and searched her books, finding a large book with the black-and-white reproductions.

The young man looked at the pictures and could not understand what the old mama found appealing. There were no color reproductions, only black and white blurry etchings. He thought they looked blurry and childish, unprofessional.

"This," the old mama exclaimed, "Sunrise. Monet. You must go and see this, it's in the new museum," she said, "you will experience the power of art!" She said and closed the book.

Soon the moneychanger disappeared into a room down the narrow hallway, and the old mama made the bed. She kissed him on his cheeks and said, "This is your home, oui?"

He slowly nodded with uncertainty. Did she really mean this? And what did her son think of her generous hospitality? He vowed to repay her kindness back one day.

He was tired, but he took out his journal and tore a page out. There was someone he had to write to.

The following morning the young man was awoken by the old mama. It took him a moment to realize where he was. "Get up, get up!" she said. "You can either keep dreaming or get up and chase your dreams!"

The young man stretched his arms. The old mama pulled the blanket off him. "Life is waiting!" She pointed at the tray of breakfast. "My son is long gone. Now you eat and go!"

The young man smiled and rubbed the cobwebs from his eyes. He visited the small bathroom, opposite the parlor, and washed his hands and face.

He returned to the parlor and ate the delicious breakfast the old mama had prepared. After breakfast, the young man hurried to the wardrobe in the narrow hallway to fetch his coat. He was excited for his first full day in Paris.

The old mama opened the five locks for him. As he walked down the steps she followed him with her gaze. "May you be blessed," she thought to herself. "Be blessed…"

She locked the door and sat down on the divan. She already missed him.

As the young man exited the apartment building, a wave of determination took over him. He was going to find the Louvre, and that other museum, even if it took him all day.

He passed by the Luxembourg gardens at the end of the old mama's street. The air was filled with the sweet fragrance of blooming flowers. In the center of the garden, the water in the fountains sparkled in the sunlight.

Two hours later, after having found a post office and sent three letters and now armed with newly converted French francs, the young man stood in front of the imposing structure of a former elegant palace, the Louvre.

He marveled at the sheer scale and grandeur. *Was this real life? Was he really beholding the Louvre?*

He saw families together. People were excited to have the museum open again after being closed since the war ended. He saw a family: a mother, a father, a son, and daughter. The brother and the sister were bickering, the brother poking his sister and running away from her. The mother looked upset about the trouble the children were causing. The young man watched as the brother ran beside him after poking his sister, which prompted the sister to sprint after him, enraged.

The young man did not understand why they were so annoyed with each other. *Didn't they realize how lucky they are to have each other?*

The young man wanted to shake the brother, to shout at him until he understood the importance of siblings, "Can't you understand that your family can disappear in an instant?"

How could they not see the unexplainable closeness of a sibling: another person in the entire world having the same blood, same features, same shared experiences?

He recalled how one time his mother gave both him and his sister chocolates. Once he had finished his chocolates, he stole some of his sister's and ate them. How upset she was! And although he apologized, his sister knew it was not sincere.

Now he would give up all the chocolates in the world to spend one more day with his sister. He could take her to the Eiffel Tower. He could walk with her to the magical gardens. And he could take her with him to experience the grandeur as he entered the museum's impressive hall.

He paid for the ticket and hurried to present it to the museum guard, then walked through the impressive arch. Large-scale oil paintings depicting grand mythological scenes met his eyes.

The *Mona Lisa* was one of the most valuable and most well-known works of art in the world—he *had* to see it.

He saw a group of Frenchmen standing by a small painting, excited. He was flabbergasted. *Was this the Mona Lisa?* He could not believe it. She was smaller than he expected.

From the faces of reverence around her, she must be the one. He felt disappointed. She looked stern, nothing like how she looked in the book. He expected a grand painting, one that would sweep him off his feet.

She seemed severe. Not smiling like he had seen in reproductions.

It seemed that as high as his expectations were, so followed the depth of his disappointment. He desperately tried to be smitten with her like everyone else was. But he could not admire her. What could they see that he didn't?

Lost, disappointed, and disenchanted, he wandered through the museum. He climbed to the second floor. The grandeur felt overwhelming.

He stopped, trying to give the *Mona Lisa* a second chance. But her gaze held no secret for him. *The Mona Lisa was presenting, modeling, putting up a front for the viewers, showing off.*

An hour later the young man stood by the Jeu de Paume. It was smaller than Le Louvre.

He walked inside. It had a different atmosphere. The colors were festive. The paintings looked as if they were created fast, almost like drafts, with thick brushstrokes.

He saw a few paintings with vibrant colors, almost violent in their coarseness. He did not recall seeing any texture while he was at Le Louvre. The paintings were flat, gentle—but in this museum, the paint jumped off the canvas, thick in texture. He saw several paintings in the same style, oleanders in a vase, sunflowers in a vase, irises in a vase, irises in a field—he was surrounded by a kaleidoscope of colors as he gazed upon the paintings. Shades of royal purple, vibrant blue, and rich greens intertwined in a dance of hues that seemed to defy the constraints of the canvas. The artist's use of color was nothing short of a symphony, with each stroke harmonizing to create a visual melody that resonated and echoed. It reminded him of intricate musical compositions.

He examined the irises, the purples, reminiscent of twilight, which varied from deep indigos to soft lavender, creating a sense of depth within the petals. The blues, like a clear sky, echoed the tranquility of nature, while the dark greens whispered of meadows and foliage. The thick brushstrokes brought the flowers to life, like breathing water, capturing the gushing waves and subtle ripples of each petal.

He felt like he could almost feel the velvety softness of the petals under his fingertips. The young man became dizzy from the movement within the painting. He could almost hear the rustle of leaves and petals, as if a gentle breeze had swept through the canvas.

He realized that beyond the colors, textures, and brushwork, the artist had poured his own emotions into the canvas, and the observer could suddenly "see" the irises—as if from the artist's eyes. It was as if he had climbed into another person's skin.

He had never seen such paintings. The paintings in his grandparents' house were always exact, lifelike, like painted photographs. But here there was something different, almost mad.

Tears welled up in the young man's eyes as he realized the colors on the canvas weren't just reflections; they were emotions, vivid and raw, mirroring the feelings that a sunrise stirred within him.

He disappeared into the painting; the museum was gone, he himself was gone, and he was the painting itself — the sunrise itself, moving eternally, stirring, turning, reflecting and glistening in the water below. The painting was moving—it was alive.

The young man was no longer a survivor of war, a desperate, lonely soul searching for meaning; he was now the sun, the water, the freewheeling boats, the fog, and the mist and the dampness of a cold morning.

This sunrise awoke something deep inside him, a feeling of new beginnings, of being alive, privileged to experience life again.

He stood there, ethereal, beside the painting. His legs were grounded, yet his presence stretched beyond, timeless and omnipresent. His body forgotten, breaths a distant memory. He embodied the soft waves, the sky's reflection, a kaleidoscope of evolving colors. Changing, yet constant. Moving, yet captured. Soaring, endlessly soaring.

The colors were *in* him; he did not know he was not one with them. He did not know he was not flying.

III

The young man left the museum, dazed.

He was drunk on the art he had seen. He levitated out of the small museum, soared through the cobblestone streets, glided past the markets, flew over the gardens, floated in the fountains, swept by the Eiffel Tower, sailed over the Luxembourg gardens, and then landed by the small street, flying into the old mama's apartment.

When the old mama opened the door and saw the red, teary eyes of the young man, she was frightened. "Did someone hit you?"

He shook his head, unable to speak, his mind still enchanted by the art. *The beauty.*

She was alarmed. *Was the young man drunk?* "What happened to you?"

He wanted to explain it all, but it was embarrassingly plain how inadequate language was. *How could he explain that for the first time in his life he had disappeared inside a work of art?* It was music itself. The notes of the colors and rhythm brushstrokes played in his mind. He could find beauty everywhere in the apartment, in the patterns of the cushions of the divan, in the velvet of the armchair, in the spines of the books on which titles were written like notes on a musical sheet — beauty in the eyes of the old mama.

The old mama's eyes suddenly shone. "Impressionism?"

The young man's eyes shone back.

She hugged him, squeezed his arms, and then pulled him away, staring at him as if she wanted to get some of the drug he had inhaled herself, and wanted to rub in the perfume emanating from his swollen heart. "Tell, tell! Dire!" she begged. "You be my eyes, what did you see?"

The young man was at a loss for words. *How could he even begin?* He remembered the flowers. The sunflowers. The irises. "Irises," he finally whispered in Yiddish.

She shook him violently. "Van Gogh!" she exclaimed. "Sunflowers?"

He nodded, tears washing his eyes.

"Tell!" she begged again, helpless, wishing to enter his mind.

What was there to tell? Of the daring brushstrokes, the violence, the loud vision, the painful, heart-aching celebration of life itself?

She saw his lips moving, but no sound left his mouth. "Yes," she said. "I know. I understand. Many do not, but I--do."

She knew she should feed him, but she was too selfish at that moment, not wanting to step away. She remembered herself on her wedding night, all the young unmarried bachelorettes coming to receive her blessing. Now this young man in her parlor was the one betrothed, the one to give his blessing, having been initiated into the intimate, penetrating power of art. He was still young, raw, uncynical, unencumbered by experience.

She gazed deeply into his eyes, and through him, she was suddenly in the museum again, her heart palpitating, fifty years younger, the world still hopeful, people still kind.

"Boats," he said, closing his eyes, seeing the sunrise. "Sun."

"Monet?" whispered the old mama in reverence.

"Orange, and turquoise, and purple...violet purple..."

"Lavender," she said, "lilac?"

"All the colors in the world," he whispered in the old language.

Her hand squeezed his with childlike awe.

"An invitation..."

She hung on his every word, thirsty. Waiting. When nothing came forth, she asked, "An invitation...?"

He tried to verbalize, forcing himself to contain the uncontainable. "An invitation to... appreciate... the beauty in the ordinary."

A poet! She mulled his words, these cherished diamonds. "The beauty in the ordinary!"

He looked abashed. "Did I lose my mind?"

She pronounced dramatically, "Did you *lose* your mind?" She pressed her hand on his chest. "You found your heart!" She smiled, her silver teeth shining again.

The young man felt embarrassed by the gush of emotions. And the apartment suddenly seemed no longer glowing, but small and narrow and bleak and stuffy, and the lady was old and her breath smelled unpleasant.

The old mama studied his eyes, seeing the young man was no longer in heaven. He seemed uncomfortable. She pulled back, adjusted her headscarf. "You must be hungry. I will get you soup."

Was he hungry? He did not even know what he felt, although he had not eaten since the morning. How did the time go so fast? The sun was setting outside. How long had he been gone? The day was gone in an instant, like the wisps of a sweet dream.

Later, he ate quietly. He could not bring himself to talk. The colors were still overloading his mind, popping on the plates, glistening when he closed his eyes.

He finished all the food, and the old mama seemed to fill up with pride like a victorious general surveying a conquered battlefield, her contentment radiating like a warm glow in the aftermath of a culinary triumph.

She refused help in the kitchen.

The young man took the dictionary and repeated the thirty words from the previous days. He began memorizing new words, but his mind was still focused on recalling sunrises, sunsets, swirling sunflowers, and irises.

He blinked painstakingly and forced himself to concentrate on vocabulary. Rather than flower gardens, he saw petals of words unfolding in vibrant hues of reds and oranges, creating a yellow wheat field of knowledge, the words swaying like golden stalks under the breeze of blue skies. He tried plucking words and savoring them. But instead he saw dancing almond blossoms, dark green cypresses, and words mixing into one another in violet brushstrokes. Each word had its own color.

A knock on the door rattled him.

The money changer came in and sat down, commending the young man on his studies, shouting to his mama about food, eating, then counting his money.

The young man tried to concentrate on the words, but could not stop glancing at the money changer who was unnecessarily adding the sums of money in long rows.

For no good reason, the young man stared at the moneychanger's paper and pen—rather than at his dictionary. He calculated the currencies. Then the young man made a terrible mistake. He forgot his grandmother's maxim that "silence is a wisdom that few people exercise." He also forgot his grandfather's warning: "People are most sensitive about their money and their wives."

The young man glanced at the numbers. He saw the moneychanger was trying to add them together, one by one. The moneychanger drew a line over each number he had counted.

The young man looked at the numbers. When he added them in his head for each row, altogether there were 257 francs, 303 reichsmarks, 32,550 pesetas, and 144 zloty.

The moneychanger was slowly calculating the francs, painstakingly adding them, and finally writing 257.

The young man said, "303 reichsmarks, 32,550 pesetas, and 144 zloty."

The moneychanger turned to him. And the young man immediately knew he had made a mistake.

Chapter 19: Darkness

Poland, 1943

Age 15

"I'm sorry. We cannot," said the maid's husband.

The boy searched for hesitancy in the husband's eyes. He saw none.

Outside, the wind howled.

The maid hurried to interject. "Now-now, this is definitely something we did not *expect*, having you as… as… company, but we are very pleased—very pleased—to have you here." Her smile turned into a glare as she looked at her husband and turned the stove heat back on under the pot.

"The soup will be ready soon," she said and took out four bowls, placing them on the table. She opened the pantry, and pulled a single, precious apple, and placed it on the table as well. She looked at the seamstress. "Please, help yourselves." She came to her husband and took his arm, walking into the small bedroom and shutting the door behind.

In the kitchen, the boy could hear the maid and her husband arguing in the bedroom. "This is madness!" the husband exclaimed. "You'll get all of us killed."

"But what do you expect me to do? Throw them out into the night? Either they'll freeze to death, or get caught…"

"Caught!" the husband said, "Here we'll all get caught!"

In the kitchen, the boy looked down at his shoes. *The husband was right.*

The maid protested, "But I haven't seen any soldiers around recently."

"Of course not, but now that they have cleared them all out and sent them away, of course they will be looking for any who managed to escape!" the husband retorted.

In the kitchen the four people gave one another a knowing look. They knew the man of the house would win, and soon they would find themselves back out in the cold. The uncle looked at his nephew, and then at the lawyer and his wife. The soup was not yet hot, but he began pouring it into the bowls. "We had better enjoy the heat while we are here."

The boy looked at the strangers. The lawyer looked healthy, but his wife did not. She was emaciated, and she slurped the soup without any etiquette, as if she had not eaten in days.

The boy was torn between the relief of reuniting with his uncle and the lingering anxiety about the uncertainty that lay ahead. Three new people made the situation much more complicated.

He wished for the warmth and privacy of his hiding place in the attic.

His uncle, sensing the boy's distress, placed a reassuring hand on his shoulder.

The boy heard the husband and the maid arguing in the room. He knew that they would all be out in the forest soon. Had he been here alone, he would have had a better chance of staying. The boy glanced over at the lawyer and his wife and for a moment felt a flash of anger toward them.

They ate their soup in silence. From the bedroom, the husband's panicked voice was loud and clear. "They hung the entire family—of that village doctor no less—for hiding one woman! What do you think they would do to us? We have *four* Jews!"

The boy drank the soup. *When would be the next time he'd have food?* He looked at his uncle and thought of his own parents. He wanted to ask about them; maybe his uncle knew something, but the boy feared the answer.

From the bedroom, they could hear the maid crying. "I cannot, I cannot put them out! I'd rather die…"

A long silence ensued. The lawyer reached for the apple at the center of the table. He pulled out a small knife from his pocket and began slicing the fruit into pieces.

The boy stared at the apple.

The lawyer slid a slice of apple toward the boy, saying nothing. The lawyer continued to slide other pieces to his wife and to the uncle. The boy took a bite. Its precious sweetness lingered in his mouth, as if there was no war, no shortage.

The maid continued arguing with her husband in the bedroom. "This is not how we, a God-fearing family, should act!"

A long moment later, the maid and her husband came out of their bedroom.

The maid looked down, blinking, her eyes red.

The boy braced himself and closed his eyes, scared to hear the anticipated verdict.

"You can stay," the husband said, resigned.

Everyone looked at him in amazement.

"But" he added, "not here."

Chapter 20: Light

Paris, 1945

Age 17

"What did you say?" asked the moneychanger, bewildered.

The young man tried to say, "Nevermind."

The moneychanger stared at the young man, then at his calculations, then at the piles of bills in front of him on the lounge table. He turned his attention to the young man again, writing what he had said. "303 reichsmarks, 32,000 pesetas? And how much zloty?"

The young man had hoped the moneychanger's knowledge of Yiddish was more limited. "144 zloty. And 303 reichsmarks, 32,550 pesetas."

The moneychanger wrote it down, his eyes distrustful. The young man suddenly feared the unknown temperament of the moneychanger.

The moneychanger spoke to himself in French, "Impossible," and went on to slowly total each currency. When he finished calculating the reichsmarks he saw, to his amazement, there were indeed 303. He gasped.

Next, the moneychanger calculated the pesetas.

The young man held on to the dictionary as if it were a railing on a boat in a stormy sea. Would he still be welcome to stay the night? What if this man wanted him out? What if he threw him out the door right now? Where would he go?

The young man thought of his valise near the door and his coat in the mahogany wardrobe. He thought of finding a place in the Parisian evening. He tried to remember how many francs he had left.

The moneychanger finished calculating. *Indeed, 32,550!*

The young man saw the moneychanger write down the sum he had mentioned. The moneychanger proceeded to count the sum of zloty.

In the young man's mind, his grandfather was snorting. "Never, ever, speak to men about their money or their wives." His grandmother stood still. "Sometimes it is better to keep quiet."

The moneychanger finished and the sum of the zloty emerged.

"Mama! Mama!" The moneychanger exclaimed.

The old mama rushed out of the kitchen. "What, what is it?" she replied.

The moneychanger pointed at the young man.

The old mama looked nervous. "What? What did he do wrong?"

The young man did not have to understand French to understand the moneychanger's excited, stuttered speech. "He…should not…be here."

CHAPTER 21: DARKNESS

POLAND, 1943

AGE 15

I

The boy did not want to leave the cabin.

He exited the cabin with a heavy heart as the husband quickly shut the door in his face. The cold night air slapped his face. Eyes seemed to peer from the dark woods.

He hurried to follow the lawyer and his wife, who walked in the snow around the cabin, following the uncle.

The snow cracked under his feet like thunder.

The uncle led them around to the back of the cabin, where he spotted the cellar door, covered in snow. The latch was unlocked.

As the uncle opened the door, the boy realized he had to relieve himself. "One moment, uncle," he whispered, and ran behind the trees, peeing quickly, a faint hiss accompanying the steam rising from the snow. He buttoned his pants and hurried to the cellar. His uncle glared at him.

The boy descended into the dark cellar. The uncle took his coat off and walked back, sweeping his coat back and forth on the snow to erase the footsteps. He came down the stairs and closed the cellar door behind him. The boy stumbled into the cramped, musty, sour-smelling, potato cellar. Although he was not particularly tall, he had to slouch to not hit the ceiling.

Potatoes covered the entire room from corner to corner, like large pebbles. He stumbled on a shovel—or a rake—that fell down, making a terrible noise.

He sat down on the potatoes.

The boy's mind raced as he remembered specters of soldiers methodically combing through each apartment, each building for any hiders, leaving no corner unsearched.

He could almost hear the panicked cries of families as they were forcibly ejected from their homes, the gunshots, the sharp crack of whips driving them forward into the relentless march towards the train platform.

Were his parents found too? Was his sister with them?

The boy could barely rest. The potatoes weren't comfortable enough to lay on. Each passing hour felt like an eternity as the boy tossed and turned.

In the presence of the unfamiliar figures, the boy felt an acute sense of unease. They served as a stark reminder of the absence of his own family.

Wasn't it only two nights ago he slept in the same room as his family in the run-down rented apartment in the enclosure?

Now they were all taken by the trains.

With each rustle of the wind outside, the boy could not help but imagine the worst—the soldiers finding him.

The silence was abruptly shattered by the sound of human footsteps. The steps became louder. Panic surged through him like a tidal wave. *They were found.*

The four figures held their breaths as the steps in the snow grew nearer.

The boy huddled closer to the wall, knowing that he could not hide. There was nowhere else to go.

The handle of the cellar door slowly turned.

In the potato cellar the four people pressed themselves into the damp walls, unsure who was coming. When the door opened, they saw the silhouette of the maid's husband in the early morning sky.

He raised a pointed finger toward the uncle and motioned for him to come out of the cellar.

The lawyer stood up as well, but the maid's husband shook his head and cut the air with a flattened palm: only the uncle was summoned.

The boy was alarmed. He did not want to remain in the potato cellar with these strangers. He stood up, hitting his head against the low beam of the potato cellar.

Wincing at the pain, he held his head as he hurried to follow his uncle. As he scrambled out into the snow, his head throbbed with every movement he made.

The husband looked at the boy emerging and shook his head disapprovingly. He walked quickly to the cabin.

The uncle closed the cellar door behind the boy quietly, and then hurried to the cabin, the boy running closely behind him.

The husband held the cabin door open for them as they entered. He stuck his head outside to make sure no one had seen them, and then locked the door. "What are your plans?"

The boy looked at his uncle. It was blessedly warm in the dimly lit kitchen.

The uncle said, "We'll walk to the bridge, and possibly sneak underneath, as we might find some boatman who'll hopefully help us across the river..."

The husband groaned beneath his mustache. "And then what?"

"We'll make our way east. We'll move at night and hide during the day."

"Nonsense," the husband moaned, "you'll be caught."

The boy looked down at his leg, which had begun to shake. *The husband was right.* There was no way one person, let alone four, could avoid the soldiers without being exposed.

The husband growled to himself. "What a mess…"

The uncle stared at the floor. "We thank you very much for letting us hide, but we do not wish to endanger you and your family any longer…"

The husband interjected. "Enough!"

Silence enveloped the kitchen. The husband let out a long sigh. "The soldiers are everywhere! You'd barely make it to the river, let alone cross it!" He inhaled deeply. "And even if you did, traveling to the eastern border takes weeks…" He stared at the uncle. "Where is your wife?"

"They took her," the uncle said, barely making a sound, "and our daughter, too."

The boy felt a lump forming in his throat as he thought of his aunt and cousin, and then of his own family. He could smell his mother's perfume, lingering on her sweater as she kissed his forehead two days earlier.

The husband shook his head and stood up. "You will need to hide."

The uncle sat up. "I'm an engineer. If we could dig a hole under the floor, somewhere—"

"Too dangerous!"

The uncle continued. "If we dig under one of the corners of the cabin, say, in the bedroom, a small hole, the depth of a person sitting and the length of a person lying, then—"

"The soldiers will tap on every floorboard," the husband said. "They will hear that hollowness."

"Not if the spot is unavailable."

"Unavailable?"

The uncle's eyes shone. "If the pit is under the bed, knocking near the bed will produce no sound… and assuming they don't move the bed…"

"Too many assumptions!"

"And even if they move the bed, I can cut the floorboards

precisely, not revealing the seam…."

The husband shook his head adamantly, his fingers stroking his mustache. They were talking too much. He wanted the uncle and the boy out before the children woke up.

He knew children could be unreliable and irresponsible. They could go to school and tell their classmates, who could then tell their parents. Then the soldiers would come and hang the entire family for display in the village square.

Dawn appeared through the kitchen's window behind the curtain. "Let me think about it," the husband said. "I have to go to the factory soon. Stay in the potato cellar until the evening. Then we'll talk again."

The boy thought it was absurd to wait. It was better than being thrown out into the forest again, but it was still too dangerous to stay in the potato cellar. Was there no other option? Why could they not be admitted into the cabin?

The husband reached for the door, indicating the conversation was over. "If they find you, you never spoke to me. You don't know who we are."

"Of course," said the uncle. The boy nodded in agreement.

As an afterthought, the husband took two slices of bread from the pantry and gave them to the boy.

The uncle bowed his head in appreciation.

The husband opened the door and looked in both directions to make sure it was safe for them to leave the cabin. "Quickly!"

Chapter 22: Light

Paris, 1945

Age 17

I

The old mama stared at her son. Rarely had she seen him so distraught.

The moneychanger repeated, "He does not belong here!"

"*Ce qui s'est passé?*" the old mama asked, glancing at the young man worriedly.

The young man tried to disappear inside the dictionary.

"I—I was counting my money," the money changer said, "like—like usual, every row, and he, from there." He pointed at the young man on the armchair. "Like that! Like that!"

I am a fool, thought the young man. Now he was about to lose the only place in which he felt at home since the beginning of the war.

The moneychanger flanked his sheet of calculations, "Mama! He is a—a—genius!"

The old mama was confused and worried her son was not feeling well. What was he saying? What was he blaming the young man for? And what was this talk of genius, about a young man whose knowledge of French was non-existent and knowledge of the ways of the world even less?

The young man was not sure whether what was happening was good or bad. Should he have not undermined the moneychanger?

Should he have kept his nose to himself? His grandmother used to say, "Talking comes by nature, but silence comes by wisdom." Should he have not bothered the moneychanger? He regretted opening his mouth at all.

"See here, Mama," the moneychanger said, wiping sweat off his forehead. "I wrote these numbers down, well, like I always do." He pointed at the young man. "And he instantaneously tallied them up! He did the figures in his head!"

The old mama shook her head. "Really?"

She hit her son on the shoulder, motioning for him to move over. Then she sat down on the divan, trying to conceal the pain in her hip as she sat. She flipped the paper over to the blank side. She wrote some numbers down. Then she looked at the young man.

The young man spoke sheepishly. "205."

She raised her eyebrows then wrote some more numbers.

He swallowed. "12,458."

She chuckled, telling her son, "Now we need to check if he's right…"

The whole evening passed that way. Together they verified each of the young man's answers.

"Were you," the old mama asked in Yiddish, "some prodigy child?"

The young man laughed. "No, on the contrary! Very dreamy, not good in school, not good in math…I liked poetry. Music maybe."

"So." Her jaw dropped a little. "How?"

The young man looked at her and her eager son. "I was lucky…I got some free private lessons…and I couldn't run away."

The moneychanger walked around the apartment's parlor. "Mama," he said, "he does not belong here! He belongs in university, in the Sorbonne, no less!"

The old mama looked at her excited son pacing.

"With such a mind! He can be a… number person, math—professor!"

The old mama turned to the young man who seemed quite uncomfortable. "Have you finished high school?"

"Only some," he said and looked down at his fingers holding the dictionary. "The war…"

"Alright. It is decided." She turned to her son and spoke in French. "Tomorrow you take him to the Sorbonne and you find out what and where and who and how and when and how much."

"But Mama, I need to work!"

"Hush it! You're married to your work!"

Her son began protesting, but then his old mama's face suddenly contorted. "See him as your brother! Had your brother not—"

The young man noticed the old mama and her son both became quiet. What were they saying?

The old mama had a stern look on her face, and she blinked repeatedly, her lip quivering.

"Alright, mama."

"Now come here," the old mama said. Her son leaned forward, and she gave him a series of kisses on both cheeks. "You are my good boy! "

In the morning the young man was puzzled to see that the moneychanger did not leave the apartment. He wore a suit that was a little too small on him. He declared to the awakening young man, "Today, you, university!"

The old mama entered the parlor and placed a tray of casserole on the lounge table. "Eat and be strong, feed that brain of yours!"

The old mama and the moneychanger looked at the young man while he was eating, as if he was a monkey in a zoo. The moneychanger whispered to his mother, "Genius!"

"Hush. We'll see what they say."

The facade of the University of Paris, the revered Sorbonne, was adorned with an array of sculptures, silent guardians of intellectual pursuits.

University students and teachers hurried back and forth, climbing the imposing staircase. A marble sculpture loomed with a commanding presence, draped in a robe, holding an open book. The entire building was adorned with sculptures holding scientific instruments, quills, and scrolls.

Above the intricate pageant of sculptures, there was a giant dome, and above it, a tower. The young man's heart pounded in his chest. Everything evoked a sense of reverence and awe, as if the very stone pulsed with the heartbeat of academic fervor.

As the young man lowered his gaze and raised his head above, he saw students hurrying inside. He pulled on the moneychanger's sleeve, wanting to climb the entrance stairs, too. He felt he was on the threshold of a new phase in life, one full of promises. He wished to climb those stairs more than anything.

The moneychanger asked one student, and they were directed

into the building. The young man followed him as they climbed the stairs and entered a hall.

The young man could barely take in the painted ceilings, grand ornamented walls, and a myriad of sculptures. The echoes of the steps and chatter reverberated throughout the imposing hall. Busts of Descartes, Rousseau, and Voltaire stared at him, daring him, challenging him.

The moneychanger finally found the admission office. He spoke to the secretary with much enthusiasm, and then to the admission Dean. The young man felt embarrassed hearing the word *"Génie"* thrown around, which he now understood to be "Genius."

An hour later, the boy followed the moneychanger to a giant library, a hall that made the young man stop in his tracks. This dwarfed his grandparents' library. The scent of aged paper and leather-bound volumes permeated the air.

He wanted to open all the books. He wanted a magic power by which he could touch a book with his finger and gain all its knowledge.

He saw the money changer talking to the librarian and handing him a note from the admission office. The librarian stood up, taking a pile of papers—a test—and led the young man to a small room.

The moneychanger hurried to follow them, but the librarian closed the door.

The young man looked down at the paper. It was all in French.

He understood nothing. His heart sank.

CHAPTER 23: DARKNESS

POLAND, 1943

AGE 15

The uncle and the boy hurried back to the potato cellar. The uncle shed his coat and retraced their steps, pulling the coat over the snow to erase them, leaving no trace of their presence behind.

The boy despised the very idea of entering the potato cellar. Previously, their refuge had been confined to the safety of the night, but now the stakes were raised even more; they were forced to hide in broad daylight.

If the soldiers came, this cellar would be their first target. The thought of the soldiers and their German Shepherds trained to detect human flesh sent shivers down his spine.

The faint light of dawn seeped through the thin cracks of the cellar door.

The boy's mind was consumed by thoughts of their impending fate. The memory of the butcher, the echoing gunshots. He knew with a sinking certainty that the soldiers were on their way, closing in to find him, to snuff out his life just as they had done to his cousin, their neighbor, the baker's son, and so many others in the ghetto.

The uncle whispered to the lawyer and his wife that they would stay for one day.

No one wanted to ask what they would do at night—if they even made it until nighttime.

The uncle gave the couple one piece of bread and split the other with his nephew.

The boy ate his bread slowly, trying to make each bite last as long as possible. He noticed that the seamstress had eaten her entire piece and was now licking the crumbs off her fingers.

Seeing this, he stopped chewing. The sight of her delicate, slender fingers brushing against her lips stirred something deep within him. Her hand, pale and gentle, evoked the softness of flowers blooming in a meadow. He had long forgotten the beauty of well-cared-for hands, as his own were marred by the grime of ghetto labor and the constant sting of bricks. She brought a whisper of a past he had nearly erased from memory—of life before the war. Only now did he notice how beautiful she was.

He looked at the remaining piece of bread in his hand.

The boy crawled a little closer to the seamstress. He lay the piece of bread on a potato next to her, and made sure she saw it.

She glanced at him, and then at the bread, and then at him again.

He nodded back at her, assuring her the slice of bread was hers to have. He then hurried to turn away, thinking of his grandmother and her many lessons, not to glee over another's suffering. He felt strangely full as he heard the seamstress chewing the last piece of bread.

A few minutes later, the lawyer had closed his eyes to rest atop the potatoes. The uncle was tinkering quietly with the tools near the cellar's stairs.

Hours later they heard steps. The boy tensed, but was relieved when the maid's husband opened the cellar door and said, "It's me." He pointed at the uncle. "Wait two minutes, then come inside."

The uncle nodded.

The boy crawled on the stone-like potatoes to be next to his uncle.

A minute later, the uncle hurried outside. The boy followed. The uncle looked at him but said nothing. The uncle closed the cellar door behind them. They walked quickly on the crunching snow into the cabin. The uncle did not wipe their steps behind them.

As they entered, the maid closed the cabin door quickly and replaced the latch. The door to the children's room was closed. The husband motioned to the bedroom.

They stood in the bedroom, the maid, her husband, the uncle and the boy. The husband said; "The children mustn't hear. They are too young to trust with such a secret, and may let something slip, even accidentally."

"Absolutely," the uncle affirmed.

The husband shifted uncomfortably, glancing between the boy and the uncle. "In this hole you are proposing to dig, how would you get any air?"

The boy noticed that his uncle suddenly came to life. He, too, was happy to see that the husband was not ruling out the possibility of them hiding inside the cabin.

"We will breathe fine," said the uncle.

The maid interjected. "But how, under the floorboards, and with a pile of clothes on top of you," the husband shook his head, "and with four of you there! Surely you would suffocate…"

"I did think about that," whispered the uncle. "I found in the cellar a metal pipe," he gestured with his hands to indicate it being long.

"We can run it all the way from the hiding pit through a small tunnel out to the garden. It will stick out from the ground. That way we'd have plenty of air."

The boy's mind raced.

The husband groaned. "And where would we dump the soil, if we dig? Everyone is looking for signs of digging these days; we cannot get rid of it easily…"

The maid suddenly shouted, "We could throw it into the old well!"

"Hush!" Her husband scoffed at her, "You'll wake the children!"

Undeterred, she repeated in a whisper, "There is a well on the edge of the property, an old one.”

The uncle raised his eyebrows knowingly. He remembered that well, as the entire family used to spend summer vacations in this very cabin and the cabins down the hill bordering the village.

The husband shook his head. “So dangerous…”

The maid said adamantly, “Dangerous or not, it is more dangerous for them out there.” She pointed outside. “At least this can give them a chance.”

The boy felt a surge of gratitude toward the maid.

The bedroom door creaked open, and the middle daughter’s head peeked in. “Mamma?”

CHAPTER 24: LIGHT

PARIS, 1945

AGE 17

I

The young man began trying to read the test. He could not understand the instructions, as it was all in French.

Outside the small room, he saw the moneychanger, standing, waiting,. The librarian was busy at his desk.

The young man knew he had to deliver, had to perform. He tried reading, vocalizing the words. He tried to recall some of the Latin he had studied in elementary school. But that was years ago, before the war started. It felt like centuries ago.

Many sentences were written — essay forms, articles, and questions — leaving room for answers. He did not know how to begin. He felt helpless.

The words on the paper looked like unfamiliar patterns, their meanings elusive. Each sentence was a puzzle, and he struggled to put the fragments together.

The young man flipped through the pages, one page after another, of the familiar yet illegible French writing, with its weird letters.

All the letters had funny hats, é, è, ê, ë—each letter more peculiar than the last, like a carnival of linguistic acrobats.

The young man sat there, desperately trying to decipher a language that seemed more like an elaborate secret code than a means of communication.

His palms and forehead were beaded with sweat.

He was flipping through the pages when he suddenly saw them—

His friends. For so many months of hiding, he had been drawing them in his mind. Equations. Numbers. There was such beauty in seeing them so majestically displayed. Each symbol dominated the small space it took on the page; each digit had its unique place, its order, its role in the greater function.

Exponents, inequalities, fractions, integers, sequences. Like a bull seeing red, he attacked one equation after another.

When he was done, he stared at all the many empty pages of French language and agonized over not understanding anything. This was his chance, and he'd squandered it.

In the evening, the young man was in a foul mood. He was not hungry. He wanted to punish himself by trying to memorize the entire dictionary at once.

The moneychanger counted his money and evaded his mother's questions regarding the exam and admission to the university.

The old mama clasped her hands together and prayed for the young man. He would be devastated if he could not start university.

Someone knocked at the door.

The old mama looked up to the heavens in careful gratitude as she shuffled to the door.

"Who is it?"

Chapter 25: Darkness

Poland, 1943

Age 15

I

"Mamma?" the teenage daughter asked, looking at the uncle and at the boy.

The maid, her husband, the uncle and the boy all turned to look at the teenage daughter, who was standing there, mouth agape.

The maid's jaw dropped, her skin turning pale instantly. The air seemed to thicken with apprehension as it became clear their plan would no longer be a secret. Time seemed to stand still as they froze, their hearts pounding in their chests.

The teenage daughter knew the boy and the uncle very well. They were from the employer's large family—the owners of their cabin, of all the cabins on the hill. Didn't the new laws prohibit them from exiting the ghetto?

What were her parents doing? Did they forget what happened to the doctor's family who helped and hid someone in their house?

The husband barked, "Go straight to your room!"

The maid said, "Now-now, it is alright. We have nothing to hide from our own children. We have educated her. It's okay. You can come in."

The teenage daughter walked into the room hesitantly, slowly, and into her mother's embrace.

The boy looked down, embarrassed about being an unwelcome

guest. He heard a quiet creak of a floorboard and saw the other two sisters peering into the bedroom.

The maid stood up and said, "Come in, you two."

Hesitantly, the two older sisters came into the bedroom. "Did you swallow your tongue?" the maid asked, and then whispered, "Good evening!"

"Good evening," the girls hurried to say, slightly bowing their heads.

"Good evening," the uncle answered, and the boy mumbled as well. He knew the girls very well. He was the landlord's grandson. They looked up to him. He was the only one who snuck chocolates out of the kitchen for the maids' daughters.

He stared at the floor. Now the roles were reversed. Now, he and his uncle were begging for their lives.

The maid looked at her husband, as if summoning him up for the challenge. Then, seeing he said nothing, she whispered in pride, raising her chin. "You remember the son of the landlady who in her *generosity* gave us this home to live in…?"

The girls all nodded.

"Well, he and his nephew…" she looked at the boy and inhaled, her chest rising proudly, "In life, there are times we are to be helped, and there are times we are to help. Now we are called upon to help. As one family."

The three daughters looked at their mother, not understanding.

The maid said, "We are going to help hide these good people, and their two friends, whatever happens."

The older daughter gasped, "But, Mamma, the soldiers, they are Jews—"

The maid turned her hands into fists. "I will hear no fear in this house! We are God-fearing people! We need fear none but God, you hear me?"

The eldest daughter bowed her head. "Yes, Mamma."

The maid walked into the tiny bedroom, where much of the space was dominated by the bed. She gently nudged her eldest daughter's chin, lifting her head gently. "You are all mature. And bright. Your younger siblings are still young. They should not hear a word of what is going on here. But I see you three as mature ladies."

Her gaze was firm yet tender as she imparted the weight of her words. "We need to hide them, as we know that if the roles were reversed, they would hide us. Is that not true?" She turned to the boy and his uncle.

"Absolutely," the uncle affirmed.

The boy nodded, although he was not so certain.

The maid continued. "We will hide them. Our fates are one. If something happens to them, it shall happen to us all."

She took a breath. "There are two more people, who are hiding in the potato cellar now."

"Mamma!" gasped the middle daughter.

The husband shook his head at his wife, disapproving of her divulging more information.

The maid seemed resolved. "With the help of our respectable guest," she looked at the uncle, "we are going to build a safer cellar, so that we can hide them safely."

"Mamma!" the youngest of the daughters cried. "But if we are found out—"

The eldest daughter nodded, and glared at the youngest sister.

The maid spoke firmly. "The blessing of the Lord is on this house. We will be safe. We will show them the blessing. We will be their blessing."

The maid continued, her voice resolute. "This should remain our secret. Not a word to the little ones. They are not yet ready to comprehend the danger. And this must remain a secret from your friends, from everyone."

"Even from the priest?" asked the little daughter.

"Even from our priest," answered the maid.

Silence followed. The boy wanted to disappear. He did not want to be the source of this family conflict.

The eldest daughter whispered. "We understand, Mamma. We

will assist you and Papa in any way we can."

The youngest daughter raised her chin, stretching her shoulders backward.

The maid said to them, "Good thing you woke up. We need your help." She turned to her husband.

The husband looked at her, not understanding. "What? Now?"

"Now," she said.

"Yes, now," the maid said, looking at her husband in the bedroom.

The boy, the uncle, and the three daughters were all looking at him.

The maid's husband shook his head and muttered, "Now? Are you crazy? Sawing the wooden floor? It will make so much noise… Too dangerous!"

The maid frowned. "Well when do you think is a better time? During the day when that old widow comes to sniff around? Or when that nosy lumberjack roams around? We have to do it now."

The boy was surprised by her determination. In his heart, he blessed her for her courage.

The husband walked about in the small crowded bedroom, assessing the danger they were in.

The boy thought that the husband seemed like a caged lion. He looked at the three daughters all standing in a row. He looked at the maid who was standing, her hands folded on her chest, awaiting her husband's words.

The uncle said nothing.

Finally, her husband spoke. "We will need tools. I will fetch them from the shed myself. We will be making noise. We must have an explanation for the noise in case someone comes. We will need to bring some logs to explain that we were chopping the logs."

The boy looked at the husband. He bit his lip, touched by the family's determination to help.

The husband continued. "We will need someone to warn us on the road leading to the forest, as well as on the other side of the house by the well. We will need you to take turns."

"Outside, Papa?" the middle girl gasped.

The maid said, "Now-now, you will dress warmly, and I will be there too. We will take turns guarding." She looked at the eldest daughter.

The oldest girl nodded in affirmation, understanding the gravity of her role. The younger sisters, though still concerned, mirrored their elder sister's determination.

The maid cast a reassuring glance at them, pleased with their maturity.

The husband looked at the uncle and the boy. "If anyone comes, you will jump out this window and run into the woods. Clear?"

The uncle consented. "Absolutely."

The boy eagerly shook his head.

The maid said, "And we need a signal in case of danger."

The youngest chimed in, "Like a whistle, Papa?"

The husband agreed absentmindedly.

The maid smiled, nodding approvingly. "That's a good idea, dear."

The room, once filled with uncertainty, now brimmed with a collective spirit, united in the face of the imminent danger that loomed over them all.

The middle daughter said, "Someone will need to stay with the little ones in case they wake up."

The maid said, "Yes. We will take turns. And if they wake up we need to make sure they know everything is alright. Papa is chopping wood, that's all."

The maid looked at her eldest daughter and said, "Help your younger sisters to bundle up. I don't want any runny noses." She, herself, opened her wardrobe.

The husband looked at the three daughters disappearing into their room. He said, "I'll bring the tools from the shed." And to himself he mumbled, "And so help us God."

III

In the depth of the night, the little cabin on the hill was abuzz. Apart from the toddler boy and baby girl, the whole family was on their feet.

In the kitchen, the maid, casting one last glance at her daughters, spoke with a blend of maternal concern and resilience. "Stay alert, and keep an eye on the surroundings. Whistle if you see or hear anyone approaching."

The girls stepped outside, the cold wind slapping their faces. The oldest daughter took the main road leading toward the village. The middle daughter took the other side of the road, toward the river. The youngest daughter stood behind the house, in the forest, near the old unused well.

The youngest sister saw her breath form a visible mist as she took her position. The dark night was frightening.

The moon barely glowed, casting shadows that danced, constantly keeping the youngest sister on her toes. One mistaken shadow of a branch could mean life or death. She shivered, partly from the biting cold and partly from the weight of the responsibility.

As she strained her senses to catch any sign of danger, the woods beyond her seemed to hold secrets, their rustlings and murmurs echoing through the stillness. A gust of wind carried a distant howl that made her shiver.

Inside, the maid was watching the children's room while also arranging buckets and assisting her husband, the uncle, and the boy. The small bedroom became a mess, and she took things out into the kitchen.

Pots and pans clattered as she hastily cleared the cluttered countertops, making space for the buckets she had brought in.

As the uncle began sawing, she hurried to close the bedroom door, the sound unreasonably loud. *What were they doing? Were they crazy?*

Was she herself crazy to allow this? The thought of her

daughters outside looking for danger scared her.

The sound of sawing was unbearably loud, and indeed the little ones soon awoke from the noise. Immediately, she rushed to their sides. With a gentle touch, she knelt beside their beds, brushing a wisp of hair from her toddler son. She whispered, "Papa is cutting lumber, go back to sleep."

The eldest daughter was by the road, wrapped in layers against the biting cold. The snow covered the ground below her feet, and the trees blew with the wind. The sound of dogs barking in the distance sent chills down the girl's back.

The middle sister was on the other side, pacing back and forth on the horizon as the road took a turn, her silhouette illuminated by the weak moon.

By the old well, near the woods behind the house, the youngest daughter halted. Beneath the usual symphony, she detected an unfamiliar noise—a faint crunching of snow that did not match the rhythm of the wind.

Her heart quickened as she strained to discern the source, breath caught in anticipation. *Why was their mother putting them in this situation? All of them could get killed for this!* Why did she have to be the one stuck in the cold outside when the boy and the uncle got to be inside? It wasn't fair! She deserved to be in her warm bed, fast asleep.

She cast a quick glance back at the cabin, wondering if she should alert the others. No one was coming. She had to decide for herself.

The dim light seeping through the curtains revealed the silhouettes of her father and the uncle, the bed having been lifted up against the wardrobe.

The footsteps drew nearer.

The youngest girl, torn between the impulse to whistle and the fear of alarming her family unnecessarily, took a hesitant step backward. Another crunch of snow echoed through the trees, closer this time, coming from the dark trees, whispering.

With a trembling hand, she raised her fingers to her lips.

She saw eyes.

Chapter 26: Light

Paris, 1945

Age 17

I

At the door to the old mama's apartment stood a man with suspenders and disheveled hair. In his hands, he was holding the test the young man took. "Madam, good evening." He introduced himself. "I'm a professor from the Math department at the Sorbonne."

The young man, sitting on the armchair, sensed something was amiss. He put the dictionary on the lounge table. The moneychanger stood up. "Please come in, come in," he said to the professor.

The professor, walking in, seemed to find what he was looking for when he spotted the young man. He began speaking to him in French, and the young man stared helplessly at the moneychanger and the old mama.

"He wants to know where you studied."

The young man explained he was from a small town in Poland called Grodno and that his brilliant uncle taught him math.

Then a long conversation ensued between the professor and the moneychanger, with the old mama intervening.

The young man wished he could understand the conversation.

The moneychanger gave him reassuring glances. He told the professor that the "young man would learn" and "will prove himself."

They spoke at length. The young man could not understand a word.

The old mama exclaimed, "University of Nancy! Why so far?"

The professor explained that he was the former dean at the University of Nancy and could recommend a trial year for the young man. The Sorbonne could not take him right away because he did not know French. But the young man's math skills were "impressive" and showed he must pursue higher education immediately.

"He solved some challenging questions only a master's student should be able to solve."

The old mama could not conceal her silver-toothed grin.

After the professor left, the old mama sighed heavily as she stared at the young man, mumbling to herself. "Losing him already!"

The young man, finally understanding what had transpired, felt his heart beating rapidly. *University.*

He thought of his uncle.

The old mama did not want to bid farewell to the young man.

She packed him food to take and kissed his cheeks several times. "You will come next Friday, yes?"

The young man nodded.

She adjusted his jacket, the collar of his shirt, and sighed.

"Mama," the money changer said, standing by the door, "he'll be back this weekend, now let him go!"

The old mama smiled a smile full of sorrow. She wanted this young man to go where he belonged. But she wanted so helplessly to keep him to herself. "Go!" she said and began hitting him, "Go, go, before Pharaoh regrets!"

The young man placed the dictionary the old mama gifted him in his valise and exited through the door. The moneychanger took the bag with the pickles, cookies, and jam, and reached to kiss the old mama. "I'll be back tonight."

"You better!" she said, and looked at the young man as he descended the stairs.

She closed the door with a sigh, locked all the locks, and walked over to the family photos in the hallway. There, she clutched a small photograph of a young man. "You keep an eye on him, you hear me?"

The train arrived in Nancy.

The moneychanger helped the young man find the university.

The campus was grand and the air was charged with the electricity of learning. Large lawns and many benches were strewn between the buildings, and students were engaged in loud debates. He suddenly felt so odd, looking at his own Polish jacket and valise, feeling he did not belong.

The moneychanger asked for directions, and then led them to the admission building. He gave the administrator the introductory letter.

The administrator began speaking in French to the young man, who could only look helplessly at the moneychanger.

The moneychanger said, "He does not speak yet, but he will learn quickly."

The administrator said, "He can enroll in the first year, and provided his grades are sufficient in all subjects, he will be able to proceed to the following year. Is that clear?"

The moneychanger said, "He will do well."

Later, the moneychanger walked with the young man to the dormitory. The young man set his valise on the bed and put the pot with the old mama's pickles, cookies, and jam carefully on the small desk. There were three other empty beds in the bare, cold room.

The moneychanger stood by the door.

The young man felt as bare as the room itself. There were no books lining the walls or shoes shorn haphazardly near the door, nothing like his childhood at his grandfather's house, where every room held a story of its own. *This* place felt like it had not been lived in. Not yet.

The young man knew he had to say goodbye to the moneychanger. *He hated farewells.*

They had never hugged before. But now the moneychanger clumsily reached over to the young man.

It had only been a few brief days since they met in the market, but in this short time they had become family. The moneychanger did not want to let go of this stranger who had become like a brother.

The moneychanger turned away from the young man, not wanting to cry. He forced himself to stop thinking of his younger brother—who, four years earlier, was taken to Auschwitz.

It was the right time to explain. How after his brother was gone, he had found an escape. The old mama had cupped his face in her hands and told him to leave her behind, that she could not bear to lose another son. The young man needed to know what it meant to them both to find him after such an incomparable loss.

The moneychanger opened his mouth. "You will visit us," he said, "Friday for Shabbat."

The young man suddenly wanted to return with the moneychanger to Paris, to the old mama, to the familiar apartment with its many books and the delicious cooking. He could not shake his sadness.

The moneychanger smiled. "Now show off to them all!"

The young man stiffened up, choking back his tears. "Thank you," he said in Yiddish, "Adank!" and then in French, "Merci," he added, "for being my family!"

Chapter 27: Darkness

Poland, 1943

Age 15

I

In an instant, the sound was heard in the cabin, and a figure jumped from the bedroom window, and then another, rushing quickly through the snow, disappearing in the woods.

The sudden whistle startled the maid into leaving the children's room in haste and running into the kitchen. She hurriedly stepped outside. She thought of nothing else but her daughters.

The boy and the uncle ran through the woods– running, running, tearing through shrubs and bushes, their feet crushing the twigs – away from the house as fast as they could.

After a few minutes, the uncle slowed down and gestured to the boy with his hand, signaling him to wait.

Breathless and panting, the uncle darted his eyes around the woods.

The boy looked helplessly at his uncle.

The uncle stabilized his breath, whispering, "Maybe it was a false alarm."

"What?" the boy asked.

"A false alarm." He put his finger on his lips to say *be quiet*, and whispered, "Let's check." The uncle stepped carefully, quietly, in between the trees, tracing their way back, until he saw the lit cabin past the woods, near the road.

The uncle drew nearer. The boy wanted him to be more careful and reached his hand to grab the uncle's wrist.

The uncle shook his head. He walked carefully through the woods, until he finally approached the trees near the house.

He saw a person walking by the house. The husband of the maid was walking back and forth, looking into the woods.

The uncle whistled gently.

The husband stopped in his tracks, looking toward the dark woods. "It was nothing," he said loudly to the woods, toward the gentle whistle. "All is well."

The uncle heard that and began walking quickly out of the woods. The boy hurried behind him, still checking his surroundings, still worrying about the potential danger.

The husband, seeing the uncle and the boy coming out of the woods, turned toward the cabin.

The uncle followed him.

Inside the warm kitchen, the maid said, "My daughter, she got scared. She must have seen a critter, I am so sorry!"

The uncle said, "Better safe than sorry."

The husband interfered and said, "Keep working. I'll be outside."

The uncle looked at him with gratitude. The boy followed the uncle into the bedroom.

For the following hour and a half, the boy assisted the uncle as he meticulously measured, marked, and cut the floorboards. Every once in a while the husband's face appeared in the window, each time frightening the boy.

Finally, they had cut the floorboards, positioning each floorboard carefully to the side. The uncle proved he had a precise hand with the saw. He meticulously cut the floorboards where the bed had stood. He flipped the boards and wrote numbers on them with a pencil, to be later joined together in the exact same order. Now, there was a brown rectangle of earth showing through the cabin floor.

The husband came inside, rubbing his hands and blowing hot

air into them. He glanced down at the hole in the ground. "Too small, how could the four of you possibly—"

"If it was any larger," the uncle said, "it would be too close to the edge of the bed. The soldiers could knock and hear the hollow ground. I'd rather not take the risk. This size will do, we'll fit."

The husband did not say anything. How could four people fit in there?

The boy began digging with the shovel, but the ground was hard and he wasn't as strong as his uncle who could dig and fill his bucket faster.

The husband began carrying the buckets outside to the old well, all the while cursing and muttering under his mustache.

In the potato cellar, the lawyer and his wife heard the digging in the ground across the yard.

The baby girl began crying. The older daughter, who replaced her mother in the children's room, reassured the baby and began singing to her.

On the way back with the empty buckets, the husband brought a few small logs of wood into the cabin to use as a cover story, so he could explain he was cutting lumber in case any soldiers came and inquired what was happening. Why at this time of night; why the girls were outside; why there was a hole under the bed—the husband preferred not to think about all that. He knew they were jeopardizing their lives.

The digging in the ground could be felt, he knew, throughout the whole hill, even though the uncle and the boy dug as quietly as they could.

Exhaustion weighed heavily on the boy as he continued to dig, the ground now reaching a depth that surpassed his knees.

"Enough," the husband finally said, "enough for one night. We'll continue tomorrow."

The uncle said, "But if we continue just a while longer…"

"No, enough," said the husband. "The girls need to sleep, if they all look tired tomorrow at school it could attract the attention of students or teachers. We'll continue tomorrow."

The uncle nodded, resigned. Every moment wasted brought them closer to death, but they could not allow their fear to outweigh good sense.

The boy dropped the shovel. He could almost taste the safety in the dirt-flecked air.

II

Daylight slipped through the cracks of the cellar door.

The uncle had taken the floorboards and was joining them together as quietly as possible.

The boy sat there, biting his nails anxiously. His mind kept trying to avoid thinking of his parents and sister.

The lawyer and his wife did not say much as they lay on the uneven potato floor. Each person in the cellar was lost in their thoughts.

By the afternoon, the uncle had finished softly hammering nails in quiet hits and was now holding a discarded metal pipe.

The boy jumped at every noise he heard outside. He wished the pit under the bed had been completed sooner; but then again, he wished that it would never be completed, that he would never have to enter that dark grave.

They heard dogs in the distance. Were they the Nazis' dogs or were they just the neighbors' dogs from down the hill?

The hours stretched like days. Anyone could come to the potato cellar with its thin door and open it—it was not even locked! That thought made the boy feel nervous.

He marveled at how unperturbed and focused his uncle was, yet he himself could not fathom a positive ending to this predicament that they were stuck in.

The boy could not stop remembering when the butcher found the family who was hiding next to them. He remembered seeing the lady and her daughter hanging at the entrance to the ghetto.

Finally, evening came.

The uncle was eager to start. He set up the joint floorboards neatly against the wall, and as he held the metal water pipe in his hand, he sat eagerly at the third stair, his head touching the cellar door, like a bull ready to launch himself at the red cape.

Finally, they heard heavy footsteps. The boy knew it was the husband.

The uncle whispered to the lawyer and his wife, "Join us, we will need your help to finish digging."

The husband came to the door and opened it. Cold air blew in from the night. He said nothing, looking to his right, and let his eyes meet the uncle's. He nodded and then left the potato cellar door open.

They waited a minute and then hurried to leave the cellar. The boy followed the uncle, followed by the seamstress and the lawyer himself, their fate looming over them like a guillotine.

Chapter 28: Light

Paris, 1945

Age 17

I

The young man stood at the entrance of the old mama's apartment building. His hand shook as he held the paper. It felt as if his fingers were burning.

Months had passed since the young man had started at the university. He went to classes daily, returned to his room, studied, and then repeated it all over again the next day.

Yet he was not progressing.

He looked at the building, reluctant to enter. The old mama had given him everything. Since his arrival in Paris, she and her son had opened their home and hearts to him. Their hopes for him were high.

He entered, trembling. The building felt smaller. The arched door to the cobblestone courtyard revealed a peeling, aging wall. He climbed the circling staircase, his heart growing heavier with each step.

Genius, their praise echoed in his head.

The young man felt like a disappointment.

In the last few months, he had loved spending weekends here, enjoying the old mama's food and the comfort of home. It was the closest thing he had to a family. Yet now he dreaded approaching the fourth floor.

Standing by the door, he took a deep breath and knocked.

He heard the old mama shuffling to the door.

She looked through the peephole. She did not expect to see him today. She opened the door. "What happened?"

Realizing the young man was distraught, she invited him in, kissing him, trying to act as if she was not seeing that something was amiss. Did his uncle die—his only relative who survived?

Or, was he in trouble? Did he gamble the little money he had? Did he get someone pregnant? Was he terminally ill? What happened?

"You must be hungry!" she said, her smile not betraying her concern—she was a professional.

The young man entered the apartment. The moneychanger was still working.

He did not feel like eating.

He felt awful. He sat on the divan, his heart heavy, the hand holding the envelope with bad news burning his fingers.

A few minutes later, the old mama came with a tray overflowing with food. He thanked her, but could not touch the food.

"I…" he began, choking.

He handed her the paper.

She took it and held it far from her eyes, for her to see. She squinted. "Semester's End Grades Report."

He looked down. He would need to pay them back for the money they were putting in his education.

"All fail?" the old mama murmured, surprised.

A heavy silence filled the room.

As the grades were laid bare, the old mama's eyes traced the journey of each mark. A knot of worry clouded her eyes as she registered the numerous failures. *Fail. Fail. Fail.*

The old mama, her heart going out to the young man, struggled to find words that would offer solace without diminishing the gravity of the situation. "I see they are very generous with their 'fails,'" she smiled.

The young man began tearing up. "I'm so sorry, I'm so ashamed. I will find a job, I will quit studying, I will pay you back every—"

"*Mon Dieu!* Don't be an idiot!" she exclaimed. "You focus on studying! You'll be a professor! One day you'll win the Legion of Honor!"

She flipped to the second page. "No, here on math, you did very well. And mechanical engineering is a pass."

The young man shook his head. He did not have the mind his uncle thought he had. He was not the 'genius' the moneychanger and the old mama mistakenly and foolishly called him. He was a failure.

She glanced at the young man, her hand adjusting her headscarf. "Why, son, these grades? You have such a bright mind…"

"I just don't understand what's going on in class!"

"But you still keep learning French?"

The young man answered in French. "*Bien sur!* Of course. I learn thirty words every day! But they speak so fast, all the professors. Everyone speaks not like in books!"

The old mama was quiet. "Now eat!" she said, and her eyes were commanding.

He ate, although it was only to satisfy her.

As she watched him, her thoughts began to churn. She recalled his arrival with that worn valise, like an uprooted tree. She remembered his awkward attempts to pay her, his eyes haunted like a frightened mouse.

She loved him. She had to help him. But how?

He said nothing, though his eyes spoke of desperation.

She had to put an end to his suffering. There was no way she was allowing any child of hers to give up, especially one with so much potential. Surely there was an easier, faster, and more efficient way for him to learn French, she thought.

Then it struck her. "Well," she smiled. "You'll have to use the most ancient trick for learning a language, son."

"What is it?" the young man looked at her, a sliver of hope, mixed with fear of disappointing her anew.

"You need to find," she smiled, her two silver teeth shining, "a girlfriend, young man. A French girlfriend."

The young man chuckled and shook his head dismissively. "I don't have time for that!"

The old mama leaned forward and gestured with her finger for him to come closer to her.

He leaned in.

She looked him straight in the eyes.

He saw her nearly hairless eyebrows, painted in with a brown pencil.

"Son of mine," she said, "let me put it into an equation for you, so that you can understand. Yes?"

The young man nodded seriously. "Alright."

"If a person has zero time for romance at the current time, then when he will *eventually* have time, he will have zero romance!"

The young man shrugged his shoulders.

The old mama's eyes widened, her finger pointing at the door. "I will not let you through that door next time you come, unless you tell me you have a French girlfriend." Her reassuring smile shone.

II

"I guess you did not find my performance appealing?"

The voice snapped him out of his book. The young man was stunned. He barely knew where he was.

He had long dreamed of owning his own books. Now that he did, he took them everywhere—to the library, cafeteria, dormitories. The heavy pile made him feel safe, shielding him from the loud, happy students around him.

He even carried them to the piano recital his roommate insisted he attend. It was not that the music wasn't beautiful—he appreciated the pianist's talent—but he had to focus on studying and building his future. There was no time for leisure.

Applause distracted him from the progress he was making with temperature, pressure, and volume on physical systems in Thermodynamics.

He applauded the pianist and was glad when the recital was over.

He was reading intently about the Equilibrium of Heterogeneous Substances, which showed how thermodynamic processes, including chemical reactions, could be graphically analyzed, and was startled when he heard a voice near him.

He noticed the pianist was standing next to him. "Did you hear what I said? I asked if you enjoyed my performance," she said in a casual tone.

He could not understand her—well, he could, but it took time for his mind to recalibrate due to her stunning beauty. "Excuse— Excuse moi?" he mumbled.

Recognizing from his speech he was a foreigner, she spoke slower. "My playing. Not good?"

"Oh no, no!" he exclaimed, embarrassed. "Good! Exquisite! Magnifique!" he said.

She flipped the cover of his book to the front cover. "But reading 'Principles of Thermodynamics' is more captivating than my playing?"

He blushed.

The young man did not know how to respond. Here in front of him stood a beautiful, confident, young woman. What was she doing talking to someone like him?

She smiled. "Are you not going to invite me to sit?"

His words rushed out of him, "Of course, s'il vous plaît," and he stood up and offered her a chair.

She laughed. "A gentleman. Unlike the rude Frenchmen," she said as she sat down.

"A gentleman would have not…" he searched for words, "read during your performance. Forgive me."

"I *might* forgive you," she said. She liked how studious he was, seeing the pile of books next to him.

There was something about how he had sat there and totally ignored the concert that reminded her of her father. "To forgive you," she said, her smile like train lights, hurting his eyes, "you will have to invite me for a picnic."

She looked at his books. "Without these."

Chapter 29: Darkness

Poland, 1943

Age 15

I

In the cabin, the buckets were filled quickly. Soon, they were standing at the height of their hips.

The husband kept peering from the window. A tangible tension hung heavy in the air, constantly urging the men to expedite their work.

A somber mood permeated the atmosphere as they tried to make no sound. But it was not only the silence. It felt as if they were digging their own grave. Finally, a couple dozen soil buckets later, the uncle leaned on the shovel with his arm. "This should do."

The uncle grabbed a metal rod. "This will create an air tunnel for us." He pointed at the sharpened tip of the rod and readjusted the angle so it angled away from the wall of the pit outward. "Once the rod is through, we'll push the pipe in for ventilation."

He tried pushing the rod into the side of the pit, on the part facing the outer wall of the cabin. He couldn't force the rod into the unyielding ground. He took the shovel and hit the back of the rod forcefully. It slowly went in.

"The noise!" said the husband, looking frantically at his wife.

The uncle seemed possessed to continue his work no matter the consequences. He said to the husband, "Please, go outside and see where the rod comes out."

The husband groaned. He had a bad feeling about the whole thing. *Should he have said no?* But it was too late now. He saw the hopeful look in the uncle's eyes, the hope reflected on the three figures in the messy, muddy sty that was once the neat bedroom. He walked outside, groaning to himself. His daughters were patrolling on either end of the road, watching. He shook his head. *What they were all doing was crazy.*

Inside the bedroom, the uncle kept hitting the metal rod with the shovel. It went further in. The loud sound reverberated through the cabin, through the woods, and through the hill.

Someone knocked on the window.

The maid hurried to open the window to her husband. Cold air blew in. The husband whispered, "You mustn't make this hitting sound!"

The boy looked at his uncle's face and saw desperation for the first time. "We only need a few more hits!"

The husband muttered, "This is madness! You'll wake up the entire village!"

The uncle grabbed the rod. "I feel it's almost out, just a few more hits."

The husband shook his head and grabbed his head with his hands, exasperated. *Were these people trying to give him a heart attack?*

With each passing moment, the boy's fear grew stronger — not that they would not complete the pit, but that they would, that he would be forced into that muddy coffin, to be in that small confined place with these strangers, to be strangled and forgotten, to be buried alive.

The husband shook his head. "We cannot continue." He looked at his wife.

The uncle looked at the husband and then turned to look at the maid.

The maid froze. "Keep going."

II

The sound of the shovel hitting the pipe reverberated through the hill. The uncle muffled the sound by wrapping a couple of rugs on its edge, but it still clanged loudly each time he hit it.

Outside, the husband of the maid agitatedly walked near the window, nearly pulling his hair out, his eyes wide, constantly looking behind him, fearing someone was going to knock at the door demanding an explanation for why it was so loud at this late hour.

The pounding continued.

He was about to storm back into the cabin and conclude the fiasco, when, suddenly, he saw the rod sticking out from the snow.

He hurried to the window. "It's sticking out!" he whispered.

The uncle, sweat pooling on his forehead, exhaled in relief.

The boy dreaded this moment. He did not want to hide in the dreadful pit, breathing through a cursed pipe.

The maid clasped her hands together.

The uncle looked at the maid, "Please, Madam, hand me a bucket of hay."

The maid hurried to bring him a bucket.

The boy looked anxious, fearing the moment he knew was coming. Near him, the seamstress grabbed her husband by the arm.

The uncle spread the hay on the cold soil. "This will insulate somewhat," he said. Then he looked at the lawyer and his wife while he handed the empty bucket to the maid. "Come, now."

No one moved. The uncle was exasperated. He turned to his young nephew and said, "Come in!"

The boy knew he could not refuse his uncle's order, even though he did not want to go into the pit. He walked slowly to the pit, and stepped down into it. His shoes rested on the soft hay. The pit reached a little above his waist.

The boy felt the hay gently yielding beneath his weight. The musty smell of soil mingling with the smell of sawdust created a distinctive aroma that lingered in the small confined space. "Sit down," the uncle told him. The uncle glared at the lawyer. The uncle did not like that the lawyer did not listen to him. He knew the lawyer and his wife did not have a choice. They had to go into the pit.

The lawyer followed them inside.

The boy moved aside, crammed into the tight space. He saw the lawyer towering over him, offering his hand to his wife.

The seamstress came down, and it was even more crowded. She sat down close to the boy, closer than propriety would allow under any other circumstance.

The husband of the maid came into the house and looked disapprovingly as the seamstress sat inside the pit. He muttered to his wife, "It looks like a grave…"

The uncle looked at the husband. "This coffin might save us from the grave."

The maid looked at her husband worriedly. *Her husband was right*, she thought. *It did look like a grave. It was not much bigger than a coffin.* How could four people hide down there? Would this silly pipe provide them with enough air? The cold intensified by the second and her daughters were still outside.

The uncle told her, "We'll need some water, wiping paper, and a bucket."

The maid, happy to walk away from the worrying scene, hurried to the kitchen cupboards.

The husband looked at the uncle and the others with pity. "Are you sure—"

"Absolutely," the uncle said, and reached toward the floorboards which stood next to the standing bed. The husband helped him bring them closer.

The maid returned with a pitcher of water, an enamel cup, yellowed newspaper for wiping, and a bucket. The uncle lowered these to the already crowded pit.

The maid ran back and handed the seamstress two pieces of bread.

The seamstress bowed her head in gratitude.

The uncle placed a hand on her shoulder and said, "thank you, we are grateful for your kindness."

He knelt down, the others making more room, and the boy yelped as the uncle stepped on his shoe. The uncle took the lid, the wooden floorboards he had joined together during the day, and closed it over them, extinguishing the last sliver of light the boy could see.

The maid gasped as the floor closed before her eyes, and the seams were barely visible—this was the art of the uncle.

The daughters were called in from the frozen outdoors. A palpable silence blanketed the family as anticipation of the possible circumstances loomed over them.

Staying inside the potato cellar overnight was one thing, as the family could always attempt saying it was without their knowledge. But this pit, under their very bed—their intentions would be unmistakable.

If their guests were found, death was certain. The gravity of the situation hung in the air like a heavy shroud. The maid hugged her daughters tightly, feeling their cold cheeks, unsure if she was doing the right thing.

A moment later the floorboards opened again. "Madam," the uncle peered through the crack, "please place as many clothes as possible above us, under the bed; the more the better. And we thank you and your husband."

The maid nodded.

Then the opening was gone.

CHAPTER 30: LIGHT

PARIS, 1946

AGE 18

On Saturday, the young man arrived at the old mama's doorstep, his heart swelling with excitement.

She opened the door but didn't let him in, standing like a guard, examining his face.

Confused by the silence, the moneychanger urged her. "Mama, let him in!"

The old mama studied the young man's face. She already knew. "Girlfriend?"

He nodded.

She raised her finger in the air, threatening. "French girl?"

He nodded. "French."

"Bravo!" she exclaimed, "Mazel tov!" She fell on him, on her young man who had graduated—not from university, but from the most important of all schools: the school of *romantique* and *amour*.

She let the young man inside and doted on him.

As he shared the news of his newfound friend with the old mama and the moneychanger, a rosy hue crept into his cheeks, betraying the depth of his emotions.

The old mama's eyebrows arched inquisitively at his revelation, her eyes sparkling with a mixture of curiosity and approval. "A pianist, you say…" her voice tinged with a hint of delight. "C'est bon! Well educated?"

With a nod of affirmation, the young man confirmed her hopes, his heart swelling with pride at the mere mention of his girlfriend's talents and intellect.

But the old mama, ever the matriarchal figure, made her stance clear. "Well, I won't approve of her until I see her!"

She seemed serious, disapproving. But beneath the veneer of zest for control, there lay a genuine mother's concern for the young man's happiness.

Suddenly, her eyes shone. "Did you kiss her?"

The moneychanger, ever the pragmatist, interjected. "Mama! He's been more than kissing her! What is he, a child?" he exclaimed, eliciting a chuckle from the young man and a playful swat from the old mama as she exclaimed, "Lucky girl!"

She wanted him to have something to compensate him for all that he had lost—something. And a girlfriend was something.

"Where did you take her?"

"We had a picnic, and then yesterday we went to a movie—"

"Picnic!" she laughed. "Picnic!"

"It was her idea," the young man said, blushing, unsure whether that was good or bad.

"Where? At the university?"

The young man nodded.

The old mama stared at the moneychanger and began chuckling, but stifled her chuckles as she saw the young man was offended. "That is a grand idea, a picnic at the university."

"It was a sunny day," the young man apologized.

The moneychanger enjoyed sizing up the young man.

"Grand, grand!" the old mama said. "Next time you should take her to Luxembourg Gardens, right here at the end of the street," her words laced with the weight of memory. "La harmonie, la mélodie, le montage de fleurs! It can be so romantique!"

She suddenly remembered the letter. "Oh!" she pointed at the letter on the lounge table. "You got a letter!"

The young man reached for the letter. He saw the name on the back of the envelope and tore it apart quickly.

He read it, chuckling, disbelieving, crying. "My uncle. He is coming to Paris!" Tears welled in his eyes.

"Family," the old mama exclaimed and slapped the moneychanger on the knee, forcing a smile out of him.

"Family!" he said.

"La famille!" she repeated. "Girlfriend, family, soon good grades. We must open that champagne!"

"Mama," the moneychanger retorted, "you said we'll save that for special occasions—"

"And here it is! If we keep waiting, the next special occasion will be when you are dancing on my grave! Bring it and open it," she said and winked at the young man who was busy rereading the letter.

She smiled and sighed. It was about time the child caught a break. Satisfaction filled her as she witnessed life's heavy pendulum swing in the young man's favor.

CHAPTER 31: DARKNESS

POLAND, 1943

AGE 15

The maid could not sleep that night, her mind haunted by the thought of the souls concealed beneath her floorboards suffocating under a heavy layer of blankets and clothes.

In the morning, she tried to put on a brave face, occupying herself with her morning tasks, making breakfast for her husband and for the girls. When they left, a rush of cold air rushed into the cabin.

She closed the door quickly behind them, locking it immediately. She wanted to check on her guests under the bed, when suddenly, she was jolted back to her duties by the whining of her toddler son, who was blissfully unaware of the drama that unfolded in the cabin and woke up more unruly and energetic than ever.

The maid played with her toddler son who was entertaining himself with a wooden dog. The dog barked loudly, and the maid patted his head absentmindedly with her thumb. His innocent curiosity heightened the tension for the maid—what was she doing? What responsibility was she taking, not only for her life, but for the life of her precious little boy? She had jeopardized the entire family. Maybe she should not have.

Her baby girl woke up, and the maid began breastfeeding her. As she fed the baby, she could not shake the nagging worry. She remembered the sealed refrigerator room at the meat factory, and how once a worker was trapped there and died of suffocation. She could not stop worrying about finding four lifeless bodies, blue, knowing that she had killed them with her own stupidity.

With a conflicted heart, the maid considered opening the pit. But her son—her toddler with the big mouth, who was the first to complain to the neighbors when his toy was eaten by a local dog, could very easily betray the people living under the floor of their household with his excitement. No. That was irresponsible.

She was hoping her toddler would finally begin his noon nap. Her son, however, seemed more energetic than ever, running about the house and telling make believe stories with his funny pronunciation. The maid was exhausted, not having slept at all the previous night and having slept but little the night before. She was agitated with her toddler's many questions about a myriad of things, and with her baby's relentless crying.

As the day droned on, the maid attempted to distract her toddler with games, hoping to tire his boundless energy. But the oblivious child continued his play, unaware of her inner turmoil.

"Now-now, sweetheart," she crooned, voice cracking. "Let's have a nap."

In her desperation, the maid tried lulling the toddler to sleep with soothing tales and gentle lullabies. She had to open the pit, giving that necessary air to the hiders.

By noon, the maid could no longer wait. Why was there no sound from under the bed? The silence haunted her. Tormented by worry, she began to dwell on the potential flaws of their hiding place, thinking of the stupidity of that narrow pipe supposed to supply air for the four of them.

What if the pipe got covered outside? Snow blanketed the ground and could easily cover the opening. What about the blankets placed atop the floorboards, covering any bit of air that might slip through the cracks?

She was finally able to lull her son to sleep, and she remained next to him, feeling her own heart beating quickly, nervously.

She walked quietly from the children's room and closed the door, her toddler and her baby both asleep. She leaned on the ground of the bedroom and began pulling away the blankets, her hands shaking, when she heard a knock on the cabin door. She hit her head against the bed, caught off guard by the surprise visitor. She did not expect anyone to knock on the door.

Another, louder knock followed. She hurried to the door, calming herself down, yet she could only think of the tanner's family and of their bodies dangling from the gallows. She asked, "Who is it?"

"Police, open up!"

Chapter 32: Light

Paris, 1950

Age 22

I

Standing there on the Paris train platform, the young man was excited.

Next to him stood his girlfriend, the pianist. He held her hand tightly.

The train was late.

A few minutes had passed, and his hands began to get all sweaty and clammy. The girlfriend, not wanting to insult him, pulled her gloves from her purse and slid them gingerly over her fingers.

"Relax," she told him.

He nodded, but he could not relax.

How could she even understand him? She had a family in France; their lot was day and night in comparison to his.

Although she did not fully grasp his anxiety, the pianist gently held his hand, rubbing the back of his palm with her thumb. He squeezed her hand tightly in return.

For months, he had been exchanging letters with his uncle, but words could not replace a smile, a hug, or the sound of a voice.

They waited on the platform, where the young man had stood alone a year earlier when he arrived in Paris. No one had been there for him then, but now his family was coming. *Family.*

As the train finally arrived, he scanned the crowd emerging onto the platform. A chaotic mix of loud exclamations and hurried footsteps—children holding parents' hands, suitcases clutched tightly, lovers embracing, and families reuniting with laughter and tears.

Where was his uncle? With each passing second, disappointment thickened the air. Anxiety twisted in his stomach.

Then, at the edge of the long platform, he spotted a tall man with two suitcases. His uncle.

He pulled his girlfriend's hand. "There!" He began running, her hand tightly clasped in his as she followed behind.

"Uncle! Uncle!" the young man cried.

All the memories of the pit rushed back. He owed his life to this one angel of a man. The endless days in the pit, though scary and uncertain, were bearable thanks to his uncle.

Family—he would never take that word for granted again.

The uncle smiled as if they had seen each other yesterday; as if they were not each other's sole relative in the entire world. "There you are," his uncle said. "All grown up. A Frenchman! And this," he said and bowed his head, taking the girlfriend's hand. "Voila!" he said in French, "You must be *la grande pianiste*!"

"Pleased to meet you," she said.

The uncle kissed her hand, "*Enchanté*."

"Uncle!" The young man said, "I didn't know you speak French!"

The uncle winked. "I prepared."

When the three of them exited the train station, the young man was the happiest he'd been since the war ended.

A year ago, a single timid young man stepped out of the train station. Now, out of the gates of the station, a family stepped out.

II

In Paris, summers turned to autumns; winters to springs.

The boy was no longer a boy, nor was he a young man. He had grown, graduated, become an engineer, and then a young scientist.

The young scientist was going to be a groom.

He had been waiting for it. He was 22 years old. His old mama and his uncle did not understand.

The old mama told him there was no reason to hurry: "Marriage doubles one's responsibilities and halves one's freedom."

His uncle, too, said, "It is not for you."

But they did not understand. Their advice for him did not take into consideration his longing for a family, for roots, for replanting the surviving remnant of what was once the grand sycamore of his family.

He earned a degree and could now begin working. At the same time, he kept studying, another degree, another mountain to conquer.

He was no longer a shy, timid young student. Now he was a brilliant scientist, having earned his degree with honors.

With his uncle nearby, life in Paris improved for the young scientist. He studied more than he ever had in his life.

While math had its fascination, soon physics, engineering, and mechanics became his passions. True, math was good for the brain; it had beauty; it could make mathematicians happy. But engineers—they could make *humanity* happy.

"Think of it," he explained to his girlfriend—now fiance—one night as they sat on the bed in his empty dormitory. "Think of it: any bridge, train, car, airplane—any building at all—they all require a precise knowledge of physics: for example, exactly how far do you need to dig into the ground to create the right foundation for a skyscraper?"

The pianist smiled. "You're cute when you get so excited."

"No, really! It has to be exactly right. If you don't do it according to calculations, you are not merely dealing with an abstract theory—like in math. Here you're meddling with people's lives! A building that is not built properly, without the necessary foundation, could collapse."

His fiance batted her eyelashes. "You could collapse too if you keep studying like this all the time!"

"No, listen, it's *everything*. Everything depends on it! A bridge has to withstand the wind, the pressure, the weight of the cars, everything. And at the same time, you want to design it to be not too clunky, not too heavy, as the bridge's own weight could be a detriment too, you see?"

She leaned closer to him. "I see!"

"Now, if my professor is right, and aviation is the future of intercontinental travel—and not ships—do you know what that entails?"

She shook her head, smirking. "No, but I'm sure you'll tell me!"

"It means that the journey of human discovery into materials and engineering will only deepen! Think of it: you want an airplane to be strong, to withstand wind as well as the engine's heat, and the overall pressure of the various altitudes, right?"

"Right."

"But you also want the airplane to be light, not to be so heavy, so you can take off easily, use less fuel, and be more aerodynamic… That's the challenge of the future, creating something so strong it can withstand much stress, and yet be light, thin, and agile…"

"Like me!" the pianist said and leaned ever closer. "Now shush and kiss me!"

III

He woke up, sweating.

The pianist, now his wife, turned to him in the darkness, exhausted. This was yet another night of his incessant nightmares. "Is everything okay?"

"I just had a bad dream," he said.

"The war?" she asked.

The young scientist *wanted* to tell everything to her. He wanted to say, 'They were so close. The butcher seized me. He almost killed me.'

But he said nothing.

He knew his wife did not like it when he spoke of the war. She wanted him to leave the past behind. She was in the present—why focus on the past and all the sad stories? Why would he still talk about what brought him sadness?

The war had ended seven years ago. Why couldn't he just leave it behind?

His young wife turned over to the other side. "Try to go back to sleep."

"Thank you," the young scientist said.

She soon fell asleep again. He could hear her gentle snores. But his eyes remained wide open.

He was not going back to sleep. He knew very well what was waiting for him on the other side.

Every night he was transported back to the heart of the war-torn city—the stench of fear and the distant echoes of gunfire reverberated through his veins: running in the forest, lurking shadows and the laughter of the butcher, a specter of death clad in uniform, his hand clasping, reaching, crushing into his skin, tearing him, death trapping him, the butcher's grip tightening, his fingers digging into his flesh and he could not run fast enough—

No.

Not sleep. *Anything* but sleep.

He lay in bed, eyes wide open.

Why were these dreams only getting worse? His life was ideal now. He had a wife. They were going to start a family. He was studying for his doctorate funded by the state and was working with people who respected him. His uncle was in the same city, doing well, and recently remarried... All was well. *All was well!*

He got out of bed, quietly exited the bedroom, and closed the door behind him. Turning on the light in the small living room, he glanced around at the tight space, which barely accommodated both his wife's piano and his study desk.

He sat by his desk and sighed.

He buried his head in his palms. "Get a grip on yourself!" he told himself. "You're a grown-up now!"

He wanted to cry.

The kitchen was shrouded in darkness. He reached for the light switch, as he always did. He scolded himself for the need for all the light. "What are you, a baby?"

He tried to quiet his mind.

"You should have gone and found the butcher. You had an opportunity."

He poured himself a glass of water.

"You should have shot them all, there, in that city. You could have taken revenge in the name of your family!"

He turned on the light in the bathroom as well, and the light by the door.

"You are a coward. Scum of the earth!"

He sat at his desk. A physics equation could help him relax. He looked at the last equation he had been working on: a bridge. The pressure exerted on a specific part of the large bridge, which had eight supports constructed deep down into the sea.

Slowly, the long equations soothed him. He wanted to understand the exact pressure exerted on the bridge and analyze the location of the key breaking points: the danger spots.

He knew his work was rife with speculation; he admitted it was mostly guesswork. The equations could never be perfectly precise. They could not truly predict how the steel in the bridge would respond to stress.

With tons of weight and a severe high-speed wind, how could he calculate that? It was only conjecture. All these impressive formulas were important for only one thing: to find the weak spots.

He mused to himself; they were like the vulnerable parts in a person's personality. Those parts could be the determining factor in whether a man would remain strong or collapse.

To find the weak points was important, vital, and crucial. A chain is only as strong as its weakest link. And a bridge is only as strong as its weakest spot.

He knew that the tendency of engineers to add more and more steel to the structure was not the answer. It was rather stupid. Maybe this could work with bridges, perhaps, but certainly not on airplanes.

He sighed. He threw his pencil down.

He clung to the equations, seeking solace from the memories and comfort from the science. But that night, the equations, once his fortress, felt fragile.

The void from his family's loss haunted him, plagued him with endless questions about their last moments. Desperate, he scribbled new equations, trying to escape his grief, but peace remained elusive.

Yet he was close—close to discovering the light illuminating the path at the end of countless equations.

Chapter 33: Darkness

Poland, 1943

Age 15

The loud knocks resounded through the cabin, causing a cold shiver to run down the maid's spine. "Police! Open up!"

She unlatched the door. Bracing herself, she put on the best smile she could muster and opened the door. Before her was her old neighbor, this time having brought with her a local police officer.

"Oh, hello officer! How can I help you?"

"Search!" The officer said in Polish. The maid was relieved he was not German. But she was aghast as he forced his way in, pushing her to the side.

Behind the police officer, the rude old neighbor followed, with pride and righteousness in her stride.

The maid glanced back in trepidation at the bedroom. She had left the bedroom door open. She nearly fainted when she saw the blankets spread messily on the floor, sticking out from under the bed, as if screaming: *Here! Search here!*

The officer headed to the children's room first.

She hurried after him, pointing at the two little ones who were asleep. "Quietly, please," she said.

The officer leaned down and looked under the beds.

The maid swallowed hard—*if the officer searched the bedroom, he would surely notice something amiss.*

Her heart beat faster.

The old neighbor stood at the entrance to the children's room, her lips curling with gleeful expectation.

The police officer methodologically moved the beds around, examining the walls and the floor.

She felt her heart failing her.

Her baby girl stirred in her cot, the noise made by the police officer startling her.

Not wanting her baby to wake up, the maid lifted her into her arms. She snuggled right into her bosom. The maid was sure her own heartbeats were nearly audible to the officer and the neighbor.

The maid felt her baby's warmth and wanted to cry. She feared for her life—if the Jews were ever found, she knew the Nazis would spare none of her family, including her baby girl.

The officer finished scanning the room and left to inspect the other room. The maid followed him, heaviness in her every step.

Suddenly she knew what she should do. The officer's head was below her as he leaned down to examine under the bed.

She prayed and asked God for forgiveness for what she was about to do.

CHAPTER 34: LIGHT

PARIS, 1953

AGE 25

I

"Aaah!" The scientist pushed the lens of the microscope away with a groan. It was a late evening in the lab. With his coworkers finally gone home and his wife out for the evening with her girlfriends, the opportunity to put into practice what he had only theorized presented itself. And he seized it.

Now armed with a PhD in plastics, he was eager to achieve breakthroughs in the field of stress measurement. But nothing came to him.

He took one last look through the lens, hoping to see the iron model of the bridge respond like its plastic counterpart. Alas, the iron model showed no color variation nor any indication of stress.

The taste of failure lingered as he stepped out into the streets of Paris. He needed to go somewhere that would make the burden feel lighter. His legs carried him to the house that felt more like home than his own. He was glad to see light at the small kitchen window.

"Son of mine!" the old mama exclaimed as she opened the door. "What a surprise!"

His face, though smiling at her warm welcome, gave away his true feelings.

"What is the matter? Are you fighting again?" she asked.

"No, well yes, but no it is not that." He sank into the divan. "I think I've made a mistake choosing plastic."

"Really? But you speak of plastic as if it was the messiah!"

"Maybe in theory. Other physicists focus on the mechanics behind airplanes or bridges! And we are stuck making plastic chairs!"

The old mama looked at him silently.

"Yet I love the colors that come with applying pressure to the plastic models. The more weight I place on the model, the stronger the colors become." His voice turned wistful as he continued, "They transition from greens and blues to darker shades of red, before finally becoming violet—indicating the most pressure."

The old mama watched him carefully, taking in the passion in his voice as he spoke about these plastics. "Son, I may not know much about what you're doing. But I know you. I know your heart."

His smile faded as he said, "There was this dinner of all the post-docs, all the physicists. This older professor asked what my doctorate was about. "Plastic?" The way he said it was as if it was… cheap. I explained I am trying to use plastic models to tell what the mathematical formulas are not telling, of where the true weak-spots are in structures."

The old mama listened intently.

"So this professor looks at me, 'Surely you don't expect steel to act like plastic?'" He remembered the way the professor smiled— a condescending, all-knowing expression. "The way he uttered that word, 'plastic,'…as if it was some venereal disease!"

The old mama huffed with annoyance. "That imbecile! Forget him. Do you believe in it?"

The young scientist paused. "I do. Plastics are the cutting edge! Metals have been studied for years. Decades! Plastics are the new frontiers. I only wish… I only wish my metal models could tell the secrets of their weak spots the same way the plastic models do."

He felt the old mama's hand lifting his chin. "Don't forget. You are a genius. I knew that from the moment I saw you in front of my door, hiding behind that good-for-nothing son of mine." She tapped his head with her knuckles, earning a chuckle out of him. "I have faith in you. Keep going."

II

The young scientist ran through the streets of Paris.

He needed to tell her.

He hurried through the large Luxembourg gardens, bouquet in hand, heading toward the old mama's street. As he approached the house, he hid the flowers behind his back. Each Saturday when he came to visit the old mama, he waxed nostalgic about his first home in Paris.

As he approached the building, he glanced up at the top floor's small kitchen window. The curtain was pulled back, barely revealing the dim figure of the old mama, looking down at the street as always.

He burst into the building. Through the arched gate inside, he saw the small cobblestone courtyard; it did not lose its charm. He ran forward, climbing the many stairs to the fourth floor, hearing the five latches opening loudly, echoing through the winding staircase.

The door opened before he could knock.

"Son of mine!" she exclaimed and kissed him many times on each cheek.

He smiled. *It was delightful to see her.* He handed her the flowers.

"Oh, look at these irises!" She inhaled the flowers, her wrinkled face lighting up with a childlike wonder. "Such beautiful irises! Van Gogh would have been jealous!"

"I'd hoped you'd like them," the young scientist said, speaking in French.

She waved her hand dismissively and welcomed him in. "You don't need to bring flowers to an old wretch like me!"

She shut the door behind him and moved to the kitchen to bring the food she had prepared. He sat on the divan and watched as she came back with the tray. She was slower than usual—her limp even more noticeable; she was dragging her foot behind her.

Guilt flashed through him. *If only he had more means to pay her back.*

"Here you go," she said, placing the tray on the lounge table.

"Mama, you shouldn't have!" He said, looking over the familiar, home-made cabbage roll that she cooked with such mastery.

"You know I like it too!" She exclaimed. She went into the kitchen, and brought back a vase with the irises. She carried the vase and placed it on the table, properly displaying the flowers.

She sat down on the armchair. Briefly, her face contracted with pain, but she quickly masked the pain with a forced smile. "Now tell me all about you. How's the wife?"

He was silent. He did not want to talk about that. Recently they've been fighting a lot about small things. The old mama shook her head knowingly. She moved the conversation along. "You're probably in that lab of yours all the time, aren't you? Tell me about that."

"I'm working on finding a development—no, it'll be a breakthrough, really. In the field of stress measurement."

She sighed. "You know I don't understand what that means…"

"I told you, remember? The advantage of plastic in measuring stress through a special lens, which shows certain colors indicating degrees of pressure?"

"Oh, that, I remember."

"Well," the young scientist began, glancing around the room, as if worried someone would hear him, "for the past several weeks I've been experimenting with trying to put plastic," his voice turned into a whisper, "on top of steel."

"Oh?"

"Think of it!" His eyes lit up. "Steel doesn't 'show' where the most pressure is placed on it, but plastic does. So what if you put plastic *above* the steel? A thin—very thin—layer of plastic, a lacquer really, on top of the steel. It could show where the steel is most sensitive to pressure."

"No. You are trying to marry a cow to a horse!"

The young scientist smiled. "I'm still developing the kind of plastic bond for the job. But," he whispered again, "I've already begun seeing some colors."

The old mama's eyebrows shot up. "Really? Is that true?"

"Yes," the young scientist whispered, "and I've also built a new kind of lens, more sensitive than the university's, and with it I can see how the weak areas on the steel respond—in accordance with all my mathematical calculations! In the same areas my calculations point at, I began seeing reds and purples when I applied stress to the steel model!"

The old mama's eyes narrowed. She played with the ends of her headscarf. "It seems you're onto something," she grinned while twitching her silver teeth.

"I think so too!"

"But," she said, pursing her lips, "if it's so simple—as simple as smearing that stuff on steel—then how come nobody else has thought of it?"

The young scientist leaned forward. "There was a physicist half a century ago who wrote of it, but back then, plastics weren't as available. The necessary instrumentation techniques weren't available either."

She studied his face. She had not seen him glow with such excitement since his first days in Paris, since he saw the art, since he got the letter from his uncle announcing he was coming to Paris.

"I have a name for it," he said.

She stared, probing him to speak. "Go on!"

"PhotoStress," he whispered. "For accurately measuring surface strains, to determine the stresses in a structure. Photo—stress!"

The old mama clasped her hands together, the clap echoing throughout the parlor. "Wonderful! You'll win the Legion of Honor for this one, I tell you!"

The young scientist chuckled, waving his hand dismissively. "It's a simple invention—an obvious solution, that's all!"

The old mama's eyebrows rose knowingly. She leaned forward, wearing a conspiratorial smile. "If it's so obvious, then why are you whispering?"

Everything shook around him. The noise was unbearable.

Yet the young scientist was not afraid, although the airplane was shaking as it garnered speed on the tarmac, soon ascending. The young scientist blessed his good fortune as the plane took off. He scratched his face, forgetting he wore an oxygen mask.

The pilot looked back and nodded at them. He unbuckled himself, and walked over to the plane's window. There were only six of them on the plane—the pilot, the young scientist, his assistant, and three other airplane engineers—testing the airplane's various systems before approving them for commercial use. A small mistake in calculations could cost many lives.

The plane was not yet pressurized, and thus not yet an approved structure. The young scientist adjusted his oxygen mask. The plane was not ready for commercial flights—it was still waiting for him to do his science, to do his *magic.*

He wondered how the wings would respond to the pressure during flight.

As he looked through the window, the tarmac becoming smaller and smaller behind them, he thought about the last year. Here he was, with a doctorate degree and two patents for his newly developed plastic-bonding technique and the pressure measurement instrumentation. They called it *PhotoStress.* Now he was working for the French Academy of Aeronautics, receiving a fine salary. The book and essays he had published about *PhotoStress* were making waves.

He adjusted the lens he and his assistant had screwed to the side of the window. His heart swelled with pride—he'd finally managed to carve a space for himself in the realm of science.

And yet an odd feeling of longing persisted. His parents should have seen him here, on the airplane, paid to conduct his experiments in the sky itself.

Even though the young scientist had received accolades and recognition, he longed for his family. He wished his father was on the airplane with him, watching fields and whole towns turn into vast landscapes from up above. He wished his mother would be there with him when he eventually accepted his awards, hugging and kissing him. He wished his sister could read his books and essays before calling him a geek.

The young scientist wished he could share his success with his family. He wanted to treat them to fancy vacations. He wanted them to be proud of him. Logically, he knew they would be if they were here, but still—their absence had left a gaping wound on his heart.

The noise in the plane was tremendous.

He examined the wing through the lens. The most danger was laid here. More specifically, the danger was laid in the *connection point* between the wing and the main body of the airplane. The wing was attached with countless bolts, but most pressure was exerted on the seam line. All the stress from the wing was transmitted through the points of attachment.

He adjusted the lens. He angled it toward the parts of the wing closest to the fuselage.

"Interesting," he muttered.

His assistant yelled over the noise, "What do you see, doctor?"

"You were right about the front bolts!" The young scientist exclaimed. "They're dark red, level three. The rear ones are becoming reddish, but only at level one. And," he looked through the lens, "interestingly enough, the center seems to show barely any pressure."

"Green?" Shouted the assistant.

"Light blue," the young scientist shouted back. He peered through the lens carefully, the lens shaking from the flight, as if the findings were exciting the lens itself. "We might be able to move some of the bolts, from the ailerons at the center to the slats at the front of the wing. It won't add more weight, and will strengthen the wing. Have a look!"

He moved from the window and held the bar. His assistant brought his eye to the lens.

The young scientist smiled at his assistant. He was already computing the changes in the locations of the bolts. They could reduce the weight of the wing by a whole five percent—the engineers would be ecstatic.

He loved his work. Especially the fieldwork. Especially in the air.

CHAPTER 35: DARKNESS

POLAND, 1943

AGE 15

I

The Polish police officer examined the bedroom. The maid stood there, watching him lower his head under the bed.

She had to do it. She prayed and asked for forgiveness for the pain she was to inflict on her own baby. Then, while rubbing her baby's back, the maid pinched her painfully.

The baby began screaming at the top of her lungs, her cry reverberating with an intensity that seemed to defy the limits of her tiny lungs. The maid pushed the baby near the police officer's ear.

Agitated, the police officer stood up and walked to the wardrobe. He opened it, beginning to feel foolish for interrupting the mother. Seeing only clothes in the wardrobe, he hurried to close its doors and headed out.

The maid was afraid to sigh in relief as she followed the officer back into the kitchen.

The baby kept crying, the maid pleased to see the agitation on the officer's face.

The officer hurried to mumble, "Well, it seems like there is nothing out of the ordinary—"

The old neighbor interjected. "The attic, the attic!"

The officer looked up somewhat helplessly.

The old neighbor said, "There's a ladder outside!"

The maid stared at her old neighbor. "Shame on you."

The old neighbor said nothing, a satisfied smile on her face.

The officer grunted as he brought the heavy ladder in.

As he climbed up, the old neighbor's hands clasped together in anticipation.

The officer looked into the tiny attic where no human being could fit. Mold attacked his nostrils. He slammed the attic door closed.

"But I've been hearing voices," the old neighbor shouted.

"My children, that is all!"

"Other voices!" the old neighbor insisted. "Officer, she has always been *friendly* with the family who owned this hill. Jews! She is hiding them, I tell you!"

The maid trailed behind them, her baby girl still in her arms.

The officer stood by the door and looked at the maid. "Sorry to have disturbed you."

The old neighbor shouted. "The potato cellar! Check the potato cellar, outside!"

The police officer circled the house, the old neighbor hurrying after him. He spotted the potato cellar door and opened it.

The police officer went down into the cellar. The maid followed them, afraid the old neighbor might notice the pipe sticking out of the snow. "Nothing but potatoes," she said.

The officer climbed out of the cellar and hurried to leave, walking to the road.

The old neighbor hurried away, muttering to herself.

The maid returned to the cabin. When she closed the door behind her, she exhaled heavily. She put her daughter back in her bed, thankful her toddler had been sleeping so deeply. She remained there several minutes until both children seemed deeply asleep.

Then, quickly, she exited the children's room. She checked the latch on the door. She entered the bedroom and closed the door.

She leaned down on the floor. Hands trembling, she pushed the clothes and blankets, revealing the narrow cut in the floorboards beneath.

She attempted to pull the floorboards, yet the resistance proved formidable. Panic seized her as she tugged harder on the boards.

"No, God, what have I done?" she muttered, her knocks on the floorboards growing frantic. She pleaded, "It is me! Open up!"

II

The maid banged on the floorboards. "God! Open up!"

As the panic tightened its grip around her, the maid's mind raced with desperate thoughts, her heart pounding in her ears. Each second felt like an eternity as she wrestled with the stubborn floorboards. Sweat beaded on her brow as her fingers struggled against the unforgiving wood.

Suddenly the floorboards moved and lifted up, moving her hands. The maid saw a pair of eyes—no, four pairs of eyes— blinking at her. "God bless!" she exclaimed. Relief flooded through her like a rushing tide. She saw their faces. She forced herself to whisper, "Are you alright?"

The uncle whispered, "The police?"

She tried to make light of it. "They have nothing else to do, so they…patrol."

The uncle seemed grateful, as did the seamstress. The maid saw the boy was embracing himself, his eyes terrified.

The uncle looked at the maid. "Madam, we will need to agree upon a secret knock," he said. "A code for us to know it is you knocking and that you are alone."

The maid thought for a moment. "How about this?" She knocked three times, paused, and then knocked four more times.

"Good," the uncle said. He hurried to close the floorboards.

They were trapped in darkness again.

The boy wanted to say to his uncle, "No, don't close us in

again!”

He closed his eyes and then opened them, hoping to notice a difference. There was none. It was just as dark with his eyes open as it was when they were closed.

The uncle noticed the boy was fidgeting. The uncle whispered, “Now don’t be discouraged. The beginning is the most difficult.”

But how could the boy ever get used to the stuffy air and the cramped space? Animals were allowed better living conditions, and he had to go to the bathroom. It had been hours since they were hidden there.

He wanted to leave, but he was terrified of the outside world. He was afraid for his life. They all were. From the moment they heard the loud banging on the cabin door an hour earlier, they all barely breathed, barely moved.

He could still hear the creaking floorboards under the police officer’s steps, his boots scratching the floor at a hand’s length from their hiding place.

How many hours had it been? They had only been there for the morning, but it felt like days.

His back was hurting. He wanted to relieve himself but could not bring himself to do it in the pot. He had to but he was too embarrassed to do it in front of other people. He chose to wait.

But how long could he hold it?

III

The boy heard the family eating and talking, chairs screeching on the wooden floor.

His bladder and bowels tortured him. His uncle had already relieved himself on the bucket. The fetid air in the pit was unbearable.

Later, they heard steps above them. Three knocks on the floorboards followed by a pause and four more slow knocks.

The uncle lifted the floorboards. The boy saw the maid, as well the legs of her husband, who was standing beside her.

The maid looked down and smiled. "I brought you food." She handed them a small pot with a piece of bread and two potatoes. She leaned closer. "We must ration the food. We don't know how long you'll be here."

"Of course," the uncle said, "this is more than enough." He passed the pot to the boy. "Thank you," he added. He reached for the smelly bucket. "Can you please?"

"Yes, yes," she whispered, "I'll get you a clean one."

The uncle lifted the bucket. It smelled so foul. The boy was happy to get it out. The bucket barely fit in the narrow space below the bed and had to be slightly tilted to slide through, its liquids tilting dangerously.

The boy wanted to ask if he could use the bathroom in the cabin. He waited for a chance.

The maid took the bucket without complaint and left.

Her husband leaned down. "How are you faring?"

"We are grateful, so grateful. In the future, if possible, it could serve us well to have a small oil lamp," the uncle responded.

The husband said, "But the smoke…the smell…"

"We'd only use it for a minute or so each time," said the uncle. "It would help us in dividing the food."

The husband blinked. "I'll see what I can do."

The maid returned with another bucket. "Here," she said and slid the new bucket to the uncle, scratching the floor.

The boy waited for the maid to look at him.

The maid's husband nudged her to hurry. "Good night. Stay strong," she said to the uncle.

The uncle nodded in appreciation and lowered the floorboards.

Darkness.

The boy wanted to go out. "Uncle," he whispered.

"What?" his uncle turned to him, his breath warm and foul.

"I…need to go."

"To go where?"

"To go…to the bathroom."

"You have the bucket."

"Uncle," the boy murmured, not wanting the lawyer and the wife to hear, "I can't."

"Nonsense."

The boy hated his uncle for his brutal honesty.

The uncle took the pot of food from the boy's hand. He whispered to the lawyer and his wife, "We'll have to divide the food equally. We don't know how much food we'll have, and the last thing we need is for us to feel competitive over it."

The couple said nothing.

He continued. "The way I see it, we are two families here. One day you will divide the food," he said to the couple, "and one day we will divide it. Yet when you divide the food, we'll get to pick our pieces first. And when we divide the food, you'll get to pick your pieces first. That way, hopefully we can avoid any…feelings of incorrect division."

"That makes sense," the lawyer said.

The boy kept his mouth shut, the insult from his uncle still burning, his uncle who is supposed to care for him, not brush his needs off as *nonsense.*

The uncle handed the pot with the slice of bread and the two potatoes to the seamstress. "You divide the potatoes and the bread, and we will pick first. Then tomorrow, we will divide, and you will pick."

The seamstress took the piece of bread in the darkness. She slowly divided it into four pieces, and then placed them back in the pot. "Here," she whispered.

The uncle said to the boy, "You pick."

The boy reached his hand in the darkness, groping, finding the pot. He took a slice of bread and half of a warm potato. Only now did he realize how hungry he was. He handed the pot to his uncle.

The uncle followed and chose his own potato half and slice of bread. Then the lawyer and his wife took the pot.

They all ate silently.

When were they going to be let out?

Chapter 36: Light

Paris, 1956

Age 28

Sitting in his lab in Paris, the young scientist had no idea that the next few minutes would change the trajectory of his life.

He was designing a new lens, one even more sensitive than the previous. Never had he imagined that by age 27 he would have a lens he designed himself, a kaleidoscope into another world.

He wanted it to tell even more secrets, to reveal more hidden codes.

He caressed the prototype affectionately.

The morning light shone into the lab.

These days, science was rewarding him. He wasn't just physically flying, but also soaring in his research. Years of countless lab hours and painstaking research had finally catapulted him to new heights.

Following the publication of his scientific book on PhotoStress, after the seemingly endless writing of research papers and the registration of patents, companies around France began hiring him to come and speak, to teach his patented technology to their scientists and improve their engineering.

The young scientist's gaze fixated on the centerpiece of his workbench: the magnificent microscope he had meticulously crafted himself. It was a labor of passion, a tangible manifestation of his relentless pursuit of scientific discovery.

He caressed his creation, pride swelling within him as his fingers glossed over the smooth surface of the heavy-duty frame. Adjusting the illuminator, a radiant beacon beneath the stage, he examined how the new coating of his patented PhotoStress was responding to the expensive alloy called aluminum under the lens.

He heard a cough at the door of the lab.

Even before he raised his eyes from the lens, he could smell heavy cologne. He looked up, meeting the stranger's gaze. The man wore an expensive three-part suit and a hefty amount of grease in his hair. When he spoke, the man's French was replete with a thick American accent: "Hurray! The famous inventor!"

The young scientist blushed and hurried to focus back on the lens. *He was not 'famous' and not an 'inventor.'* Inventors were Edison, Bell, the Wright brothers… He shut his left eye as he refocused on the lens. *He had just happened to stumble upon a useful technology, that was all.*

The American continued, "You look much younger than I had expected!"

The young scientist did not know what to say. What did this man want? He looked back up. After a moment, he replied, a bit reluctantly, "Please, have a seat."

As the American settled into the chair, he began to express his admiration for some of the young scientist's multiple articles in a couple of American science magazines. "You know, I've been following your work for quite some time."

Somewhat distracted, the young scientist said, "Oh, I didn't realize my work had reached such an audience."

"Absolutely! Your ideas, your inventions—they're cutting-edge. I had to meet the man behind it all."

The young scientist raised his eyebrows. "I appreciate your interest, but I wouldn't call myself an inventor. Just a researcher who stumbled upon something interesting."

"Modesty, my friend! How refreshing. Regardless, let me tell you, you've got something special here. Something the world needs. And that's why I'm here."

The young scientist's curiosity piqued, he finally tore his gaze away from the microscope and looked directly at the American.

Over the hour that followed, the man with the grease in his hair explained that he was a headhunter and wished to introduce the young scientist to a few companies in America.

The young scientist tried to smile cordially, but anxiety festered in the pit of his stomach. *What would he have to do in* America *of all places? He did not speak the language. He and his wife were expecting a baby.*

He took a deep breath. "Thank you very much," he began, "but I am afraid I'll have to decline your kind offer."

The headhunter did not seem taken aback. Instead, the man took a piece of paper, wrote a number on it, and slid it across the desk to the young scientist. "Perhaps you'll reconsider. This is what you could expect to be paid, young man, for just one year!"

The young scientist grinned and returned the paper to the headhunter. "I'm already making more than I need to support my family. I also don't speak English. It took me years to master French. I cannot see how this would be of any advantage…"

"Well, you could become famous there," the American headhunter said, his eyes studying the young scientist. "Think of the recognition, the banquets, the great receptions, the awards!"

The young scientist's face remained impassive.

The headhunter tried another angle. "With all due respect to the French industry," he said slowly, "I do believe that America offers great advantages in terms of technology…"

The young scientist tried to keep a passive expression on his face, but the headhunter caught a glimmer of interest in his eyes. The young scientist's blink was subtle, but the headhunter recognized it for what it was. He continued enthusiastically, "Yes, America offers great advantages in technology! And think of the great motor companies, changing the world… Edison, Ford! Who invented the first cars? Who invented the first airplanes? Think of Tesla! Einstein! No one cares if you speak English or not, on the contrary, not speaking English adds to your sex appeal."

The young scientist winced.

After a long speech, in which the headhunter tossed in the air the names of the leading scientists in the United States, many of whom he claimed to know personally, the young scientist said, "What is *your* interest in this, and what will *you* get from this?"

"A 10 percent commission, as is the custom with talent headhunters."

The young scientist nodded. "Well, I'll have to consult with my wife—"

"I'm not asking you to relocate! All I'm asking is for you to come with me for a month-long tour, and let me introduce you to potential companies, great companies!"

The young scientist thought for a long moment. It sounded fair. But he would have to wait. "All right, but it will have to wait for at least a year."

"A year! Why on earth is it so long?"

"Firstly," the young scientist said, "my wife is due to give birth in two months. There's no way I would miss out on the first few months. Secondly," his hand caressed the lens, adjusting the knob of the coarse focus, playing with the fine focus, "there's a small… construction project… that I have to oversee personally."

The headhunter looked baffled. "Surely someone else could oversee a 'construction project!' Let's schedule the visit for two months and two weeks from now. You'll be with your wife and the baby for two weeks, *hurray!* Then fly to meet me in New York." The American seemed insulted, muttering to himself, "Construction project!"

The young scientist shook his head, lost in thought. "You see," he played with the prototype microscope, elevating and lowering the stage, "this construction project…it's more like a debt that I have to settle, involving an old lady who has been like a… mother… to me."

The headhunter sighed heavily. "So can we agree on five months from now?"

"Six—and only if my wife agrees. And," his voice suddenly engaged, as if the child within was bursting out. "You'll have to promise me time to see the Eiffel Tower in New York."

The headhunter was confused. "The… Eiffel Tower is here, in Paris!"

The young scientist smiled. "You probably call it, the Liberty Tower—no, the Liberty Statue?"

The headhunter looked puzzled. "The Statue of Liberty? But isn't that the work of the great artist Bartholdi?"

The young scientist took his hands off of the microscope lens and leaned forward. "Bartholdi *designed* it. But Eiffel *built* it. Without Eiffel's iron truss tower, Bartholdi's design could have never been manifested."

The headhunter studied the shining eyes of the young scientist.

The young scientist murmured, "Eiffel understood stress, strain, pressure…. Most people think a heavy-duty structure, weighing millions of tons, would be better. But Eiffel chose *not* to use a completely rigid structure—which would have led to cracking and breaking—no! He designed a skeleton, to enable the statue to move in the winds of the Atlantic…"

"I didn't know that!"

The young scientist's eyes shone. "Most people notice only the skin, the outer appearance of the sculpture, and think of Bartholdi. Yet, without Eiffel's engineering, there wouldn't have been a Statue of Liberty; without the *scientist*, the artist could not erect anything."

The headhunter smiled knowingly. "You will do very well in America."

Chapter 37: Darkness

Poland, 1943

Age 15

I

It was night in the pit.

The boy thought of his parents and his sister. *Had they been taken too? By the trains?*

His heart burst at the thought of it.

He felt his uncle's breath close to him. "If you keep thinking about it, it will drive you crazy."

The boy moved away from his uncle. *How did he know what the boy was thinking about?* He felt a huge lump in his throat. He wanted to scream.

The uncle spoke to the lawyer and his wife. "We don't know how long we'll be here."

The lawyer whispered, "Right."

"It might take time until the Eastern Front is here. It might take weeks, it might take months. It might," he sighed, "take even longer than that. Therefore, we must learn how to live together in this small space without becoming crazy."

The boy recalled the days playing in the sun.

The uncle continued. "Sitting here is uncomfortable, as you can tell. The dimensions are ideal for lying down, not for sitting like this with our heads bent."

They agreed.

"And so," the uncle sighed, "I think what we should do is have three of us lie down and have one of us sit where our legs are and use the bucket."

The boy wanted to cry, '*How long do you think we'll need to be here?*' But he kept silent.

"Of course," the uncle said, speaking to the lawyer, "my nephew and I will not lie next to your wife. You can always serve as a buffer" The lawyer mumbled something like, "Right."

"But," the uncle said, "there should absolutely, unconditionally, be no sex here."

The boy's cheeks reddened. He hurried to cover his face, then realized no one could see him.

The lawyer whispered, "Of course…"

"Otherwise," the uncle said, "we'll end up killing each other. It is not to be."

The lawyer said nothing. The uncle took a big breath and whispered, "If we're not careful, we will develop unreasonable behavior here. One must not get attached to any spot or position. Every couple of hours we will switch places. The person who was sitting on the bucket will lie down, the person who was lying on one side will move to the center, and so on…"

They all said nothing.

The boy wanted to hear his uncle speaking some more. It distracted him from his own thoughts. But the uncle said nothing else.

Finally, after a few more minutes of them all still sitting, cramped, the uncle said, "Let's do it now." He whispered to the boy, "Do you want to sit on the bucket or lie down?"

The boy needed to go to the bathroom so badly but could not imagine doing it there. He said, "Lie down."

The uncle did not say anything, but just took the position on the bucket. They shuffled around.

The boy lay down on the side, near the lawyer. He felt the hay sticking under his pants. He felt the cold soil wall next to him. He felt the lawyer lying close to him. *Was this really how it was going to be?*

They heard the bed screeching above them. It seemed like the maid and her husband were going to sleep.

The boy felt the scratchy hay beneath him. It was so uncomfortable. And yet, it was more comfortable, he knew, than both the attic above the kitchen and the potato cellar with its bumpy floor. Still, he could not find any solace in that. What scared him the most was how long they could have to be there.

The claustrophobic space seemed to close in around him, suffocating him with its oppressive presence. He longed to break free from the confines of their makeshift prison, to feel the warmth of the sun on his face once more.

But as his thoughts turned to escaping, he thought of the butcher. A cold shiver ran down his spine. He tried not to think of the soldiers, not to think of where they took his grandfather, not to think of the way his cousin's body collapsed to the ground after she was shot before his eyes, not to think of the blood gushing from her once beautiful face. He did not want to think about the butcher's sadistic smile.

The boy regretted having asked his uncle to lie down. His body desperately urged him to relieve himself on the bucket.

It took hours. First, the uncle was on the bucket. Then the seamstress. The boy heard her peeing. Then the lawyer took his turn.

The odor of feces permeated the air through the closed lid of the bucket, which did nothing to isolate the stench.

Finally, hours later, came his turn. He was dizzy and weak, and the smell from the bucket was nauseating.

His bowels were unable to hold it any longer. The constricting quarters offered no privacy, no dignity, no escape.

He wanted to be finished with the foul task he had to complete. But he could not bring himself to do it.

The pangs of urgency transformed into a relentless ache, throbbing, making it hard to concentrate, a persistent reminder that he was mortal, carnal, beast-like. An animal in captivity.

He was no longer the boy that was praised by his teachers for his musical talent. He was no longer the grandchild walking proudly with his well-to-do grandmother in town. He was but an animal reduced to its basic instincts.

As the boy shifted uncomfortably on the bucket, the stench of his fellow inmates crawling from below, his muscles cramped with every subtle movement.

In the darkness, the boy's hands trembled as he clutched at his abdomen. The urgency, a relentless drumbeat in his ears, drowned out the world beyond his body.

He could no longer avoid the demands of his body. Yet he knew the seamstress was listening, and so was the lawyer, and his uncle too.

He tried to hold back the tears of shame and humiliation. He had to choose between his self respect and his body's demands. He shivered, sweat crawling on his skin. Survival, in its rawest form, required a renegotiation between dignity and necessity.

A cynicism towards the human race spread through him, a disdain for all men, and a scornful rejection of vulnerability, of weakness, of shame, as he succumbed to his body, tears rolling down his cheeks.

III

The boy shivered.

He could still hear the echo of his bodily function in the bucket below him. He cleaned himself with the pieces of old newspaper the maid gave them. He pulled his trousers up. He poured water from the pitcher on his hands, trying to wash away the stench—to wash away the shame.

How long had it been? Minutes? Hours? Finally, the uncle said, "Time to switch."

They shuffled positions in the tiny pit, and the boy crawled to a lying position next to the wall, his uncle next to him. The uncle lay near him in the center, with the lawyer on the other side, and the seamstress now on the bucket.

The boy wondered how his uncle knew when to switch. His uncle did not have a watch.

He thought of his sister. Of his mother. Were they alive? Did anyone lend them a helping hand? What about his father? And his grandmother?

Earlier that year, there were rumors circulating about the grim fate awaiting those that were deported. Of mass murders.

Guilt gnawed at him for making the heart-wrenching decision to escape that day when the Nazi guards were not looking, after he heard they were rounding up everyone in the enclosure.

He did not notice his leg was fidgeting.

The uncle turned his head toward him. "Don't think about it!"

The boy hissed, "Enough telling me what to do!"

Silence ensued.

A breath away, the lawyer, hearing them, twitched

uncomfortably.

The uncle was undeterred. "Which grade are you in now?"

The boy did not want to reply. "Should have been in tenth."

The uncle nodded. "Which grade did you finish?"

"Finished? Actually graduated?" the boy asked.

"Yes."

"Seventh grade," the boy said, "before the war…"

"I see." The uncle said. "What did you last study in math?"

"I don't remember," the boy said. He could see no point in this conversation.

"Did you learn proportional relationships? Integers? Rational numbers?"

"I don't remember," the boy answered, irritated.

"How about multiplication and division of negative numbers? Inequalities?"

The boy wanted to scream at his uncle. Why, of all things, was his uncle speaking of math?

The boy hated math. His favorite classes were orchestra practice and literature.

The uncle moved around. He seemed to be concentrating. Thinking. "Do you think birds are lazy?"

Was his uncle out of his mind?

"Answer me!" the uncle whispered. "Are birds lazy?"

"Birds?" asked the boy.

The uncle nodded in the darkness.

Were birds lazy?

The lawyer moved uncomfortably. His wife was silently sitting on the bucket. Only by her smell did the boy know exactly where she was, near his feet.

Birds. Lazy?

The uncle continued. "Why, then, do they fly in a V-formation?"

The boy thought of birds. He missed looking at the sky. *Why were they flying in a V?*

He suddenly knew the answer. "To follow the leader!"

"Is that so?"

"Yes, the leader shows them their way…" The boy was no longer certain, "showing them the way as they migrate following a change of season…?"

"Why, then, does their leader change all the time?"

The boy did not know the bird at the front was not the same throughout the journey.

"Yes. They change leadership. Then, why do they fly like that? In this structure? Geese, pelicans, some cranes, even mute swans?"

In the boy's mind's eye, the birds kept flying above the pit, one type of flock after another. The boy could almost reach his hands and touch them.

The uncle whispered, "Why, then, the V formation?"

The boy thought hard. *If they were changing leadership, why the strange form?* "Is it because it is like an arrow?" he asked.

"Maybe."

The boy moved slightly, agitated, wanting to guess it correctly.

The uncle finally spoke. "Have you ever heard of Bernoulli's principle?"

The boy felt stupid. Ignorant. "No."

The uncle began whispering, but no word came out of his mouth. Instead, he blew air at the boy.

The boy felt his skin tickle.

The uncle blew air again from his mouth. It gently hit the boy's face.

"Air," said the uncle, blowing yet another soft wind through the stuffy pit's stillness. "Air is like water. It moves and swings and twirls. Like liquid."

"Like liquid," repeated the boy, wanting to find out the answer to the riddle of the birds. *Were they lazy?*

"If you drop a stone in water, what happens?"

"It sinks?"

"But what happens to the *surface* of the water?"

"It ripples?"

"Exactly. Air—it ripples too. When a stone hits the water, it forces the water down. But the water doesn't remain passive. It fights back. This is the ripple. They are like tall waves; you push the water down, but it fights, it retorts in waves higher than the static level prior to the stone hitting it."

The boy listened intently. "And?"

"Patience. The ripples go the opposite direction of the direction they were hit. Did you ever drop a stone into a well and see water springs back at you?"

"Yes. Drops jumping out."

"Precisely. Good, your mind is a bright mind. The water fights back." Suddenly the uncle made the sound that annoyed the boy the most. He yawned. "Good night."

"No, uncle, finish!"

The uncle smiled to himself in the darkness. "I forgot what I was talking about."

"You were talking about the splashing water!"

The uncle sounded confused, feignedly so. "Why was I talking about that?"

"Because…" the boy began, "because of the reaction to the stone, there are ripples, the water pushes in the opposite direction." He then added, seeing that the uncle was not responding, "And the air is that way too."

The uncle yawned again, a long, exaggerated yawn.

The boy thought hard. "And, if air is like water, then it also 'fights back.' It retorts."

The uncle's silence seemed to slowly draw the answer from his nephew.

The boy thought of how the air was hit. Like stone. But he could not see how it had to do with birds being lazy or with the V formation.

"Tell me, uncle!"

"Think about it," the uncle said. "Now I really need some sleep."

In the darkness, the boy could tell the uncle was not sleeping. In his mind, he could also hear the flapping of wings. He thought of birds, of air and water, of strange forces retorting and responding to one another. Of ripples.

CHAPTER 38: LIGHT

PARIS, 1956

AGE 28

I

The young scientist's heart was beating fast. *He had to receive a 'yes.' He had to.*

The moneychanger looked puzzled at the young scientist. "What is so urgent?"

They were not in their usual place. They always met at home, on Saturdays. But now the young scientist asked to meet him in the only cafe in the Luxembourg gardens. They were drinking coffee. The young scientist tried to conceal his excitement. "I'm sorry for all the secrecy, but I had an idea that I just had to tell you."

"I am intrigued," the moneychanger smiled.

"Well, I have been reflecting a lot about everything that has happened over the past decade, and I am eternally grateful for everything that your mother has done for me. Over the years, I have desperately wanted to repay my debts."

"We know, you have tried!" the moneychanger chuckled. "But my mother is a stubborn woman."

"Yes! And I have been at a loss with what to do, until now."

It had been a decade since he first came to Paris and met the moneychanger on the very first day. But now he was a scientist who made lots of money. It was time to repay his debts.

The old mama had refused to take his money and threw a fit each time he offered to pay her back for the tuition fees she had paid.

He still wanted to pay her back.

"Your mama," he said, "she always looks so eagerly at the street."

"I've asked her to move a million times."

"I know…"

"The stairs, her hip."

"I know." The young scientist tried not to sound too eager, to sound dismissive. Disinterested. "Did you ever think of an elevator?"

The moneychanger nearly choked on his coffee. "An elevator?"

The young scientist nodded, his face angled down at his coffee, only his eyes carefully studying the moneychanger's eyes.

"But," the moneychanger gasped, "the money…!"

"Forget about the money."

"But it costs so much! Only the wealthiest—"

"Forget about the money. The city said we need to procure approval from everyone in the building."

"You've already gone to the city?"

The young scientist sipped his coffee. "If we procure the approval of all the building residents, we could build an elevator in the back of the building, in the courtyard, with the door facing outward; therefore, it will not tamper with the facade, not harm the exterior of the building, nor the narrow staircase, you see?"

The moneychanger was completely stunned.

They sat there in silence.

The young scientist had asked the old mama many, many times why she and her son would not move. She would never listen. He tried to convince her that an apartment at street level would let her step outside, be in the fresh air, and go to the gardens… But she always refused, saying, "This is where I hid during the war, and this is where I'll die. This is my home!"

Her hip, and now her knee, made it difficult for her to walk, especially on the stairs. The young scientist knew she had not been out of the house for some fifteen years.

The moneychanger smiled. "An elevator! I cannot believe I never thought of it myself."

The young man shrugged his shoulders dismissively. He did not want to tell how he had spent months weaving this in his brain. He imagined it could be a surprise – that the old mama would not be told about the cause of the reconstruction; they would tell her it was just regular construction, mandated by the city, to reinforce the building. She would believe it, would she not?

And he knew they should do it on her birthday in six months. But time was of the essence, and they needed to procure signatures from all the neighbors in the building soon.

The moneychanger shook his head. "But… expensive!"

"I have the money. But I need your help."

Today was the day.

He had worked on this project for six months.

In fact, he had worked on this for a decade, ever since the end of the war.

The young scientist examined the brass sign and the buttons indicating: first floor, second floor, third floor. He lovingly placed his finger on the last button. Fourth floor.

Downstairs, in the small locked building garden, everything was finally ready. He held tightly to the flowers, unable to calm himself down. *What if the old mama hates it? What if she blames him for going behind her back? For insulting her?*

The elevator climbed up. It slowly made its way to the fourth floor. The door opened, revealing nothing but the white tarp covering the elevator door. With one hand holding the flowers, the young scientist moved the tarp out of his way, then allowed it to fall back, concealing the creme-colored metal door.

He stepped through the narrow ledge to the only door on the floor. He took a deep breath, glancing back, ensuring the tarp was covering the elevator.

Then he knocked on the door.

He could hear the old mama shuffling through the house. Then he saw her looking through the peephole.

She opened the door. "Son of mine!" she exclaimed, adjusting her headscarf. "What are you doing here in the middle of the week?"

"I was just passing by and wanted to say hi!"

Suspicious, the old mama pouted her lips. "I did not see you coming down the street!"

"I arrived some time ago," he said as he entered the house.

"Some time ago?" the old mama asked as she locked the door. "What's all this secrecy? And what do you have behind your back?"

The young scientist handed her the flowers.

"Oh! Irises…" the old mama exclaimed with joy. "What have I done to deserve a visit with irises in the middle of the week?" She smiled with all her teeth, illuminated with pride and curiosity.

"It's your birthday, Mama!"

She smiled and blushed. "I knew that, but I did not know *you* knew that! Nor did my ungrateful son," she spat on the floor, "who said *nothing* to me this morning!"

"I don't think he forgot."

"Of course he forgot!" she said, holding the bouquet. "I must put these in water!" She suddenly seemed stressed. "Oh my, you must be hungry…let me see what I can make…"

"No, Mama!" The young scientist laughed, his eyes becoming moist from the gravity of the moment. "No, I have a surprise for you…"

"Surprise? More than the bouquet? What surprise?" She walked to the kitchen slowly.

He followed her in the narrow hallway. "You remember telling me about the building's reinforcement—"

"Oh, don't let me speak of that! Stupid city!" she said as she pulled out the vase, staring at him from the kitchen. "The noise I had to bear over the past few months! And they opened a hole in the wall in the stairway! The dust! The mess! Merde! Merde! Merde!" She spat on the floor. "What a stupid policy! I would have preferred no reinforcement at all!" She looked up to the ceiling. "May there come an earthquake and take the building down with me!" she tut-tutted, "All this mess and dust and noise…!"

The young scientist could not conceal his excitement any longer. He searched for words, but had none. He saw the old mama was fixing the irises in the vase. He reached for her hand, murmuring, "Come."

"Where?" she said, confused, following him through the narrow hallway.

He reached the apartment door, undid the five locks and opened the door wide. "Mama, I want you to come with me."

"Fool! Don't you know already I cannot handle the stairs!" She saw him reaching for the tarp. "Have I not told you a thousand…what's *that?*"

In the hallway, the young scientist pulled the tarp down and folded it, a cloud of dust appearing. As if by magic, he revealed the metallic creme-colored door, framed by a thick metallic door frame, as if it was a piece of art.

The old mama looked startled upon seeing the glossy creme door. "What's that, son?"

The young scientist had tears in his eyes. "It's your surprise, Mama!"

The old mama looked at the shiny door, at the door frame, at the button in the wall. She had seen these in the finest hotels of Paris, years before the war. "An… *elevator?*"

The young scientist pointed at the button. "Press here!"

The old mama shuffled to the wall button, her eyes examining the button, and then looking at the young scientist, then the button again, then at the young scientist again. Her hand shaking, she pointed her finger forward, like a figure from a Michelangelo Sistine Chapel scene, and pressed the button on the wall, her face alarmed when its light turned on.

She heard a sound.

The elevator door opened. *"Merde!"* the old mama muttered. The young scientist, smiling, tears in his eyes, gestured for her to enter. She walked in hesitantly.

The elevator door closed, and the elevator suddenly began moving. "Merde! Merde!" the old mama exclaimed and pointed at the young scientist's face. "I should have thrown you down the stairs that very first day! Wanting to give me that filthy money! I could have saved myself the agony of…"

It was then that the elevator reached the bottom floor, the door opening into the small courtyard. The voices shouted in unison, "Happy birthday!"

The old mama stared at the courtyard, seeing all the old neighbors, her son, a table, and a cake.

These were the neighbors who had, during the war, sealed their lips and told the occupying army's soldiers the woman upstairs was long gone. There were the neighbors who had brought the old mama food and made sure she was safe. There was the baker and his wife, the accountant, the factory manager, the philharmonic cello player, and of course, the wide-eyed lady who, with her late short-haired partner, had bribed the soldiers to keep them from searching the apartment on the top floor.

Seeing all of them, the old mama gasped and adjusted her headscarf.

She made a miserable face and whispered to the young scientist standing near her in the elevator, "But I'm not properly dressed…"

The money changer walked to the elevator from the table and exclaimed, "Mama, look at all your friends, they've come to celebrate with you! Now come out!"

Slowly, the old mama stepped out of the elevator, overwhelmed: overwhelmed by the smiles of her neighbors, overwhelmed by the way she had made it downstairs, overwhelmed by the bright sunny day, by having no rooftop above her head after years of glancing at the sky from an angle. The sky opened widely above her, locked between the buildings.

As the minutes stretched into an hour, the group gathered around the table and indulged in the sweet decadence of the cake that served as a centerpiece to their shared memories.

With each bite, layers of nostalgia and camaraderie unfolded, weaving a tapestry of stories that spanned the tumultuous years of war and the halcyon days of peace that came after.

They spoke of the crazy artists who had once graced their lives with their eccentricities, their imaginations breathing color into the monochrome canvas of everyday existence.

The short-haired lady, with her avant-garde sensibilities and infectious laughter, had been a constant source of inspiration and amusement, her presence a reminder that even in the darkest of times, creativity flourished like a defiant flower in the cracks of adversity.

And then there was the baker's wife, her warm smile a beacon of comfort in a world plagued by scarcity and uncertainty.

With each loaf of fresh bread she delivered to the doorstep of the old mama, she offered not just sustenance, but a gesture of kindness that resonated far beyond the confines of their shared neighborhood.

In the simple act of breaking bread together, they forged bonds that transcended the boundaries of time and space, united in their resilience and their unwavering belief in the power of community.

Soon, the old mama regained her composure and began pleading with them all to eat more and finish the cake.

When they finished, the wide-eyed lady stood up slowly and said, "Now, we shall all walk to the Luxembourg Gardens."

The old mama was stunned. "No…!"

They all nodded. "Yes, yes, come on!"

"But," she breathed heavily, unable to contain the gravity of the proposal, "I… cannot walk that far!"

The moneychanger was pleased and hurried to bring a wheelchair from the back of the yard. "We thought of that, Mama, so we prepared this…"

The old mama stood up at once and said, "Take that thing and shove it up your tush!"

They all laughed. She exclaimed, "No, you sit on it, and roll yourself into the Seine!"

They all laughed again. The old mama began walking. "Come on, you all!"

Eyewitnesses at the Luxembourg Gardens that day saw a procession of older people, led by a stubborn old lady, supported on either side by two younger men, her eyes filled with tears.

Chapter 39: Darkness

Poland, 1943

Age 15

I

"So tell me. Are birds lazy?" the uncle whispered.

The boy hesitated. "When the birds flap their wings, is it like hitting water with a stone?" the boy whispered.

"Maybe…" the uncle replied.

The boy had a guess, but it sounded ridiculous. "Can it be that the ripples are like waves, and that it is easier for the other birds to ride that wave?"

"Bernoulli's principle," the uncle whispered, "is an idea of fluid dynamics. It says that as the speed of the fluid increases, pressure decreases. The leading bird, at the front, carries all the blunt of the heavy lifting. But the second one needs to work less hard."

"Because of the thrust from the leading bird?" asked the boy.

"Yes. It is called the 'lift.' Now, if the front bird carries the most burden, who carries the *least* burden?"

"The last bird?" guessed the boy.

"Very good. Why?"

The boy thought. "If the first bird creates a 'lift', then the second adds to it? And then each one, making it grow?"

The uncle's voice betrayed a smile. "Like a pure mathematical sequence."

The boy said, enchanted, "Like a pure mathematical sequence."

The uncle mentioned Newton's second law of motion, and force, change, momentum, object, and time.

The boy was used to dozing off in math lessons, never realizing there was a beauty and elegance in numbers and equations. But somehow, through the uncle's words, there seemed to be great beauty—and clarity—in the mathematical sequence.

A few hours later the boy was almost able to forget he was in the same crammed pit. The uncle whispered to him riddle after riddle, each time adding a new layer of complexity, a new hint to unravel. Mass, velocity and speed introduced themselves to the boy, each new element complementing the previous.

The uncle stretched. "And so, in the flock, flying, where would the strongest healthiest birds be positioned?"

"At the front."

"Yes, changing, taking turns at the very front. And where would the older birds, the baby birds, the sick birds be?"

"At the back!" The boy finally understood the beauty of the riddle.

"Is it easier to fly alone, or fly in a flock?"

"In a flock!"

The uncle chuckled. "So, you tell me now. Are birds lazy?"

The question hung in the air. The boy roamed the sky, his wings flapping, the air hitting his beak, his heart soaring. The pit was airy and spacious, and his mind was boundless to infinity and back.

"No," he said. "They are not lazy. They are just smart."

The uncle laughed.

"Uncle, another riddle, please!"

II

"Can you picture a pinecone?"

The boy thought of times before the war, when he used to go with his uncle on a walk during the summer vacations. One summer he collected pine cones. He could still recall their sweet and earthy smell. And the sap that stuck to his fingers.

"Yes, Uncle."

"Now imagine you are walking in the forest. And you stumble upon a pinecone. A special one. This pinecone holds a secret, a hidden pattern that connects it to something greater than itself."

The boy furrowed his brow in the darkness. "What do you mean?"

"Imagine this," said the uncle. "If we were to carefully examine the spirals on the surface of the pinecone, something remarkable would become apparent."

The boy's eyes widened with curiosity. "What?"

"We would discover that the number of scales and their pattern goes in a unique sequence, both clockwise and counterclockwise. It is a secret only mathematicians know."

"I want to know!"

"It is a sequence. A series of numbers where each number is the sum of the two preceding ones," whispered the uncle. "It starts with 0 and 1, and then each subsequent number is the sum of the two before it."

The boy's eyes lit up with a spark of comprehension. "Like adding numbers?"

"Yes, exactly," said the uncle, nodding. "Let's see if you can complete it. We begin with zero, then one. What is the sum of zero and one?"

"One!"

"Well done. So now the last couple of digits are one and one. What is the sum of one plus one?"

"Two."

"Good. Now we have one and two. What is the—"

"Three!"

"Exactly. And then?"

The boy hesitated.

"Always add the last two numbers in the series together."

The boy added three plus two. "Five?"

"Well done. And then?"

The boy added five plus three together. "Eight?"

"You are very bright."

The boy added the numbers in his head, finding the sequence challenging, yet not impossible to calculate.

"Here's the fascinating part: if we count the scales on the pinecone, we'll find that the scales are *exactly* like the mathematical sequence we calculated."

"What? How?"

"Nature knows," the uncle responded quietly, mystery in his voice. "The pinecone knows exactly how to grow from the moment it is but a seed. The formula is ingrained in it. Have you heard of Fibonacci?"

"Fibo—?"

"Fibonacci."

"Was that a composer?" the boy inquired.

"He uncovered this hidden sequence in nature."

As the boy's fascination deepened, the uncle continued to unveil the mysteries of what he called the *Fibonacci sequence*, with sequences spiraling clockwise and counterclockwise, dazzling the boy's mind in the darkness.

The uncle explained it was not only in pinecones, but also in the delicate spirals of seashells to the graceful curves of flower petals.

With wide-eyed wonder, the boy began to see the sequence's imprint in his mind. He followed his uncle's guidance, finding order in the branching patterns of trees or the arrangement of leaves along a stem. He was no longer confined to the pit. Nature, it seemed, was a symphony of beauty and order—audible for those willing to listen.

CHAPTER 40: LIGHT

NEW YORK, 1956

AGE 28

I

"Liberty lady. Take me to her, please," said the young scientist as he met the headhunter at the Idlewild airport in New York.

The headhunter hesitated for a moment, trying to comprehend the urgency of the young scientist's desire to visit the statue.

But the young scientist insisted. He wanted no rest nor food.

Two hours later the young scientist climbed the narrow stairway up the Statue of Liberty, with the panting headhunter behind him. He marveled at the spiral staircase, built so meticulously in times when technology was still taking its first steps, at the twilight of the previous century.

His fingers traced the contours of the walls. The cool touch of iron and the familiar scent stirred memories of his arrival in Paris and his first love—the Eiffel Tower. In both structures, he recognized the unmistakable fingerprint of Gustave Eiffel himself.

As the young scientist hurried up the stairs, his thoughts lingered on his baby girl at home—her wondrous eyes, tiny fingers, and rosy lips. He missed her coos, her smile, and the way her little hands would reach for his face after a nap. He cherished the professional photos he had sent to the old maid and her family. Though he hated leaving his baby, the chance to experience America, with his flight and hotels generously covered, was an opportunity none of his peers had received. His wife was surprisingly unbothered about him leaving for a month. She asked her mother to assist with the baby. She was almost happy to see her husband leave.

His uncle, too, encouraged him. Much like a decade earlier when his uncle had nearly forced him to go to France, now his uncle said that he'd be a real fool not to at least give America a try.

The young scientist ascended the stairs, glancing through the narrow windows at the bustling city below. He thought of the countless immigrants who had *begged* for a chance to be here, while this country had invited him.

Through the windows, he saw a vibrant city, a mosaic of cultures and stories stitched together by resilience. In the quiet of the stairwell, he reflected on his own journey, his mind filled with memories of those who had come before.

He knew that he had been given a rare gift, a chance to make a difference, to leave his mark upon the world in ways both big and small.

For in this strange new land, anything was possible, and the young scientist dared to dream of a world where barriers were broken, and boundaries dissolved in the pursuit of a brighter tomorrow.

The headhunter read the sign above the stairs, panting, "We…are…almost there, fifty more stairs…"

The young scientist began climbing two stairs at a time. "I'll see you up there!"

From the top, looking through the large windows in the crown of the statue, the sea was vast. The city was shining in the afternoon sun. There was the Empire State Building. And so many other grand skyscrapers. *What a nation*, he thought, *to build these buildings stretching to the heavens, a triumph of man over gravity.*

He saw the headhunter panting, leaning on the railing. The

headhunter tried to smile. "Breathtaking, isn't it?"

The young scientist smiled. "Literally."

They quietly gazed at the stunning view.

The scientist seemed lost in thoughts. Finally he said, "Thank you for bringing me here."

"You are more than welcome."

"Now, please show me more of America."

II

The young scientist was sitting in his uncle's apartment in Paris. The uncle had remarried. He and his nephew met regularly to discuss politics, science, the future—anything but the past.

As they sat in the uncle's home, the atmosphere was tinged with both nostalgia and anticipation. The uncle, a man of few words but full of wisdom, leaned back in his chair, sipping on his tea while his nephew, the young scientist, fidgeted with his cup, lost in thought. In the kitchen, the uncle's wife was making supper.

"There is no question here," the uncle said. "Of course you should emigrate! Give up an opportunity to go to America? People would kill for that!"

"But, Uncle," the young scientist protested, "I don't even speak the language."

"You'll learn it!" the uncle said. "What exactly did that American headhunter offer?"

"A generous salary working in Philadelphia for a large manufacturer, as the Director of Research."

"You'd be a fool not to take it. What is your wife saying?"

The young scientist sighed. His wife was unwilling at first: what would this mean for her career as a concert pianist? And how could she get by as a new mother in a foreign country? But she relented. She still believed in their relationship, no matter how difficult it had become for the two of them.

"She is amazing," the young scientist said. "She is willing to try."

The uncle gestured with his hand casually, as if to say, 'So what is the problem?'

The uncle's wife emerged from the kitchen momentarily to place a plate of freshly baked biscuits in front of them. She looked at her husband and said, "Take it easy on him."

The uncle rolled his eyes playfully at her, and she smiled at him. The young scientist watched this small interaction as a pang of longing hit him. He missed such moments with his own wife. He watched as the uncle's wife went back to the kitchen, softly humming to herself.

The young scientist was torn. He looked toward the kitchen. "Is there any chance you two would join us?"

The uncle shook his head. "You're not a boy anymore. And neither am I. My life is here. You still have the future ahead of you…"

"So do you, Uncle!"

The uncle was quiet, as he so often was. He looked at his nephew with his sad eyes. "I promised your parents…in my heart." He looked away, strained, blinking rapidly. "I promised them I'd watch over you." He inhaled slowly, "This is an opportunity…You have to give this opportunity a chance."

The scientific discoveries in America were too tempting to not go and take part in.

Would he have the courage to leave everything behind again? To leave the language that slowly had become his second nature? To leave the city that embraced him with its large avenues, its iconic tower, and it's beautiful cafe and gardens?

Could he not rest on the laurels of his success and choose home over an unknown future? Would he forever be running away from anything that resembled home and stability?

Chapter 41: Darkness

Poland, 1943

Age 15

The seamstress bewitched him.

They received a small oil lamp from the husband of the maid. They only used it for a minute each day, to divide their food. Each time the oil lamp was lit, the boy had to cover his eyes. After weeks of darkness, light felt unbearable. The only benefit for the boy was seeing the seamstress; she was not much older than him—maybe only a decade—and the boy blushed every time he looked at her.

Those thoughts were sweet, intoxicating, and poisonous. He had to unwillingly shake them, for the more he dwelled on them, the more he felt embarrassed by their presence.

Days morphed into nights, nights into dark days. The hours in the hole became days, and the days became weeks.

The boy had gotten used to relieving himself on the bucket. They all had.

Food was scarce, but the lawyer had some gold coins in his shoe, of which he gave to the maid every few weeks. In turn, she was able to buy a few vegetables and get bread for the many mouths in the cabin, above and below ground.

The boy did not leave the uncle alone, asking constant questions. The uncle did not seem to be bothered by it.

The boy thought a lot about the world outside. They knew what time of day it was according to the noises in the cabin. The most noise was made in the cabin in the morning and in the evening. Once in a while they heard a farmer or a neighbor coming to visit.

Although it was still stuffy, the spring air penetrated the pit. The boy yearned for the sun's warm caress, a distant memory fading like an old photograph.

He longed for the symphony of nature that accompanied spring—the gentle hum of bees, the melody of songbirds, the taste of fresh air of blooming apple trees.

Every passing day in hiding heightened his appreciation for the simple pleasures he once took for granted. The crunch of gravel underfoot, the arguments he used to have with his sister, the comforting scent of his mother's cooking, and the lively discussion shared around the family table—all became vivid in his mind, haunting him in his solitude.

The boy thought constantly of the mathematical questions posed by his uncle. It was not enough of a distraction, though. He began attending, in his mind, practices with the youth orchestra he used to play in.

In his mind, he pictured the conductor, that peculiar man with large spectacles, whom the kids in the orchestra used to mock. Before the war, the boy had played the violin—until soldiers stormed their cabin, one of them smashing the instrument against the wall, shattering its delicate neck.

Desperate to escape the memory, the boy found himself back in the youth orchestra rehearsals. Mozart. Beethoven. Bach. He heard the music clearly, knew exactly when his violin should join the others, when the oboe, when the clarinet… He replayed the melodies in his head, over and over. If only he had another chance to feel the violin under his chin, to move the bow along its strings, stirring all the souls that stood witness. Making his mom proud.

There was the ache of thinking of his mother. And of him leaving her that morning when the Nazis took everyone to the trains. He couldn't think of his betrayal.

"Uncle, give me a new equation!"

Chapter 42: Light

Philadelphia, 1958

Age 30

I

It was time to take an airplane to start a new life.

Thirteen years after he had first stepped foot in Paris, the young scientist was leaving his beloved adopted city. Sitting on an airplane with his wife and precious two-year-old daughter, he made his way across the ocean again.

Even though he had moved before, after the war, something about this move felt insurmountably difficult. He had settled in Paris and had started a family. He did not want to uproot them only for the sake of his career.

But America whispered of opportunity. Of a better life—a better life for his daughter. She, too, could become a scientist, in the land of possibilities. A scientist—or anything else she would one day choose.

He did not remember much of Philadelphia, one of the many cities he had visited with the eager headhunter. But one thing he did recall: a bell. A *cracked* bell. One that represented liberty.

He liked that.

He also liked the crack itself. He smiled to himself. Had they used his methods and technology two hundred years earlier, then maybe—just maybe—they could have identified the areas of the bell most susceptible to pressure. Using the unique plastic coating he developed, they could have pinpointed those weak spots, and then corrected the design, making the bell thicker where needed, making sure it would not crack.

He smiled again. Then, however, the bell would not have been the same bell. *What made the bell so unique*, he mused, *was* the crack. The crack threatened to break the bell, but instead it had only made it more unique: of historic importance!

The crack 'made' the bell.

He bit his lip as he looked through the window at the clouds. He liked that thought. 'The crack made the bell.'

Years passed. The city with the cracked bell smiled at the young scientist. Now thirty-three, he was the chief scientist for the large manufacturer who had brought him to America.

The work was interesting. The manufacturer was involved in several realms: the train industry, the automobile industry, and even the budding space industry.

More excitingly, the young scientist now had a family. A real family, like the one he had dreamed of for years, ever since the war. His eldest daughter was now six years old. His wife had given birth to two more children: another beautiful daughter and a sweet baby boy.

He ignored the difficulties in communication he had with his wife and marveled at her strength and charisma. She had left her beloved country and her family for him, and it was not something he took lightly. English was a challenge for him. But he made it his habit to learn thirty new words each day like he did when learning French. He forgot many words, yet some stuck. After a couple of years he could speak the language fluently. True, he had a heavy accent and made many grammatical errors. But still, he spoke the language.

He loved traveling to different factories owned by his employer, the multimillion-dollar company, and using the equipment and technology he had developed to create improved designs that were both lighter and stronger. He loved demonstrating to the designers and engineers the beauty of his *PhotoStress* technology. He had also developed, with the help of his team of scientists, an electronic measurement device. After connecting it to the lens, they could immediately find the corresponding mathematical pressure associated with each variation in color.

Yet this electronic device had one small problem that frustrated him. He could not ignore it.

It was the same problem many fine precision devices had. After prolonged use, there were glitches in its performance. This didn't matter for most electronic products. Nor were the glitches in the results important for anyone who was not a scientist.

The glitches vexed him. He asked his colleague, an electrical engineer, to explain to him how the electric system worked. That's how he learned that the problem arose from a part in the electric cycle that would heat too much. This part, called the 'resistor' consisted of a metal wire that played a crucial role. Much like a valve restricts the flow of water, the resistor was responsible for restricting the flow of electricity.

His colleague explained that the only problem with this metal piece was that it naturally got hotter when the current passed through it. When it got hotter, it expanded and grew, like all metals do. And when it became longer, its resistance to the current became a tiny bit stronger.

"But can't you just use a different material?" he asked the electrical engineer.

The electrical engineer snorted. "Well, they've tried. Back in the day, resistors were made from all kinds of metals. But they found that only this kind of metal from carbon composition does the job pretty decently."

Pretty decently. The young scientist did not want a "pretty decent" resistor. He wanted an excellent resistor. "Pretty decent" might be okay for a toaster or a radio, but not for his extra-sensitive measurement device.

And surely, if he had problems with how resistors varied in their performance over time, others must have experienced this as well.

He thought of it often.

At night, he heard his baby boy stirring in his cot, about to cry. The young scientist hurried to get out of his bed, not wanting to wake his tired wife.

He fed his baby boy the milk, then rocked him to sleep. After watching his baby fall back asleep immediately, the young scientist could not go back to sleep.

He turned on the lights in the living room. Quietly, he pulled out his notepad and drew the electric circuit. The resistor was a crucial component, varying the electric current, manipulating it to become exactly the right amount for the specific component. *The exact amount—no more, no less.*

He drew the resistor—the metal wire wound around a small cylinder. The electric current forced the wire to heat up. Heating forced it to expand. Expansion resulted in a slightly stronger resistance to the current.

He sighed. He knew it was only a fraction of one percent change in the resistance. But it was still a change. He sensed it. *Others must sense it too, right?*

He drummed the notepad with his pencil. No ideas. He'd better go to bed and get some sleep before morning comes.

Little did he know that this tinkering with this little electronic component was going to cost him his job and the stability he had worked so hard to gain.

Chapter 43: Darkness

Poland, 1943

Age 15

Weeks became months. The boy felt more and more helpless. It became ever more hot and stuffy in the pit. The air stood still, and he was itching from lice.

The more the time passed, the more bitter he felt about his plight, and his family's, and his people's.

The boy's thoughts soon became a bitter, venomous brew threatening to boil over.

Even the equations could not distract him from the hatred growing inside him.

He wanted to take revenge. When the war was over, he thought, he would go to the heart of the occupying army, and he would have a revolver. He would gun everyone down.

Everyone.

At times, he would remember the horrific things he had seen. How the soldiers had herded his whole community, tens of thousands, into a tiny segregated ghetto. How the damned officer, nicknamed "the butcher," shot at people for no apparent reason.

He remembered the butcher very well.

It was summer now, and instead of enjoying the sun, he was locked in darkness.

Sometimes in the pit, when the boy heard noises coming from the outside, he thought it was the butcher with his soldiers, coming to look for him.

He knew danger was there, always.

One day they heard a knock on the door.

The old neighbor visited and obviously gravitated toward the bedroom.

Under the floorboards, the boy and the others clearly heard the neighbor exclaiming to the maid, "Where *are* they?"

"Where are who?" asked the maid. "My daughters are at school!"

"Don't pretend you don't know," they heard the neighbor saying. "Where are you hiding them, those damned hat-wearers?"

"What?" the maid exclaimed. Then she yelled, "You are accusing us of hiding such people? Never would I do that!"

"Don't act so innocent, everyone knows how you got this fine house!"

"Well—" the maid stumbled over her words.

"And where is that family now?" the neighbor interjected. "Seems like a pretty convenient time for them to cash in a favor!"

Under the floorboards, the boy's body tightened.

No one dared moving.

"Oh please!" the maid scoffed, regaining confidence. "I haven't heard from that family in years! Why, for you to even suggest—it's preposterous!"

"Swear in the name of God!" they heard the neighbor saying.

The boy swallowed his saliva. The maid was extremely religious. Would she desert her belief in God to help four lowly Jews?

"Swear in His name!"

Silence followed. The boy's heart sank. *It was over.*

Chapter 44: Light

Philadelphia, 1961

Age 33

I

"I have it!" the young scientist exclaimed triumphantly as he entered the electrical engineer's office.

The two had been working together, and the electrical engineer knew of the young scientist's lack of understanding of electrical engineering.

"What?" the electrical engineer asked.

"The resistor! I have a way to design it so that there will be no variations whatsoever in the electric current!"

The electrical engineer smirked. "Really?"

"Well," the young scientist smiled, "when you think of 'resistor,' you think of a metal wire, right?"

"Right."

"But in essence, any form of metal could do. Even, say, a piece of foil, right?"

"Right…?"

"So, if you take some foil, and you use adhesives to bond it to a material that does not expand or contract, say, a piece of ceramic…then, in turn, the foil will not expand when it gets hot, nor will it contract when it gets cold."

The electrical engineer stared at the young scientist.

The young scientist spoke fast, with his heavy Polish-French accent. "It is simple! Being bonded to a material that does not expand, will lead to no expansion." He paced excitedly around the small office. "No variation of size, therefore no variation in resistance. Voila!"

The electrical engineer chuckled. "But it won't work."

The young scientist frowned. "Why?"

"Because, it's too simple an idea. They would have invented it already."

"Simple isn't a bad thing. *PhotoStress* has been criticized for being too simple!"

"Yes, but the adhesive, how can you be so certain it would stick to that metal foil in the long run? And how can you be sure that the metal will not expand just because it's glued to some non-expanding surface? And how can you be certain that gluing it won't mess up the resistance altogether? It sounds too complicated."

"Wait, are you saying it is too simple or it is too complicated?"

The electrical engineer shrugged.

The young scientist recognized this shrug. He had seen it before. Whenever he tried developing something new, he faced skepticism from everyone.

He was determined to prove himself to everyone who ever doubted him.

II

The young scientist tinkered for weeks with various materials. He wanted to build a new resistor, something that would be more accurate. A resistor that would not heat, not expand, and therefore not create annoying variations in its electrical current. He wanted to make sure his resistor had precision. It had to be perfect.

Again, he stayed in the lab late into the night. The lights of Philadelphia shone through the window.

He tinkered with ceramic. Glass. Graphite composites. Carbon fiber composites. Aluminum silicon alloys. Anything that had non-expanding quality.

He did not have it *yet*. He knew it would take a large team and a few months of research to nail down the exact combination of the right foil, the right non-expanding material, the right adhesive, the right size, and a few other small details.

But he knew he was *onto* something. And he knew there was a need for it. If he *himself* needed such a resistor, others surely would be interested....

He finally managed to schedule a meeting with the big boss, the CEO.

Sitting in the big boss' huge office overlooking the city, the young scientist introduced his idea. For fifteen minutes, he explained the concept behind the new resistor.

The big boss, chewing on his cigar, tried to follow the explanation.

The young scientist finally concluded, "It can create a revolution in resistor technology!"

The big boss leaned back in his big chair. "I can see the logic in your words…But you're a scientist, not a businessman—a very good scientist, mind you—but still, a *scientist*."

The young scientist stared at him. He needed this to become a side project taken on by the company, funding the research—and the company would in turn reap huge returns.

The big boss continued. "For this to be explored further, we need to do market research. The last thing I need is an obscure electric component for which there is no market demand, gotcha?" He put out his cigar and watched the scientist.

"I see," said the young scientist, "but I can assure you that if I need such a component, then surely—"

The big boss called his assistant into the office. "We'll need the marketing team to look into market demand for this—" He looked at the young scientist. "—What did you call it?"

"Temperature-impervious resistor. A resistor whose resistance level doesn't fluctuate with use."

"Yes. That."

The assistant wrote it all down.

The big boss sighed and looked at the young scientist. "I hear you are leaving for a short trip to France, is that correct?"

The young scientist nodded.

"I hear you are to receive some prize there…?"

The young scientist nodded again.

"Well, congratulations!" the big boss said and leaned forward to shake the young scientist's hand, marking the end of the conversation. "We'll give the marketing team a month or so to do the research and then we'll see…"

The young scientist shook his hand eagerly. "Yes, yes, thank you for your time!"

Chapter 45: Darkness

POLAND, 1943

AGE 15

I

The boy heard the neighbor repeating again, "Swear in the name of God!"

"I swear in the name of God!" the maid shouted. "I would never hide those terrible people!"

Then there was silence.

In the pit, they dared not breathe. Nor even blink.

"Well, we'll see about that!"

They heard the neighbor leaving.

They spent the rest of the day in silence. There were no math exercises. They did not even switch positions.

When evening fell, and after the children went to sleep, the maid knocked on the floor.

The uncle lifted the floorboards.

They all saw the maid and her husband.

Would the husband tell them to leave?

The boy was afraid that this was to be their farewell. That the couple would explain that they could no longer hide them. That it was too dangerous.

The maid and her husband said nothing. They looked at the

uncle and the other three scared faces inside the hiding pit.

The uncle looked at them. It was the longest of moments. The maid's eyes seemed as if she had been crying.

The uncle said, "We are so appreciative of your courage. You've been so kind to us."

The maid sighed and shook her head, "Now-now, don't mention it. You would have done the same for us."

There was silence again. The boy moved uncomfortably.

The husband whispered, "They've caught—the Germans caught, a family in the village, who hid one woman. They came with dogs, finding out the hiding place."

The husband usually spoke faster. But this time he spoke slower. "They shot her then and there. And they hung the whole family, the two sons, too."

That following night, when the maid brought them their food and took the heavy smelly bucket, the uncle said, "Madam?"

"Yes?"

"We need to get a dog."

"A dog!" The maid looked at him as if he had gone crazy.

"Yes, a dog," responded the uncle.

"I can barely feed us all, eleven mouths! And now you want me to feed a dog, too?"

"A dog," said the uncle, "could distract the soldiers' dogs, if they come."

The maid corrected him. "*When* they come."

"When they come," the uncle said.

The maid and the uncle looked at length at one another. She sighed.

The uncle looked at the lawyer and placed his open palm before him, asking him for money.

The lawyer reluctantly reached for his shoe and pulled out a coin.

The uncle handed the maid the gold coin. "We can help you pay for a dog. And a doghouse. It'd be outside, near where our air pipe is, so that his presence there would diffuse our scent. Any dog of theirs would easily smell us out. But," he paused, "a dog, with a doghouse near the pipe, might save us."

The maid said, "Let me see."

The uncle smiled. "Thank you. We are grateful for you all."

The maid took the coin, sighed, shook her head, looked with pity at the four faces, and then stood up.

In the darkness, the uncle turned on the lamp. They divided the food silently.

The boy was always hungry, but now he could barely eat.

His thoughts were invaded by the feeling that the neighbor had surely realized where they were hiding but had not yet said a thing. Was it a silence intended to protect them, or to deceive the maid? So when the soldiers did come, there would be no escape for them at all.

II

The days were all the same. Dark, damp, dreary.

Summer arrived The pit was warm. The air was full with the smell of fields. Intoxicating flowers: roses, lavender, wildflowers. The distinct earthly smell of grass, crisp, lung-filling crops, forests, trees stretching their branches. Soil, hay. Warm earth.

He missed those smells. He missed the world outside.

He thought things could not get worse. But they did.

There was less food, and oftentimes the maid brought them nothing but potatoes.

The smell was appalling. The maid and her husband bought a dog and placed his doghouse and chain right in the yard by the narrow pipe. The pipe brought the pit the much needed air, but now there was the stench of another animal, occasionally barking and rattling its chain.

Like the dog, the boy, too, was in chains. But the dog had more freedom than they had in the pit: the dog could see the night sky, chase butterflies, see birds and squirrels, and roll in the grass.

In the darkness of the pit, learning had become the boy's escape. He reprimanded himself for not having paid more attention in school. Now he wanted to learn everything, not just math. His uncle's knowledge of the world was limited—he mostly knew math and physics. And the boy was hungry for more.

He asked the lawyer countless questions about law and humanities. But the lawyer was always reserved. And the boy did not want to upset him. And he knew better than to talk to the seamstress.

Talking to her would only have intensified his thoughts of her. He already thought of her too much. Feeling her presence in the hole, smelling her scent, glancing at her in the few moments of light they received… It drove him crazy.

He'd never kissed a girl before.

What would it be like to kiss the seamstress? She wasn't much older than he was. And he was quickly becoming a man. Surely the lawyer would not mind…

He brushed the thought away, but similar thoughts persisted.

It was immoral to think about someone else's lawfully married wife in such a way; his upbringing compelled him to stray away from such thoughts.

But they kept coming and occupied his mind almost entirely.

Concentration, he learned, was his only way out. Grappling with complex theories and complex mathematical equations were the only things that kept him sane. It distracted him, kept his thoughts away from the seamstress, his family, where they all were. They could distract him from thinking about the butcher and from the immediate fear the thought of him elicited.

It was the middle of the day when they heard the family's dog barking loudly. They instantly became alert.

What was happening? The dog never barked this loud.

The maid frantically ran back and forth inside the cabin, exclaiming loudly, "Now-now, it's okay, children! It's just a nice soldier at the door!"

Chapter 46: Light

Paris, 1961

Age 33

I

The young scientist inhaled the Parisian air. He had missed Paris.

He walked into the old building. Everything seemed smaller in Paris compared to America.

He walked to the cobblestone-enclosed yard, and thought of the surprise party he had organized for the old mama before he relocated to America.

He pressed the elevator button and was pleased to see it was working well. The door opened, and he entered hesitantly. He did not like elevators, nor other confined places. But this was the old mama's elevator; he had to ensure it was working.

He examined the date of the elevator's last inspection. He pressed the button for the fourth floor and adjusted his collar, glancing at the bouquet in his hand.

A minute later, the caregiver opened the door.

The old mama sat in her wheelchair, rolling herself to the door. "Here he is! Here he is! Son of mine!"

The young scientist tried to conceal his shock at how old and small she looked. "Mama!" he exclaimed, "You are looking so well!"

"Liar!" she said and smiled a large smile, two silver teeth glittering as her face shone. "My hero!" she said and reached for his face.

She kissed him endlessly, wetting his face. "You smell like America!"

He handed her the flowers.

"Irises," she said and shook her head violently from side to side, as if she had just tasted the sweetest of chocolates. "You shouldn't have!"

He smiled and sat down. She introduced the caretaker to him. The young scientist did not want to offend her by reminding her that he had already met the caretaker. Nor did he mention the payments he was making directly to the moneychanger to assist in paying for the daily help.

She instructed the caretaker to bring her "boy" all the food in the kitchen. When the caretaker disappeared into the kitchen, the old mama said, "She's not a good cook. But no person has *everything*. Tell me, tell me. I want to know everything!"

The young scientist spoke excitedly about his three kids, showing photographs and telling of their unique interests. The oldest daughter—a future biologist! The second daughter, an artist. The youngest boy, a curious bee.

"And the wife?"

The young scientist sighed. "She is a good mother."

A dark cloud emerged in the old mama's eyes. "I see." She heard him speak with excitement about a measuring device, a "resistor" he wanted to develop. He believed the device would be a profitable asset to the company and to the many scientists who struggled with keeping the pressure and temperature consistent in their equipment.

"I want to repay the company for bringing me to America."

Finally, the old mama asked, "Now what is this ceremony you want to flaunt my beauty in?"

"A prize, a small recognition for…the discoveries."

"Is this for the Legion of Honor?" she looked pointedly at him. "Because if it isn't, I'm not coming!"

The young scientist grinned. He absolutely adored her. "It's the

Order of Merit, for Research and Invention."

"So it's not the Legion of Honor!" she sighed and said, "You will have to beg me to come."

"I'm begging," the young scientist smiled and kneeled on the floor.

"All right, all right! I'll come," she said, blushing. "Come here and let me kiss that handsome face of yours. A man! A grown-up man!"

II

The Parisian auditorium was full. The atmosphere in the ceremony's grand hall echoed with anticipation.

The scientist stood in the wings, wearing a suit, holding a sense of excitement in his heart—a sense, as always, mixed with sadness.

They should have been here too.

In the audience sat his four guests: The old mama in her wheelchair, the moneychanger, the uncle, and the uncle's second wife.

The scientist thought of home. He missed his children in Philadelphia. And although he did not want to think of it at that very moment as the ceremony commenced, he missed his parents.

As the master of ceremonies welcomed the Minister of Education and the Minister of Commerce to the stage, cameras flashed, and the audience applauded.

The old mama blew her nose loudly, her silver teeth showing.

The moneychanger whispered, "Mama, the whole audience doesn't need to hear your nose blowing!"

The old mama turned her head to him and blew her handkerchief loudly in his ear.

"Very mature, Mama."

Several winners were announced. Each person walked proudly to the stage, shaking hands with a row of dignitaries. Then it was the scientist's turn. The master of ceremonies read all of the scientist's achievements in contributing to the French industry and science.

The old mama felt a surge of energy bolting in her and insisted on standing up. Her surprised son helped her rise. "Bravo!" she applauded. "Bravo!"

Her face shone with maternal pride. She had made a pact years earlier, on the divan, with the frail refugee whose eyes were the size of an owl's. "You, family?" she had asked him on the divan. "No Mama? No Papa?"

She remembered clearly his reluctance to speak, to utter the words. She had made a pact then and there that she would always take care of him.

"Bravo!" she cried, long after the other applause subsided. "Bravo!"

As the Minister of Education and the Minister of Commerce shook the young scientist's hands, the old mama's eyes followed her adopted son. The moneychanger, standing and supporting her, exchanged a knowing glance with her.

A momentary silent acknowledgement passed between the moneychanger and his mother—an unspoken recognition of the pure joy of offering a helping hand: a hand to a poor immigrant, a war refugee, gaunt and pale, scared of his own shadow.

The moneychanger looked at the young scientist on the stage and whispered to his mother, "Didn't I tell you? A genius!"

"Yes, congratulations," she said dryly, "for once in your lifetime you were right!"

As the young scientist stood, holding the medal for the photographs on stage, he could not help but feel time's inexorable march. In the audience stood the once vibrant figures in his life, now marked by the passage of years—the wheelchair-bound old mama's frailty, the moneychanger's graying hair, and the uncle's shorter frame.

As he reminded himself to smile, he felt not only the weight of the medal, but also the weight of the collective journey that had brought him to this moment. One person was responsible more than anyone else—his uncle—the one teacher who saw potential in him. He was glad to see the uncle holding hands with his wife.

His heart swelled with gratitude to the old mama and her son for easing his way into a new life, from the ashes of that empty train station in Poland, the station to which his family never returned.

His heart expanded as he remembered the warm, approving look of his father upon seeing his son sharing a game with his little sister.

The young scientist wished he could have seen them among the many pairs of eyes in the audience. Sometimes, he still foolishly hoped that they would emerge; in the years after the war, he was still hopeful, reasoning with the silence, haggling with the facts: his father was strong. His mother was industrious, resourceful.

This was his sister's moment to see what had become of her pony-tail-pulling brother, her brother who did not know how to say "I love you" or even "I'm sorry." And when he finally learned how to share his feelings, it was too late.

In the audience, he glanced at his uncle, the only one who could decipher that gloomy half-smile, that ocean of sadness in his nephew's eyes. Everyone in his family–even his grandparents–should have been embracing him now, shouting 'Bravo!' and embarrassing him by cheering for him too loudly.

The uncle's eyes shone in understanding. They glanced at one another from across the hall, from the stage to the seat, with an understanding they forged together as two who shared a pit for a never-ending winter. It also set them apart, far from each other and from the world of the living, each carrying his own ghosts, his own regrets–each burning in his own unique daily, quiet hell.

The uncle nodded at his nephew.

The nephew blinked for a long moment, not wanting to open his eyes and release the dam of tears.

The uncle's wife, feeling the grip of her husband's hand, suddenly sensed that she did not really know her husband—her husband who had another wife and a daughter before the war, who had a life he always remained eerily silent about.

She knew her husband was often emotionally disengaged. She glanced at him as he gazed toward the stage, his eyes leaking tears he tried to blink away in rapid succession. She had never seen her husband shed a tear before. Until now.

Chapter 47: Darkness

Poland, 1943

Age 15

In the deafening silence of the pit, they could hear the family dog's frenzied barking. The chain by the doghouse rattled violently, threatening to snap, as the dog ran back and forth outside.

They heard the maid's voice, frantic, "It's okay, children! It's just a nice soldier at the door!"

They were paralyzed by what they knew would come: their very last seconds in hiding. The air was thick. It trapped the acrid stench of the bucket filled with excrement and urine, the smell of the damp soil walls, and, above all, the unmistakable scent of human fear.

The boy pressed himself against the cold pit wall. The lawyer laid in the middle beside him, his wife on the opposite side. The uncle, frozen in place, remained perched on the bucket. The imminent danger paralyzed them.

The dog's relentless running outside sent the chain rattling, sending vibrations through the ground and shaking the soil wall. The boy knew the chain would not hold. The dog was strong, and each time it reached the chain's end, it pulled on the hook the maid's husband had installed in the ground. The chain's ear-piercing clatter foretold the dog breaking free and exposing their breathing pipe to the savvy military dog's probing nose, trained to find humans.

Trained to find *Jews*.

They heard the maid running back and forth inside the cabin. The boy understood; she was losing her mind, afraid for her children. Everyone would be killed now.

As the maid opened the cabin door, the soldier's harsh commands echoed through the air, confirming their fears. This was no ordinary visit, no local police officer. The staccato speech–the barked commands–made it crystal clear.

German.

The boy felt the arm of the lawyer silently shift, as his hand reached into his pocket, pulling his knife out.

CHAPTER 48: LIGHT

PHILADELPHIA, 1961

AGE 33

I

The young scientist was finally back in Philadelphia. He was eager to discuss plans for the component he was developing.

He sat in front of the big boss. The two people from marketing finished their explanation. The Head of Marketing placed copies of the report in front of the big boss and the young scientist.

The young scientist was stunned.

"Therefore," the Head of Marketing said, finishing his speech, "we see no marketability, no viability for such an innovation, in the foreseeable future."

The young scientist was stunned.

The young scientist had come to the meeting wanting to discuss a possible percentage—a tiny fraction of the success he envisioned for a new precise resistor. Instead, he was told there was no 'marketability' or some other nonsense.

His eyes, filled with disbelief, watched as the big boss reached and poured himself a glass of hard scotch.

The young scientist read this as a sign that the conversation was over. He forced himself to speak. "This cannot be!" he exclaimed. "There is a need for it, there must be demand for it! I know, I need this resistor myself! This company needs it!"

The Head of Marketing looked puzzled, "Well, we've asked—

we've asked all our retailers; there's no need for such a component."

"But…" the young scientist cried out. He saw the idea he had been laboring over for months now quickly dissipating into thin air. He could not let that happen. "But they…they don't know what they are talking about!"

The young scientist had a feeling his behavior was unprofessional, but for once in his life, he did not care. He had to defend his dream. "I'm sure, I'm absolutely certain, that if we simply develop it and release it to the market, then the demand will be found!"

"Enough." The big boss felt frustration tugging at his collar but remained composed as he took another puff from his cigar and turned to look at the marketing experts. "Thank you, gentlemen."

The two men left the room.

The big boss leaned back in his chair. "You are a bright young man. And I hate to disappoint you. But I simply cannot approve research that will lose me money."

The young scientist bit his lip. He had been working on it for months. *Months!*

How wrong they all were not to see the truth in this!

"Come back to me," the big boss said, "in a year or two. We'll see then."

Crushed, scared, upset, defeated—the young scientist left the office.

There was only one thing left to do.

II

The young scientist knew how incredibly expensive international phone calls were. But he had no other choice.

A day earlier, he had telegrammed Paris.

The disappointment of the conversation with the big boss still pained him. "Come back to me in a year or two. We'll see then."

A year or two!

How preposterous!

This was a new decade. The 1960s. A new speed to things—a year or two!—the big boss might as well have said a decade or two.

The young scientist picked up the receiver and dialed O for the operator. "I need to make an international call."

A series of clicks and tones followed. "International Operator, how may I help?"

He had never phoned overseas, as it was a waste of money. A letter could take a few days, and you would get an answer. One could even telegram and have answers in hours. But he had to talk this through. He would pay the money.

"I need to place a call to France," he said.

The international operator said, "I'm connecting you to France, please hold the line."

A series of clicks and tones and echoes followed. Finally, someone picked up the phone in France. The young scientist said, *"Bonjour, je voudrais passer un appel à Paris."*

The operator connected him to the operator in Paris, and two more operators were required before he reached the post office of Place de Vosges. He asked to speak to his uncle. When, a minute later, his uncle's voice was heard over the phone, the young scientist felt a decade older.

"What did he say?" the uncle asked, skipping the niceties. He had received the telegram a day earlier from his nephew. "Manager nixed resistor research. Urgently need advice. Initiating call 1700 hours French time."

The voice of his uncle sounded metallic and distant. "He said there is no market for it, and had some marketing 'specialist' prove no one wants it. I…"

The young scientist paused, hating himself for wasting the precious money on a pause. "I don't know what to do."

His uncle's voice was choppy. "What are your options?"

"I can try and go on my own, develop this, see if there is anything in it." He gulped. "Or I can put in it the drawer, but I would hate—"

"This is what you should do," he heard from the other side.

He was not sure what the uncle answered—to go the independent business route or to save his job and forget about the cursed resistor. "What?" he asked, helpless.

He waited for what felt like a lifetime. He wanted to speak again, but he knew that one more sentence from him would lead to an entire backlog of sentences interrupted mid-sentence, creating havoc. He bit his tongue, patiently waiting.

If there was one thing he learned in the dark months, it was this. *Patience.*

Finally, the voice came from across the ocean. "Go on your own," came the short, decided answer from the uncle.

The young scientist held the phone close to his ear, trying to hear it all. But nothing followed. "Really?" he finally asked, hating his unpreparedness. He should have talked to his uncle in statistics, through facts, in numbers of feasibility and risk.

Ages later, the voice came. "I just don't see, what do you have to lose?"

"Everything," the young scientist hurried to answer. He lowered his voice. "My wife thinks it's crazy. So do my colleagues. 'You don't just walk away from this kind of position,' they say."

Another agonizing moment. Was the uncle silently deliberating?

"Nonsense," the uncle's muffled echo responded, "You've always been an entrepreneur."

The young scientist chuckled, "Me?"

"Of course. In the war," the uncle said and began coughing loudly.

The young scientist waited quietly, worried about his uncle.

"In the war," his uncle continued, "how did you know to come to the cabin?"

"Well, I guess…I knew in my gut that no other person would…"

"And after the war, how did you know how to develop

PhotoStress?"

"I guess I just knew…"

A long trans-Atlantic silence followed. The young scientist was afraid the call had dropped.

Then the uncle's voice reemerged. "Remember: you are a survivor. You've been through the war. Those who did not go through it will never be able to understand it. No one!"

They were silent. The uncle added, "Can you keep working in the company, and do the research on the side?"

"It's a giant undertaking," the young scientist answered. He had mulled it over in his mind for a long time. And there was the non-compete clause. "I'm afraid not."

The uncle's voice came loud and clear. "I think you can't *not* do it. You'll regret it for the rest of your life."

The young scientist sighed. "But…what if I lose everything?"

"What do you mean if you lose everything? You already lost everything when you were fifteen! We lost everyone! So don't be dramatic like those American friends of yours, you hear me?"

"Yes, uncle," The young scientist said.

"You should—I want you to go after it as if your life depended on it. You hear me?"

"I do, uncle…Actually, I already have a name in mind."

"What is it?"

The metallic sound of the line being disconnected was suddenly heard, and the muffled sounds disappeared. "Uncle? Uncle, can you hear me? Uncle?"

It took all the young scientist had in him to file the resignation letter.

It took all he had to take the loan.

It took all he had to go from a lab researcher, a doctor, to a lab owner, a businessman, really.

He had clarity on only two things: he knew that if he needed such a good resistor for his electric lenses and measuring devices for PhotoStress, surely other scientists and industrialists needed better resistors too.

And he also knew the name he wanted to give the enterprise. A surreal name. A name that meant something. A name that needed commemoration.

Four months later, the young scientist glued the sign onto the door.

"VISHAY"

He sighed, proud, trembling. He looked up and closed his eyes.

His grandmother's sentences went with him all these years. "To be kind is more important than to be right. People need not a big brain that chatters, but a big heart that listens."

Vishay.

He remembered his grandfather once telling him, "You city kids don't know what work is; back in our little village, back in Vishay, you would have learned that work is not a man's punishment, but a man's reward!"

The young scientist looked at the sign on the door. *Vishay. Vishay.* It was almost like a prayer.

His grandfather came to his mind again, making him smile unwillingly. "You might have some Vishay sense in you after all."

He chuckled. His grandfather's praise may not have seemed like praise to others.

He remembered how, once, he stayed the summer with his grandparents. Guests were expected to visit, and there was no chocolate in their house to offer the guests. His grandmother was on one of her excursions to the poorhouse or to visit the elderly. His grandfather became anxious about having nothing to offer the guests. He gave the boy money and sent him to the store. "Make sure to get the Rübezahl bonbons, not any other kind. Rübezahl chocolate bonbons. Now go!"

The boy ran to the store. He asked the grocer there, but there were no Rübezahls—none at all, only another kind.

He was determined not to disappoint his grandfather and ran quite a few blocks to another store, even though his grandmother would not have approved of him going so far away on his own. *How old was he? Eight? Nine?*

In the new store, he asked, panting, for Rübezahl bonbons, but the store owner there did not have any either.

Frustrated, he knew he had to return to his grandparents. But should he return with nothing? *No. His grandfather would disapprove.*

He therefore paid and got the lesser kind and hurried with the bonbons in his hand, running through the streets.

Before entering the house, he hid the package of chocolates inside his coat.

His grandfather snorted when the boy entered the house. "What took you so long!"

He answered, his voice high–it had yet to change. "There were no Rübezahls, Grandpa, so I ran to the other store, but they didn't have any either!"

"Well," his grandfather grunted, "you should have gotten the other kind then, foolish boy!"

The boy smiled "I did, Grandpa!" he said and pulled the package of chocolate bonbons from his coat and handed it to his grandfather.

His grandfather looked at him strangely. "Well, you might have some Vishay sense in you after all…"

The young scientist looked at the plaque on the door to the little lab he was renting. "You might have some Vishay sense in you after all!"

That was quite a compliment, he thought, coming from his grandfather. Now he had to prove he deserved it.

He looked at the plaque. The name bore a legacy. He had promised all those who had been murdered that he would live, that he would somehow make their memory last, that he would not allow them to be forever forgotten.

The plaque echoed the voices of laughter and tears, of singing and mourning. Vishay.

He would have to make this lab work and this business succeed. He had given it the one most sacred secret of his life: his past. So often he tried to forget his past; with this name, he would always be reminded of where he came from and what he represented.

His grandmother always spoke of Vishay, the village in which everyone knew everyone, where Jews lived for centuries. Vishay was wiped out, but the memories must not be erased.

His grandmother had saved him; not only in spirit, but physically, too. It was her kindness toward the maid years before the war that cemented the maid's resolve to help his family.

This lab was in his grandmother's honor.

Chapter 49: Darkness

Poland, 1943

Age 15

They heard the soldier's harsh staccato commands.

German.

Shivers ran down the boy's back. It was a Nazi soldier. And the boy was a smelly Jew.

He tried to listen to the voices over the sound of his pounding heart. The Nazi was shouting. The maid's responses were feeble, a desperate attempt to maintain an illusion of normalcy.

A new sound emerged: the rapid tap of paws on the cabin floor. A sniffing dog was now in the house.

They did not breathe.

They heard taps in the other room, quick, and the boots of the soldier following, thumping against the floorboards.

The boy, once resentful of the pit's walls, now begged to stay here—to stay here forever. He desperately wanted to stay, to remain sheltered, concealed, hidden from what he knew was to come.

The four huddled together, their breaths suspended between life and death.

The commanding footsteps of the soldier's boots echoed throughout the cabin.

The sniffing dog's footsteps grew louder as it neared the bed.

The boy imagined himself a million miles away. He imagined his mother, he imagined reuniting with her, and the thought offered him a fleeting moment of solace. *Mother. Mother. Mother.*

There was silence, broken only by the loud sniffing right above them, as the nose of the dog grazed over the floorboards.

The dog had detected their presence. The boy's heart sank.

He thought of his mother. Of her arms around him. The way she smelled. The sound of her laugh.

Mother, Mother, Mother.

A sudden loud bark shattered the silence. The boy gasped and trembled—it was a loud, signaling, detecting bark.

The loud thuds of army boots followed. The army dog barked in their ears.

The pit, a sanctuary just moments before, now felt like a trap closing in on them, crushing them. The boy braced himself for the bullets, shivering. *Mother. Mother.*

Outside, the dog was still barking madly.

The boy braced himself, but then—

The army dog above them did not bark again, but instead seemed to choke—or sniff—or gag—

The rapid tap of the dog's paws ran through the floorboards to the kitchen. The soldier's boots followed, walking away from them.

The soldier shouted, his boots pacing in the kitchen.

The boy strained his ears to hear, but the barking of the family dog was loud and continuous, and the sound of the rattling metal chain obstructing the sound.

Then there was nothing.

Was the soldier taking the maid?

They heard the dog's barks becoming even louder, going crazy. There was much noise, then the dogs barking at one another. He heard the soldier, and the maid too, in the yard.

They heard the potato cellar door open.

Through the loud barking and chain sounds, they felt the ground reverberating by the heavy boots of the soldier.

Hope—strange hope—began filling the boy's heart.

He strained his ears, trying to determine where the soldier was heading next. Was he to return to the cabin? Was the pipe outside going to be discovered? The loud barking and growling intensified his fear. And yet—hope.

They heard a few more words being yelled by the soldier.

The sound of his boots stomping again throughout the house rattled the boy to his core. They heard the soldier search through the kitchen, opening the cabinets, knocking items over without care.

The boy squeezed his eyes shut, heart pounding in his ears.

Then, a few moments later, the barking stopped.

None of the four of them dared to move at all.

They heard the maid's steps, walking into the cabin, locking the door.

They heard her walking to the other room. Her toddler son was crying, and so was the baby girl—only now did the boy hear them.

They heard the baby's loud crying coming closer, nearing them, in the maid's arms. "Now-now, children, it's all right! All is well! God bless! God bless!"

It was close—so very close—their brush with death.

For now–it seemed–they were saved, spared yet another day.

Nevertheless, they did not dare to change places in the pit. At night, long after the family's dinner above, the boy heard the maid knock on the floorboards.

She handed them two potatoes.

They all looked at her, eager to hear what had transpired.

The maid's husband walked back and forth in the kitchen.

The maid whispered, her eyes shining in the dimly lit bedroom. "It was close."

The uncle nodded. The seamstress looked with admiration at the maid.

The maid shrugged her shoulders, enjoying the sudden moment to pause and finally relax. "There, I saw him, through the window. With this big dog!"

The boy listened to her story intently. They all did.

"I said 'One minute! And then I grabbed a handful of pepper, like this," she held her fist loose, "and ran in here and sprinkled pepper all over the floor, all the way to the bedroom door."

Was this the sound the boy heard, someone running in the cabin?

"Only then I opened the door, 'Guten Tag!'" she smiled.

The husband, standing near the door to the kitchen, muttered, "Hurry!"

The maid glared at him. "I must tell them, they were probably terrified!"

The husband groaned.

"In any event," the maid continued, her eyes shining, "the dog came inside. The soldier asked how many people live here, where is your husband, what does he do, all that. The dog came here and barked, I thought I was dying! But right when the soldier followed the dog, the dog got irritated by the pepper!"

She laughed.

The boy smiled. *How courageous she was!*

"The dog quickly left the room for the kitchen!" she continued, "And the soldier looked at the room for half a second and then went after the dog. 'People say you buy too much food, that you are hiding Jews!' I told him, 'Of course I buy food, I have five children and a husband bigger than you!'"

She laughed again. But then her eyes widened. "When the soldier was outside, his dog went to the pipe, and I nearly fainted, but then the dogs began fighting and the soldier thought nothing of it!"

The uncle looked at the maid in appreciation. "You are a courageous woman, Madam!"

The lawyer nodded, and his wife said, "Very brave!"

The maid's husband hissed from the kitchen, "enough already."

The maid took the bucket from the uncle. "People talk, we need to buy food in different places, at different times… But may this be our only problem!"

The boy smiled. She reminded him of his grandmother, who often said, "In Vishay we used to say, 'May this be our worst problem!'"

The uncle smiled, lowered the new bucket into the pit and hurried to close the floorboards above them, not wanting to upset the maid's husband.

The boy wished the pit had remained open for just a few more minutes… Every moment of light was like tasting freedom. But the floorboards were placed back, and they heard the maid pushing the clothes and blankets on top of the floorboards.

The boy thought to himself how, if they survived, he would do everything possible to express his gratitude to the maid and her family. *They are heroes*, he thought, *all of them*. In his heart he thanked her. And he thanked his grandmother, her silky, wary voice echoing in his mind. "In Vishay we used to say, it is not what you have that is yours; it is what you give."

Above them, the weight of the bed squeezed as the maid lay down.

The maid knew she could not endure another search.

CHAPTER 50: LIGHT

PHILADELPHIA, 1962

AGE 34

I

"I think we got it."

Six months after starting "Vishay Labs," the young scientist and his small group of fellow scientists working in his new lab felt they had nailed it.

It was a small component. The smallest resistor ever. In fact, it did not look like a resistor at all. It was small and flat. And inside the tiny plastic box was a surprise: not a metal wire, but a piece of metal *foil*.

Curiously, it was glued to a piece of glass. The experiments they conducted showed that glass functioned better than ceramic or any other material under heat.

The result was a resistor with no fluctuations in its performance. There had been nothing like that available in the world of electronics.

The young scientist registered three patents involving the use of glass, the unique adhesive, and the way the foil was laid in the tiny plastic box.

Holding the tiny piece in his hand, he smiled at the other tired scientists, who had worked days and nights for months with him.

The young scientist lifted the tiny resistor up high. "Friends, it's showtime!"

For the young scientist, 'show time' meant that he had to put aside all his fears. He hated public speaking; he hated making calls. He hated "selling." He was the opposite of a salesman. He was a shy scientist who preferred to muse about the formation of birds rather than to speak to strangers.

Yet he had to do it. Not for himself: he now had employees to take care of. He simply had to make it work.

And not only was his name on the line—there was also another name. The name of his ancestors. The honor of his ancestral village, the family's roots, was on the line. Vishay–a mostly Jewish village, industrious, festive, and a historical community.

A community that was wiped out completely. A deserted synagogue, a forgotten graveyard, looted houses, erased names, vanished hopes.

A village that once thrived, a village with the sounds of children's laughter, that now had an unmarked mass grave deep in the adjacent forest, bodies pressed against one another in that frightful night.

He had to correct what happened. He had to make his ancestors proud, to prove to them they were not forgotten.

He set to work. He wrote professional essays about the new resistor and sent them to relevant academic magazines. His team sent samples out to key companies that cared about precise measurements: electronics companies, airplane manufacturers, navigation component makers, and even companies in the budding computer industry.

He hated public speaking, but nevertheless, he gave several lectures about the new resistor. He hated calling big firms to solicit their interest, but he dutifully sat by the phone and dialed.

The companies were always skeptical. The young scientist flew to their various headquarters, saying, "Just try it. Give it to your scientific team. You'll see there is nothing on the market quite like our resistors."

Soon the findings of the scientific teams in these large companies showed that the Vishay resistors were indeed more precise than any other.

Orders slowly began coming in.

More and more people were needed for the assembly line. Soon, the labs expanded, and the name of the company changed to 'Vishay Intertechnology.'

No one knew of his growing anxiety.

II

Vishay Intertechnology began growing. Various companies began finding that indeed the tiny Vishay resistor was more precise and reliable than any other on the market.

Orders began pouring in. An assembly line. Expanding labs. And over it all presided one young man, one scientist who hid a big secret.

To many people, the young scientist-turned-businessman seemed like a regular person. A polite man. A husband. A father of three. A boss.

No one knew why, whenever he visited a new building, he would quietly walk around, studying the "architecture."

Only his eyes showed his true study: emergency exit doors. Escape routes. Fire exits, evacuation staircases, emergency stairwells.

His brain kept drawing emergency exit maps, just in case.

No one knew why he preferred meeting in the lobby or on the bottom floor, rather than going up to one of the fancy top floors, from which jumping would mean death.

No one knew why he chose a small room with a small window for his office, rather than the CEO suite with the large, beautiful view. No one noticed that the small room had a small window which opened up to a small roof, from which one could escape if necessary; the CEO suite had no proper escape from the large window with the vast landscape view.

The young scientist kept reminding himself he was now in the free world. *The war was over.*

He scolded himself each time he woke up sweating at night from yet another nightmare. He reproached himself for not being able to adopt the carefree nature of his American colleagues.

He kept telling himself he should just *relax.*

But his mind was always on the lookout for danger.

One day, his fears proved themselves right. They came for him. *And it was too late to escape.*

Chapter 51: Darkness

Poland, 1943

Age 15

All the boy wanted was to be out. In the open.

He wanted to roam the forest. Play his violin as loud as he could, in the center of the city square. He wanted to shout out loud. He wanted to see his family and kiss them. He wanted to apologize to his sister for having been so mean to her at times. He wanted to dance with the maid's eldest daughter.

A few weeks earlier, after that terrifying visit from the soldier and his dog, the maid made up her mind. "We are going to have a party."

They all looked at her, puzzled.

"Madam?" the uncle asked.

She looked at the four scared people under the bed. "Everyone is talking. Let them come here and see for themselves we are not hiding anyone. It's a holiday in three weeks. We will celebrate here."

They looked at her, frozen.

The boy wondered if she was mad.

She said, "I already told the neighbors at the village."

The uncle nodded slowly. "Brilliant idea, Madam."

The boy wanted to shout. *What was so brilliant about it? It sounded like a suicide, like an invitation for an examination, a more thorough search,*

The maid took the bucket and said, "We have to. We have to show we have nothing to hide."

In the darkness that followed, the boy saw in his mind the maid's eyes shining. *She must have gone mad.*

As the days progressed, the boy tried busying himself with math. He tried replaying the rehearsals at the orchestra in his mind. He tried reciting poems he loved. He tried writing poems in his mind. He tried everything.

Each day, as the maid handed them the bowl of food, he hoped for her to tell them she had changed her mind. He hoped for her husband to put some sense in his wife.

"Uncle," he whispered, "the party."

"We will be alright."

"Uncle! What if someone searches under the bed?"

"The maid is clever. You saw what she did with the pepper."

"But what if—"

"What if, what if!" the uncle sounded upset. "What if—that is probability. Have you studied statistics?"

"Uncle, I don't want another lesson—"

"Just listen. Statistics are everywhere. It's true beauty. It may be the most beautiful of all the disciplines."

The boy did not want to hear his uncle's lecture. His uncle was always saying, about every lesson, that it was "the most beautiful of all disciplines."

Could his uncle not see that this was no time for riddles? Their lives were on the line!

"It's in agriculture, guessing the probability of crops. It's in health—the probability of a patient healing with one medication over the other. It's life or death."

"Our situation is life or death!" the boy cried.

"You love music. You can guess the next note based on statistics, taking into the equation the metric, melodic and harmonic structures. Anything that you love, you can take statistics and use it to get a better understanding of what is at stake."

The boy sighed heavily.

"Say I tossed a coin. You, also, tossed a coin. Here, in the darkness, we each need to guess each other's coin."

"Uncle, enough!"

"If we guess correctly, the war would be over."

The boy did not respond. Sometimes he hated his uncle—especially when his uncle did not listen, especially when his uncle was cruelly manipulating him, treating him like a fool.

And yet his uncle's question hung in the air, echoing in the boy's mind. "Will the war end?"

The uncle responded, "If we both guess each other's side of the coin correctly. What are the chances?"

"I don't know?"

The uncle sounded disappointed. "Maybe."

The boy moved uncomfortably. He knew he should not have answered. His uncle had led him into another trap.

He hated that his uncle was smarter, that his uncle thought him stupid.

He thought hard, coin flipping in his mind. "Was there not a fifty percent chance with each coin, heads or tails?"

"Yes, with each coin. True."

The boy thought hard. His uncle's response kept repeating in his head. 'Yes, with each coin. True.'

He heard the subtle emphasis on the word 'each.'

The boy whispered slowly, "So if each coin has fifty percent chance, then both happening together—"

"That's a good direction. Go on."

"Is it addition, subtraction? How do I…?"

"You multiply."

"Fifty percent times fifty percent, or, one half times one half, is one quarter? 25 percent?"

The uncle seemed pleased. "Well done."

"Only 25 percent chance that the war would be over?"

The uncle smiled through his words. "There is a hundred percent chance the war would be over. All wars end eventually."

"But, when? And, will we be alive?"

"Do you want to break this into an equation?"

"I do. I have to know."

The uncle said, "Very well. How would you begin tackling such a question?"

Over the next few days, as summer began feeling more like fall, they tried tackling the question from a myriad of directions, leading them not only to math, but to history, geography, even biology. Each time, just as the boy felt he was approaching the answer, his uncle added more factors.

"Don't forget to read every sentence of the universe's book. As in reading, you stare at letters and you know how to turn them into words, sentences-- drawing meanings, conclusions. Math is to numbers what reading is to letters."

The boy grunted but continued calculating.

Then the day came. The maid took up the bucket. She did not seem cheerful at all. "Tomorrow."

The uncle nodded. "How can we help?"

"I will pick up the bucket in the afternoon. If you can hold it, so that the smell…"

The boy blushed. It felt demeaning.

"Absolutely. Anything else?"

The maid looked up towards the heavens and dragged the bucket on the floor. "Pray."

The following day, bright sunlight hurt the boy's eyes when the maid knocked. She pointed to her lips and whispered, "The children are sleeping." She took the bucket and handed the uncle a new one. She handed them a bowl with potatoes and leeks, as well as a pitcher of water. "Pray," she said again.

The boy moved uncomfortably in the pit.

In the afternoon, the uncle whispered, "We will not switch tonight. We cannot risk any sound."

The boy laid next to the lawyer. He did not like the lawyer's smell. Everyone smelled foul in the rotten pit, in the cage that was his home for more months than he wished to admit.

He did not want the evening to come, but it did.

Instead of the usual dinner sounds of all the children, he could hear loud, congratulating sounds from men entering the kitchen–

The footsteps of men walking above them–

The creaking of the bed as people sat down.

The boy knew their fate was to be discovered in public, scrutinized in a celebration of execution.

Then it happened. One man lowered his head and shouted just above their floorboards, "You are hiding them under your bed, aren't you!"

Chapter 52: Light

PHILADELPHIA, 1962

AGE 34

I

The young scientist took another look at the paper.

The three men waited in his office, staring down at him.

He glanced at the title again. "CLASSIFIED"

Then below, at the bottom, in small letters, it stated:

"National Aeronautics and Space Administration."

His heart skipped a beat. "NASA?"

Excitement surged through him. This was the opportunity of a lifetime! To work with the leading space agency in the entire world—rivaled only by the Russians, who had already put a dog in space six years earlier. He had been following the Telstar project closely, which aimed to place a communication satellite in space. What an incredible human achievement!

Skimming through the contract, already envisioning the groundbreaking discoveries he would help make, he signed. He was not going to argue. He was ready to take the plunge, no matter the risk. "Now, let's talk about what kind of resistors you may need. Shunt resistors?"

The man took the signed paper and nodded to the other two men. "When will you be able to come with us?"

"Come where?"

"It will require a flight to an undisclosed facility."

"I… don't know, maybe next month, I need to look at the calendar."

The man said, "How about in an hour?"

"I… I will need to speak to my wife first."

The man reached rudely to the black phone on the desk, lifted the receiver and handed it to the young scientist. "Remember," the man said in a low voice, "you have signed under Congressional Law, unauthorized dissemination will lead to Criminal Consequences."

The other man said, "Speak and you will not see the light of day again."

The scientist's mind was a whirlwind of thoughts—excitement, fear, anticipation. He dialed his home, his hands shaking.

The young scientist sat with his eyes blindfolded, the roar of airplane engines echoing around the giant hangar. "We got the doctor," one of the men escorting him said.

The young scientist was helped upstairs into a small airplane. "Gentlemen," he said, "is this really necessary?"

No one answered him.

He was directed to a seat, and his seatbelt was fastened.

Four hours of agony later, he heard the pilot from the cockpit.

"Ellington Approach, this is Cessna 170B inbound to Houston from Philadelphia. Currently, over Lake Charles at 5,000 feet. Requesting permission to land at Ellington Base. Over."

Houston?

He had not heard of NASA being stationed in Houston—but then again, he had not heard much about it at all—the name NASA was spoken in hushed conversations by scientists, always fearful of divulging sensitive information.

Twenty minutes later, sweat permeating on his forehead, the young scientist was sitting in a quickly moving car. Two men sat on either side of him.

The blindfold was uncomfortable for him. "Is this level of secrecy necessary?" he asked.

Again, no one answered.

The young scientist sighed. He did not like it at all. He did not like the blindfold, and he did not like the secrecy.

The car began slowing down. It passed over traffic spikes. Then some more. The driver rolled down the window and there was a shuffling of papers. Then the car started forward rapidly, the driver squeezing the accelerator to the maximum.

Two minutes and two turns later, the car suddenly halted. The doors opened at once.

The two men led the young scientist into a building, his eyes still covered. Only once they had sat him down did one of them untie the blindfold.

The other handed the young scientist a glass of water. "Here you go, doctor."

"Thank you," the young scientist said and sipped the water gratefully.

The door opened, and an old man in a white lab coat came through the door. "My gosh! Could you really be the man behind Vishay? You look so young!"

The old man's demeanor was disarming. The young scientist smiled. "I am. And...you are?"

The old man shook the young scientist's hand and introduced himself. "Mission Director. Telstar 2."

The young scientist perked up in amazement. "Telstar 2!"

The Mission Director sized up the young scientist. "I must admit you look quite young. If I may ask, how old are you?"

"Thirty-four," said the young scientist.

"And *you* are the brain behind Vishay?"

"Along with my team."

The Mission Director exhaled. "Well, good for you. We've been examining your resistors, and I must say, we've never seen anything like them."

The young scientist could not conceal a smile.

"Now," the old man said, "you probably heard about the president's ambition to land a man on the moon—"

"...By the end of the decade," the young scientist interjected.

"Well, for that to happen, we must first manage communication. Otherwise," he smiled, "we might be able to get a man on the moon, but not get him back." He stood up. "Please follow me."

The young scientist followed the Mission Director through two long corridors and three doors requiring special codes. Then a large hall appeared.

Flooded in light, it looked to the young scientist like a scene from a Jules Verne book. A few large monitors and two giant mainframe computers for punched cards engulfed the fluorescent-lit hall. Some thirty people in white lab coats milled around.

A large, round structure stood at the very center of the room. A fragment of the imagination, a fabrication coming to life.

He found himself in the presence of a technological opus—the legendary Telstar 1. This pioneering communication satellite commanded attention with its spherical frame, an outer shell of lightweight resilience meticulously crafted to endure the rigors of both launch and the vast vacuum of space.

Solar panels adorned the satellite's surface, new technology designed to capture distant sunbeams and transform them into the power that sustained Telstar's operations. For any other person, this would be awe-inspiring. For the young scientist, it was as if he stood in a temple, witnessing the holy of holies. As the young scientist stood in quiet communion with the Telstar, he marveled not just at the satellite's physical form but at the embodiment of human achievement it represented, a testament to the collective ingenuity of those who dared to bridge the boundaries between Earth and the cosmic expanse, between reality and imagination. *Reaching to the stars.*

The Mission Director laughed. "I can see you are converted!"

The young scientist looked up closely. "7075 aluminum."

The Mission Director gawked. "And you can tell that from looking?"

The young scientist ignored the question. "I must participate. What can I help with?"

The Mission Director nodded. "As you can see here," he said, pointing at the solar paneled wings, "each and every solar cell requires a shunt resistor to work properly. But," the Mission Director sighed, "we don't have an allowance for—"

The young scientist completed the sentence, "an allowance for any more *weight*."

"Correct. And our surface space is limited, too."

"Which is where I come in…?"

"Could you mount one resistor for each solar cell, and fit them on the wings, without the weight or space other resistors require? We have a generous budget."

The young scientist smiled and suddenly wanted to make a call. *If he could call and tell his uncle!*

If only there was no damn confidentiality agreement. His uncle would be so proud! His crazy uncle, the one who insisted that his nephew must emigrate to America, for it had "more opportunities." Had the young scientist remained in France, would he ever have been given an opportunity to change—shape—participate somehow in mankind's quest for space, in humanity's quest for the galaxy?

The Mission Director looked at him, anticipating his answer.

The young scientist wanted to jump up and down and respond along the lines of 'Willing, would I be willing? Seriously? I would be willing to do this for free!'

Instead, he somehow managed to restrain his enthusiasm and said, "I believe we can work it out." His shining eyes made it impossible to hide his excitement.

"You won't regret it," said the Mission Director.

His heart beat violently. "I already don't."

II

"Ten. Nine. Eight..."

The young scientist had to pinch himself. He stood alongside hundreds of the most esteemed minds in the United States and from across the globe at Cape Canaveral Air Force Station. They were about to witness the launch of their cutting-edge satellite.

"Seven. Six. Five."

Tremors coursed through the young scientist. It was May 7th, a date from his past. Eighteen years prior, on this very day, amidst the ruins of war-scarred Poland, he and his uncle had clung to a radio, listening to news long-awaited and prayed for since his eleven-year-old self heard about the war. The German Third Reich's unconditional surrender, a conclusion of humanity's six bloodiest years.

And now, on this same day, his resistors, the embodiment of his labors, his family's pride, were to ascend into the sky. Every resistor on the satellite was from his lab—the fruit of his lab's toil. These were the same resistors his previous boss refused to finance research for, resistors that his electrical expert colleagues scoffed at, resistors the world resisted.

Now they were launching into space.

"Four, three…"

The young scientist blinked rapidly, endeavoring to stop the tears from blurring the clarity of this historic moment. The satellite's exterior was adorned with 2,512 minuscule solar cells, each cradling an even tinier resistor made of foil and glass—a concoction forged by late-night alchemy with his devoted team.

Upon each resistor, the lab's name was etched—a microscopic signature bearing its name. Vishay.

"Two..."

Now there were to be thousands of Vishay's in space. This was to be his modest triumph. The best revenge: massive success. Someone sought to erase his family, to annihilate his lineage: burying them in pits, flinging their bodies on trucks, suffocating them with gas, burning them in crematoriums. Yet, his family endured, his village outlasted, his kin triumphed. His grandfather. His grandmother. His sister. His parents. Were they observing this now?

"One."

The Delta D rocket encompassing the satellite shook violently as a bright haze of fumes blurred the scientists' view of the rocket, while below, colossal engines ignited with a roar. A brilliant burst of light erupted from the rocket's engines in a thunderous roar, painting the valley with a blinding glow, a vast conflagration of red fire and smoke—a controlled eruption, a storm of scientific wrath and destruction—*would it work? Would it launch successfully?*

A loud explosion reverberated through the plains as the rocket departed the base, ascending skyward, declaring humanity's defiance against the bonds of Earth. Giant bubbles of smoke unleashed, a massive gray cloud spilling like a champagne of carbon dioxide, as the rocket rose up in a perfect trajectory straight to the heavens.

Chapter 53: Darkness

Poland, 1943

Age 15

The man's voice echoed through the pit. Any smart man, understanding anything about acoustics, could decipher that the floor under the bed was hollow. "You are hiding them under your bed, aren't you!" the man shouted and hiccuped.

The maid's loud laughter was dramatic. "Now-now, someone here had too much to drink!"

"I haven't drank that much!" protested the voice.

"Then here is another glass," the maid walked to the bed, her steps decisive. In her hand, she held a glass with diluted wine that she was able to buy in the black market. It was expensive, but the maid wanted to curb all the talk about her harboring Jews. "Sounds more like you want to be hidden under our bed, you silly pervert!"

Everyone laughed. The maid exclaimed, "Who wants more wine?"

Under the floorboards, they could hear the people moving to the kitchen.

Music came from the children's room. Violin. The boy recognized the song. Brahms. He learned how to play it on the violin as a child.

His body resisted the urge to move, to dance.

Floorboards above them shook in the other room, in the kitchen, rapid steps entering their room and then leaving. This lively piece had a folk-like quality, associated with the barefoot travelers' music he heard in the city square one holiday years before, when the world was sane and people were not killing each other.

He remembered the warmth of his mother in the city square—his shy mother who was always timid and soft spoken. In that city square, he saw a different mother, a mother whose hand gripped him with excitement. He could feel the pulse of her heart in her palm, the beat of the music in the way her fingers closed on his.

He remembered once, on Passover, when his father was drunk, how his parents danced in the dining room. He remembered how he and his sister tried mimicking their parents, twirling and twirling.

The world used to turn in the right direction then.

The music from above the floorboards rattled the cabin, the sound of footsteps scratching, drumming, vibrating through the floorboards, moving them like strings.

The violin was lively and energetic. The boy recognized each tune. These were the sounds of his childhood, of living, of celebrating lives. They were in his blood, pulsating loudly through his veins. His fingers echoed with the tunes, tapping against his will.

Lost in the music, he shifted slightly, struggling to contain the emotions surging through him. His body ached to move, to dance, to escape the oppressive confines of the pit. Inching upwards unconsciously his head brushed against the floorboard above him, releasing a muffled thump as it settled back into place—the noise startling the other frozen dwellers of the pit.

The boy froze, heart pounding, terrified that the creak might betray their hiding place. His uncle's hand shot out, grabbing him and pulling him down to the floor, the grip tightening with panic.

Holding their breaths, the pits' prisoners listened intently for any signs of alarm from above, praying that the boy's moment of carelessness had not doomed them all.

Above them the party continued, the rhythm of life pulsating through the wooden beams. They remained still, hoping against hope that their secret sanctuary would remain undiscovered.

The music kept intoxicating him. The use of syncopated rhythms, rapid tempos, and virtuosic passages gave the piece a playful quality.

The boy realized that life above was continuing. People kept dancing. Life went on without him. People fell in love. Got married, gave birth. And he was to be stranded here forever. No one cared about him and the stench-filled pit with excrement and the piercing smell of urine—even with an empty bucket they were worse than street rats. No wonder the world had forgotten about them.

His thoughts turned to his sister. His beautiful sister—she was no rat, although he made sure to call her names when they were younger. But she was beautiful.

If the soldiers had done anything to her…! The boy vowed he would avenge her. *She deserved to live.*

The music pierced through the floorboards, knocking on his ears, tugging at his heart, luring him out, to the open. Outside. Outside, where life continued.

Life!

The folk music continued, the compositional melodies weaving into one another, simple yet captivating. Brahms was a genius at weaving these simple tunes into one tapestry that made sense.

The boy recalled how, a few weeks earlier, the maid told them–

"People are suspicious," she said. "A boy from class told my daughter that he 'knows'…"

The thumps of the heels and shoes made the boy feel terribly vulnerable. *Why on earth had the maid let the party spill into the bedroom?*

He heard much laughter and conversation and dancing above. *Life* was taking place.

The boy desperately wanted to dance with the girls. *God damn it!* He was fifteen! He wanted to live, to enjoy what life had to offer… Not to be stuck in this stinking pit, with three ghosts, barely talking, with an uncle who could only speak of math and science, nothing else. He wanted to pull the floorboards away– to get out and yell, "Here I am! Shoot me if you want! Call the soldiers if you'd like! But, for now, just give me that violin, and let me play!

Just one song! One dance!"

But he said nothing, barely moving, barely breathing.

Chapter 54: Light

Israel, 1969

Age 41

I

As the years unfolded, the young scientist turned forty-one. Vishay Intertechnology forged deeper connections with NASA, intertwining its destiny with the exploration of the cosmos.

The first triumphant touchdown of a spaceship on the moon, a monumental achievement, brought the young scientist to the pinnacle of emotions—he felt grateful. His company had left an indelible mark on the space race, a testament to human ingenuity and technological prowess. He was on the moon.

Back on Earth, Vishay was growing. Operations grew in America, and there was much demand from manufacturers of electronics in Europe. Business was doing well, and he could allow his management team to do more of the managing while he began concentrating on the two things he loved most: science and his children.

When his eldest daughter was about to turn twelve, his heart swelled in pride and sadness: his daughter was the age his younger sister was when he last saw her, when they were parted forever.

He could not explain the sadness to his daughter, for he knew he must keep the shadows at bay. Don't talk, don't stir up, don't wake the demons of guilt and shame for having survived while the purity of his sister was taken to the slaughter.

His daughter, however, saw the sadness and knew it had to do with her father's nightly murmurs, his harrowed eyes upon waking up from a bad dream.

She was approaching the age of the traditional rite of passage. Twelve, a momentous age in the life of a Jewish girl, when she turned from a girl to a woman.

"What would you like, as a gift?" he asked his daughter.

He expected her to say that she wanted a large party. A couple of presents, a big party with a fancy dress. Maybe a visit to Disneyland, the park which had recently opened.

For his daughter, there was one dream for the rite of passage. "I know you will not agree," she said.

"Try me," he said, and in his heart, he vowed to do all he could to fulfill his daughter's wish.

"I want a trip, dad."

"To where?" he asked. Every summer he took the family to France, to see his uncle and visit his wife's parents. But it was not France that his daughter wished to travel to.

Over the years, she had heard him speak of a distant land, a land whose name sounds like magic. An oasis in the desert. A land of ancestors, of roots, of rebirth. Her father always trembled when he mentioned its name.

"To Israel."

Her request surprised him. "Really?"

She nodded.

He had wanted to go to the Holy Land for years. Somehow, it was never the right time for the pilgrimage: when he was young, there was the war; when the war ended, there was university; when university ended, there was parenting, and work, work, work.

But he could not seem to think of a good enough reason to refuse his daughter's wish. He looked at her beautiful eyes—his curious baby, his little girl who first crawled and stood up and walked and ran and now had grown up to be a beautiful, strong young lady of twelve. "Is that really what you want?" he asked again.

"Yes, dad."

He nodded slowly. There was no turning back: *This was her will.* He was overcome with emotions. *Israel.* When he was young, there was no State of Israel, but the Holy Land—British Palestine—a land of which the mere mention brought tears to his grandmother's eyes. It was but a fable. A far away, unattainable, hazy dream.

True, some people did emigrate there, but those were crazy people, odd-balls, who moved there before the war started—crazy forerunners who saw what his parents and grandparents did not, who saw the Nazi beast's claws gripping when most people did not.

He thought of the friends of his parents who emigrated to Palestine; that couple—the two accountants, who left to live on a farm—no, an agricultural community—a "kibbutz", in which Jews were farmers, working the land, herding the cattle, and self-governing in a utopia-like society.

"What would you do there?"

The accountant had answered, "We've undergone training over the last month. They don't need more farmers right now. I was given a crash course as a welder."

His father had tried to suppress a smile.

The man's wife, the accountant, had said, "And I was told with my background in biology I can be a veterinarian, they have cows and other livestock—"

His mother had laughed. "You would give up accounting for milk cows?"

Remembering these memories, the scientist cringed. At the time, he had bought into his parents' incredulous views of the ridiculousness of this will to leave the good life in Poland to live in the harsh conditions of the Middle East, in a rural agricultural community. How wrong they were!

He suddenly wondered about this couple. The accountants-turned-welder and the veterinarian, these academicians turned farmers. He began to feel this itch to know what had happened to them. Were they still alive?

His eyes were looking at his daughter, but his mind was drifting through time, drops of moments, streams of seasons, years like rivers flowing steady and fast. Life was passing by. *When would it ever be the perfect time to visit the land of his people?*

"Very well," he said to his daughter.

"Really, dad?" His daughter jumped on him, disbelieving that her workaholic dad might say yes to such an outlandish request.

He nodded and wrapped his arm around his daughter's little shoulders.

"Dad, can it be for just you and me? Just the two of us?"

When the scientist landed in Israel, he felt a peculiar sensation. He had never been there—not physically, at least. His heart had been there, many times, but this was the first time he had set foot in the country. He had dreamed of this moment for decades.

It was the same year that a man landed on the moon: "One small step for man, one giant leap for mankind." But for the founder of Vishay Intertechnology, landing in the Holy Land was his personal giant leap.

Every step taken down the beaten cobblestone paths of Jerusalem made the scientist feel a bit lighter. Like a wanderer who had carried a heavy sack on his back for years, finally returning home, letting the sack down. Lighter. Free. Home.

His daughter had never seen him like that. He was happy. They had never bonded as they did over these few days.

As they walked by the ancient walls of Jerusalem, the stones whispered of tales long gone– of temples and pilgrimages, of desert nomads, of slaves released from Egypt.

The stones seemed oddly familiar, as if he had seen them, as if he himself had worshiped there a millennia before, as if he was a tree suspended in the air, finally planting roots in the ground again.

The trip was a time of reckoning, a midlife examination of what he had been through and where he would like to be. He wanted more of this. This—being with his daughter, spending quality time with his kids, visiting the Holy Land, maybe even buying a house in Israel.

There was so much goodness to be had. So much to be celebrated.

One evening, after a day of exploring, they found themselves in a bustling market. Stalls overflowed with vibrant produce, but the grime of the city was evident in the dust that coated everything. Vendors shouted their offers, their voices competing with the honking of impatient drivers. The scent of spices mingling with the fragrance of freshly baked pita bread and sizzling meat filled the air, overwhelming their senses. They came across a small falafel stand tucked along a quiet side street. The stand was simple, barely noticeable compared to the vibrant stalls at the street's center, but the smell wafting from it was irresistible. The owner, a small man in his later years, greeted them with a kind smile. "Welcome, welcome! Falafel? Best in Jerusalem!" he proclaimed in broken English with a twinkle in his eyes.

"Daddy, I want one!"

The scientist said, "We'll have two, please."

The falafel man skillfully prepared the falafel, shaping the chickpea mixture into perfect balls before dropping them into bubbling oil. "First time in Israel?"

"Yes," the scientist replied, watching the man's skillful movements. "We've been exploring Jerusalem all day. Beautiful!"

"My family—" said the falafel man "—ten generations here! From the time of the Turkish Empire!"

The scientist was stunned. "They came from Spain? Sephardic Jews?"

"Oh no," the falafel man grinned, "Muslim, Sufi!"

The scientist's face froze. He had never had a first-hand interaction with an Arab.

The scientist nodded and was anxious to leave. The falafel man handed them the mouthwatering falafels. And as the scientist was about to pull his daughter's hand away, the falafel man seemed disappointed. "Take a bite!"

The scientist's daughter took a bite, and her father, though reluctant, did not want to seem rude, so he took a bite as well. The first bite was an explosion of flavor, the crispy exterior of the falafel giving way to a warm, grainy inside, with the creamy tahini and pickles.

"This is amazing!" his daughter exclaimed, her eyes wide with delight. She seemed to be fascinated. "What are the Sufis?"

"Oh, now that is a question!" the falafel man exclaimed. "The seekers."

For the remainder of the hour, as they ate the falafel— "delicious!"—the three spoke of Sufism and Kabbalah, religion and dogma, war and peace. "Inshallah," said the falafel man, "peace comes in the holy land, for you, for me, for all."

"Amen," said the scientist and was surprised when the falafel man hugged him.

Later, at night, as the scientist kissed his teenage daughter good night, he thought of the falafel man's kindness. This land, so rich in history and culture, had given him a precious gift—a deeper connection with his daughter and a renewed sense of home.

But as always, the shadows gnawed at him. Everywhere he looked, people reminded him of his father, his mother, his sister. Older ladies in the street had his grandmother's royal nose, his aunt's probing eyes.

He enjoyed the days of vacation in a place that felt more like home than Philadelphia. He enjoyed sharing fun memories with his daughter, swimming in the Sea of Galilee, floating in the Dead Sea, and camel riding in the desert.

Yet bitter thoughts lurked in every corner, thoughts of what could have happened had his family been as stupid and as crazy as the two odd accountants who preferred tending to cows and steel over the comfort of their life in Poland.

He could not stop thinking about his grandparents possibly still being alive like these ancient-looking women and men, sitting in a carefree cafe, sipping coffee, laughing. He could even hear Yiddish being spoken by elderly people the age his grandparents would have been.

Bitter—bitter—bitter, and sweet. A mirror to his entire life, a home far away from home, an alternative dreamlike la-la land of conflict and strife but also sovereignty and strength.

Before the trip, he had called his uncle, trying to locate that couple, his parents' friends. He could not remember their names, nor the name of the kibbutz, only that it started with the word Kfar.

It turned out that there were dozens of kibbutz's beginning with the word Kfar, Kfar simply meaning "village." Without names, it was like searching for a needle in a haystack.

All he could recall was their faces and the vague understanding they'd left for an agricultural collective, Kfar-something.

He turned to his daughter, who was soaking in the sites of the land around her. "How would you like to visit a kibbutz?"

They drove to a kibbutz in the south of the country, in the middle of the desert, an oasis growing amidst dunes.

They ended up in the welcoming office, near the entrance. The scientist marveled at the green lawns in a land that had a water shortage.

"Recycled water," a man, who, a few minutes later, turned out to be the secretary of the kibbutz.

The scientist knew there was no chance, and yet he had to try. "Do you happen to know, by chance, a couple, from Poland? They should be now in their sixties, they immigrated to Israel in 1939, I believe. They were both accountants— they were trained back in Poland to go to Kfar-something. I don't know the name."

"Wait," said the secretary of the kibbutz. He picked up the phone.

Chapter 55: Darkness

POLAND, 1943

AGE 15

I

It had been weeks since the party. Summer was gone. Fall was here. The smell of crisp air. The sound of leaves crunching underfoot outside as the dog chased a bird, his heavy chain following him.

There was a lot of smoke emerging from chimneys in the village as the nights grew colder. Rain. Damp soil. An earthy scent in the air. Snails after the rain.

Fall.

The maid looked forlorn.

"What happened?" the uncle asked.

The boy looked at the maid as she held the bowl of food, peering at the four of them. He could see she had been crying.

He thought of the worst outcome. *Would she ask them to leave?*

The maid said nothing. She mustered a brave smile. She handed them the bowl. There was potato and bread. She took the bucket quietly and handed the uncle a clean one. She looked at the four of them and sighed.

The uncle looked at her, urging her to speak. "Madam," he said softly.

"There's been an uprising."

"An uprising?" asked the uncle.

The boy leaned forward. The lawyer cranked his neck. The seamstress gazed at the maid.

The boy wondered. *An uprising?*

Did this mean they would soon be free?

If it was good news, why was the maid upset?

"Yes, in Warsaw," the maid said quietly. Her face was contorted. "Led by the Resistance. By your people."

They were thirsty for news. "And?" the uncle said eagerly.

Her lips quivered. "They burned them. Alive."

The boy rarely saw his uncle's eyes respond that way; a second earlier there was fire in them; then, an ocean of sorrow.

The maid's voice could barely be heard. "Thousands. They say some thirteen thousand. Children, mothers. The army lit the entire ghetto on fire."

The boy's eyes widened.

"Those who tried to escape were shot." The maid's eyes seemed hollow. "I shouldn't have told you."

The boy saw the uncle's fist tightening. "No… news, any piece of news is good for us to know."

It was the first time, if not the only time, he saw his uncle look that excited.

The maid nodded silently.

A rattle came from the yard outside, spurring the boy to nearly jump, heart pounding in his ears. Immediately, the dog let out a couple of booming barks. Without a word, the uncle hurried to close the floorboards above them. The maid quickly placed the clothes and blankets back on top, the barking slightly muffled.

The boy strained his ears, listening to the frantic footsteps above his head. A silent understanding resounded throughout the stagnant pit, and no one dared to move.

That night the boy lay as stiff as a board, barely breathing. Minutes dragged into hours, and the boy could not bring himself to sleep. In the cold night, fire ate him alive, melting his flesh. He could hear the screaming from Warsaw, a capital of the world, a city known for its civility, for its culture. The heat suffocated him, his oxygen running out, the fire forcing him to keep his eyes wide open. Children. Mothers. Thousands of innocent people.

What kind of person would want to burn people alive, to extinguish families as if they were wood?

Now, more than ever, he felt that at any moment, he could be discovered. What was the better option: staying in the cabin and being engulfed in flames or running outside only to be killed by bullets?

Fasting? The boy thought the lawyer's suggestion was ridiculous.

It all began in yet another one of those dark days. In the endless darkness, the days mixed into one another. So did the months.

One day the lawyer whispered, "We've been here six months now."

It felt longer.

None of them responded. The boy thought these six months felt as long as his entire life, and more.

The end of the war seemed farther and farther away. There were no signs of any defeat of the occupying army; only of resistance being crushed—burned alive.

"If I'm not wrong…" the lawyer said and then paused for a long moment, "yes… if my calculations are not wrong, the day after tomorrow should be the Day of Atonement."

The boy knew that holiday very well. Each year, they would fast, not eating nor drinking at all, beginning in the evening and ending the following evening. Each year, he would spend many hours in the temple with his family and the whole community, all dressed in their best white clothes.

The uncle sat up. "We should celebrate it."

The boy shook his head in disbelief. *A day of fasting?*

Every day seemed like a fast!

None of them responded. The uncle persisted, "It's our holiest day. *Yom Kippur.*"

The boy knew that the uncle was only remotely religious, his mentions of Jerusalem only a vague memory. In fact, the uncle himself never had observed any holiday, now that the boy thought about it. The boy considered mentioning that, but then thought better of it.

Was his uncle losing his mind?

The uncle kept whispering, "I do not particularly believe in the concept of atonement, but tradition is tradition."

The lawyer sighed. "And, right now we need any help we can get. I believe that God hears our prayers the most clearly during this day. We ought to pray for forgiveness."

The uncle added, "And for liberation."

The lawyer added, "If we are to celebrate it properly, we ought to ask forgiveness from one another. To make amends."

The boy could not believe what he was hearing. Have they all gone mad? He was already malnourished. The seamstress looked like a living skeleton. An entire 24 hours of not eating could be detrimental to his health. His favorite moment during each day was the blessed meal, the lingering taste melting in his mouth, settling his rambunctious stomach. He had to say something! He was not going to join a fast when every day was a continuous fast.

He mustered the courage to speak. "But," he mumbled, "Uncle, you said you do not believe in God! We do not even observe the Sabbath!"

The uncle smiled. "You are right. But, tradition. Not for religion... but... out of respect." Then he added quietly, "To them..."

The boy did not understand who 'them' meant. And besides, must they really *fast* to show respect for tradition?

A spark of defiance flickered within him. Was this fasting ritual truly the answer they sought, or merely a futile gesture at trying to appease God, like a gambler throwing the dice once more with no odds of winning?

The boy knew his opinions did not matter at all for any of them. He wanted to agree with everyone else for the sake of solidarity in the pit, but not on the expense of their actual survival. Everyone else in the pit needed less food than him as they were all grown ups. For him, each meal vanished before he even began to enjoy it.

Ever since he'd moved into the pit, his legs had been growing. In the beginning, he could lie in the pit without his fingers touching the wall near the bucket. But now he had reached it. He needed food; could not they see it? Could they exempt him?

And so, as the Day of Atonement loomed on the horizon, the boy steeled himself for the stupidity ahead, knowing that salvation lay not in starvation, but in wisdom, which his fellow pit mates lacked.

The thought could not let the boy rest. He hated them for taking the food from him.

At night, they heard the maid walking to the bedroom. The uncle, knowing the daily food was coming, said, "I will ask her not to bring us food tomorrow night, but before sunset. Unless any of you protest?"

The boy wanted to protest. He wanted to be exempted! He wanted to speak up, but did not find the words. He was afraid they would look down at him as if he was a baby—

The maid knocked on the floorboards.

The boy noticed she seemed tired. She had bags under her eyes. Her face seemed to have become older over the recent six months, creases like moats near her mouth, plowed fields in her forehead. She listened to the uncle as he was speaking, explaining.

At first, she nodded while he spoke. Then her face froze. She glared at him. "Are you out of your mind?"

The boy's fist tightened. He knew the uncle was no match for the maid's will; in this boxing match, he was an ally to the opponent.

The uncle simpered. "We can have the meal earlier, if possible, tomorrow before sundown, and then proceed not to eat until the night the following evening."

The maid shook her head in disbelief. "But anyhow I barely give you any food … You fast every day!"

The boy wanted to say, 'She's right!' He hoped she could reason with his uncle's craziness.

The uncle looked at the maid, blinking, defiant. She stared back at him.

The boy hoped the maid would win against his uncle's bizarre idea.

III

The boy stared at the maid, who glared at the uncle as if he was one of her daughters having a tantrum.

Yet the uncle blinked, unmoved—somehow he was able to seem both defiant and yet oddly respectful, poised, like a seasoned diplomat skillfully navigating the minefield of tact.

The maid finally blinked, ever so subtly.

The uncle knew. He proceeded to hand her the smelly bucket. "Thank you for understanding."

As night became day and as day slowly ebbed, the boy counted the hours. With every position change, he hoped someone would want to change the plan.

Yet he also noticed something.

Something was different in the pit.

The atmosphere had somehow changed. There was a strange calmness.

What was it, exactly?

It wasn't only the holiday that made them feel so elated. The boy knew that neither the holiday nor keeping the tradition made the difference he was sensing.

It was the choice, he felt: the day before, they had been prisoners in this dungeon of torture, accepting life as it was, being led by men's cruelty.

But now, anticipating the fast that would begin following sunset, they felt…*he* felt…like a part of something bigger.

He felt like they were taking *responsibility*—that, though their freedom had been taken from them, though they were confined to live in inhumane darkness, bothered by lice, never seeing the light of day—they still had a choice, however limited it was.

Exercising this choice made them feel… *different*.

It was as if each person was preparing. They were no longer passive, but proactive. The boy had begun waiting for the unusual time of the pit's opening—before sunset. He wondered how the world looked with its natural light and what the bedroom looked like.

He began anticipating not eating that night and the following day. Usually they kept some of the food from each evening for a tiny meal the following day. This time they would not.

Not to do so—out of choice. Not because they had run out of food. But because they had *decided* to.

While at first the boy had thought this idea of fasting ridiculous, as the day passed, he felt more and more excited, eager for the hourglass to proceed. A strange wish to reclaim some dignity spurred him. He had forgotten he was the child of his parents, the grandson of his grandparents.

The boy thought of the maid. The maid had been respectful to them—however, how much longer could she be respectful to the cockroach-like bucket-filling lice of the earth? Surely their dignity was eroded in her eyes. Surely the propaganda got to her as well. Surely at times she wondered why she was doing this, hiding these pitiful slimes of the earth. This fasting, however, somehow made the boy elated, knowing that somehow, in the maid's eyes, they might look different.

He replayed the stand-off battle of stares between the maid and his uncle again and again. He suddenly respected his uncle more— even more than before. His uncle was elevating them all somehow.

The boy *chose* to fast. Not because his uncle and the lawyer and his wife were fasting. But because he *wanted* to.

He still had some dignity left in him. He could still choose. To others, he thought, it might have seemed foolish. But for him, the choice made him feel—all of a sudden—like a human being again.

He never wanted to admit it, but over the past months his mind was a battlefield. He was busy crafting revenge.

In the realm of his mind, he was not merely a frightened child fleeing from danger; he was a hero of his people, a savior, a fighter.

The decision to fast was finally something he could hold to, in the realm of reality, an action of defiance, an act of—as small as it may be—heroism.

The knock of the maid came too early, too soon.

The uncle opened the floorboards.

The light hurt the boy's eyes. Real light, not an electric bedroom lamp. The maid's face glowed in the afternoon.

He turned to see his companions once again clearly though briefly. They were the same—the sallow face of his uncle, the overgrown lawyer, the soft look of the seamstress. Although somehow, they didn't look like the same people at all.

The boy's gaze trailed over the seamstress as the maid exchanged their bucket for a bowl.

She wasn't particularly different from the women he knew, and was made worse for wear by half a year. Rather suddenly, the boy realized he was calm. That heat which roiled beneath his skin and prickled down his neck to his fingertips seemed to take a breath. Postponed, he thought, under the clarity of an empty stomach and focused mind.

The uncle smiled at the four potatoes and two whole slices of bread. "Thank you very kindly."

The maid exhaled. She pushed the clean bucket under the bed.

Later, in the darkness, the uncle lit the oil lamp. They divided the food: a feast!

The boy's instincts told him to save some of the food, to put aside some of the whole potato he was given and save it for later— for the dizzying sickening feeling of not eating an entire day. They ate quietly, each savoring the food. The uncle poured the water from the pitcher into the enamel cup, passing it around. "Drink. Let's finish the water."

No one was lying, they were all sitting, hunched.

The boy felt full—uncomfortably so. His belly had gotten used to eating little, in small sustainable doses. The uncle turned the oil lamp off..

In the darkness, the seamstress spoke out loud for the first time in weeks.

Chapter 56: Light

Israel, 1969

Age 41

I

The scientist and his daughter were looking eagerly at the secretary of the kibbutz, who had picked up the phone in his office and begun talking in Hebrew.

The scientist's daughter wove her fingers into her father's hand. "I have a good feeling, Dad."

The scientist knew not to get his hopes high—if there was anything that life had taught him, it was to be realistic—pessimistic even. What were the chances? Statistics were against him. "Come!" the secretary said, and went to his tractor. "Climb up!"

The daughter was excited to go on the bumpy ride atop the open air tractor. They circled the kibbutz, and the secretary led them through the fields. "It's three kibbutzim over."

They rode through dunes and semi-cultivated fields, orchards of date-palms, and one of those strange red fruits with a crown at its top—a pomegranate orchard. Finally, they arrived at a kibbutz. The sign echoed something deep within him, evoking age ten, sounding as if it could be "Kfar Menahem."

In the shared dining room, an elderly couple awaited—although decades of sun wrinkled and tanned their faces, the scientist knew he had found them.

This was nothing short of a miracle.

How do you recap 30 years?

Where do you begin?

His memory did not betray him; the beautiful lady with the white hair was the kibbutz veterinarian, and her husband was now running the kibbutz metalworks factory.

They spoke of his parents. The veterinarian looked at his daughter. "She has your mother's eyes."

He smiled and wanted to add, 'And my sister's.'

"And you…you look exactly like your father," she added.

"Nonsense," her husband said, "a spitting image of his mother!"

The conversation was jubilant and lasted way into the evening. They ate together at the kibbutz dining hall, speaking about life, politics, agriculture, as if they had known each other for years. They talked about the present, the future, and the years after the war.

Only one subject was skillfully avoided at all costs, lest the daughter heard, lest the pain resurfaced. The scientist and his parents' friends carefully avoided any mention of what should not be spoken about.

Although she was tired, the daughter wanted to hear more about the grandmother she never had the chance to meet. She observed the pain the three of them had whenever she or the others who were killed were mentioned. Her father and the two elders were careful, evasive, hopping from topic to topic, like juggling hand grenades of their shared loss.

As night drew closer, the veterinarian and the welder offered the scientist and his daughter to stay overnight.

The daughter knew her father to be extremely polite, reserved, and never wishing to burden anyone. She knew he would decline and that they were to somehow make the drive back to the first kibbutz, then take their car and endure the long drive to the hotel. She was, therefore, stunned when her father said, "Are you certain it won't be a burden?"

"Of course not!" the lady said, and began making the beds for her two guests in the modest kibbutz home.

The welder poured wine and sat in the enclosed veranda, the screen keeping away the mosquitoes. It was easier to talk over wine. The scientist could not avoid the subject anymore.

"Can I ask you a personal question?" he asked the welder and his wife. His daughter was already asleep on the bed in the living room.

"Of course," the veterinarian said, as if she had expected it all along.

The scientist tightly closed his eyes, forcing himself not to tear up. "How did you know?"

It was late at night; the scientist sat in the enclosed veranda with the white-haired veterinarian and her welder husband. They seemed so Israeli, their skin tanned, a certain roughness to them, an unassuming air. The welder wore simple khaki overalls, and his wife wore a short sleeve shirt. Nothing about them reminded the scientist of the sophistication and strict etiquette conduct that were so prevalent in his parents' age group, which he recalled from his childhood in Poland.

The veterinarian looked at the scientist. "How did we know…?"

"How did you know?" the scientist asked again. His thoughts haunted him. He was now a father to three children, and in his mind there was a constant fear that the tide would turn in America; that Philadelphia would not be safe; that he would become comfortable and complacent and would make a grave error in judgment. That he would lead his family astray, the same way his parents did not see the violent train rushing toward them, a train wreck with whose aftermath he was still grappling, decades later.

The veterinarian, holding her wine glass, glanced at her husband. He shrugged, the way of Israeli men, men of few words and many war scars.

Yet she saw the scientist's big eyes, his eagerness to hear—a pathetic look in his eyes, as if somehow an explanation could miraculously bring back his deceased parents.

She stared at the lawn of the kibbutz through the mosquito screen. She sipped her wine, its bitter tang spurring courage. "Did you ever feel uninvited to a party?"

The scientist nodded.

She continued, "I felt uninvited in my own country. Unwelcomed. I believed in Poland. But Poland did not believe in me. We had to leave." She looked at him and thought of her friends, his parents. "It was easier for us, we did not have children."

The scientist murmured bitterly, "It should be easier if one has children—choosing to protect them."

The veterinarian studied him and answered carefully, "Your parents thought they were doing the right thing, staying where they were, waiting for the storm to pass."

"But how did you know?" the scientist asked, unwilling to let the subject drop. He wanted his parents to be alive, healthy, strong, like their friends in front of him. He wanted his family back.

The scientist grew angry at the silence. The writing was on the wall and his parents—his father—refused to see it. The scientist had spent years trying to forgive, trying to let it go, trying to move on. But that thought gnawed at his mind.

He could have been an Israeli, tanned, working in a kibbutz now. He could have had a family, holidays together, Saturday meals, big Passover meals instead of his small family consisting only of his wife and children. His children could have had cousins, uncles, nephews, nieces, grandparents—a world that was spared from them, taken from them. Taken from him.

The veterinarian looked at her husband and noticed he poured himself another glass, and was now drinking it rapidly. He poured a third glass for himself. He looked at the red substance in the evening's dim light. His voice was hoarse.

"Sometimes—" he cleared his throat. "Maybe your father was smarter."

The scientist stared at him, waiting.

The welder's words were barely audible. "You don't know what it feels like to leave your… parents… behind."

The scientist suddenly felt stupid, insensitive.

The welder continued. "It's a sin I reminisce about every day. Sometimes I think," his voice turned into a murmur, "it would have been better to end up—end up—with them—than have the blame of—"

He did not finish his sentence.

They sat there in silence. Each was lost in their own thoughts. A dark cloud seemed to have descended on them; the euphoria of being reunited after 30 years seemed to vanish, leaving each person surrounded by ghosts from the past.

The veterinarian looked at the two forlorn men, and her

nursing instincts kicked in, as if they were injured calves needing a tetanus shot.

"Your mother would be very proud of you." She saw the 41-year-old man perking up. "Of the way you are with your daughter," she pointed into the house. "She looks up to you, and you seem like a good father to her."

"And of your work," the welder said, staring into his wine glass. "Electronics. That's good work. Your parents would have wanted that for you."

"Thank you," the scientist said.

The welder realized he did not know what exactly his friends' son was doing in America. "You were saying you work in electronics…An electrician?"

"Sort of." The scientist had learned not to boast of his successes.

"What? Repairs, fixing televisions, radios?"

The scientist tried playing it down. "I have a—" *What should be another word for company?* "team, we produce chips for industry. Resistors, and other parts."

"You don't say! Do they pay you well?"

"Not complaining."

"It's hard to work for a boss, though," the welder said, cherishing his own profession and independence. "You work in a factory?"

The scientist felt he must not hide what he did any longer. It was somehow disrespectful. "I studied engineering, and was fortunate to make a few discoveries, and started this small lab. Thankfully, we now have our own factories."

"You don't say!" the welder turned to him, and then looked at his wife, "You heard that? Factories!"

The veterinarian smiled. "Wonderful."

Encouraged, the scientist thought of this visit to Israel, a once-in-a-lifetime trip, of feeling at home in this land, of wanting to return. "Who knows, maybe one day we'll establish a factory here."

"Wouldn't that be something?" the welder said, animated, turning to his wife again. "You heard that?"

She smiled.

The welder said, "Well, why wait? The country needs work, needs factories."

The scientist felt pressured. "One day, not now," he had to give a plausible explanation. "We're now expanding into Europe."

"Europe! Europe is a spit away from here! We have seaports. One day and your chips are in Europe!"

The scientist felt overwhelmed. This was a dream, not an option for the near future.

The welder stood up. "I can arrange a meeting with the minister of industry. We need a factory. When are you leaving?"

"In two days."

"I will call him right now."

The veterinarian looked at her unreasonable husband, "It's too late at this hour!"

"It's never too late! Factories!" the welder got up. "What's the name of your company?"

The scientist inhaled, swelling with pride. "Vishay."

The welder looked at him strangely, and then at his own wife. "What did you say?"

"The name is Vishay, like the village, not far from our city—"

"I know Vishay, I was born there!"

The scientist swallowed hard. "My grandparents came from there too."

The welder said, "No survivors from there, I hear."

The scientist nodded. Even from Grodno, which had 30 thousand people, barely a hundred people survived.

The old welder breathed heavily. "Vishay," he seemed as if he was about to faint. "Vishay. What a name. What a legacy."

This was the first time someone had recognized the scientist's lab and business as a 'legacy.'

The welder exclaimed, "This was meant to be. I'm making the call right now!"

The scientist and the welder met with the Israeli Minister of Industry. The scientist told him of Vishay, its factories in the United States, and the need to expand to Europe. "Europe is more urbanized, organized, and industrialized."

The Minister said, "That's ridiculous. Whatever you can get in Europe, Doctor, we'll get it for you here."

The scientist nodded hesitantly.

The Minister looked at the map of the country on the wall, and squinted his eyes deliberately. "We'll be able to give you considerable tax breaks—if—you help us develop the south, the desert."

The Minister expected the scientist to recoil. Yet the scientist, thinking of the kibbutzim and the villages he had seen in the desert, the resilience of the people there, agreed. "I will get the funds, and you will help me with the permits. But there is one more thing."

"What is it?"

"We will need to hire local people."

"Why, this is our hope, Doctor!"

"Local people, from all of society, regardless of their religion."

The Minister seemed taken aback.

The scientist stared at him. "We will train people that will pass our tests, men and women. Everyone will be welcome; Arabs as well as Jews."

The Minister stared back. He folded his hands together in agitation. "You are a very peculiar person, Doctor."

The scientist reached his hand forward for a handshake, feeling a momentous weight as he did—he was doing something for his people, for the land of the ancestors—and for the people who lived in the region.

The Minister reached out his hand and they shook hands firmly. The scientist said, "Now, let's talk about the details."

And so, without intending it, without planning it, the scientist traveled back and forth to Israel for two years. As the factory was planned, foundations of the building were poured, and constructed, and it was finally opened two years later.

The electronics factory in the desert began training workers from all religions. Jews, Muslims, and Christians. The factory became a haven of peace, a desert oasis in the Holy Land.

In his life as a scientist, he had achieved goals beyond his dreams. Satisfaction and grace followed him in all endeavors.

But in his personal life, his family life, and his marital life, there was turmoil; and the turmoil was about to explode.

Chapter 57: Darkness

Poland, 1944

Age 16

I

The seamstress said, "Day of Atonement. I…"

She paused.

"I feel ignorant," she said.

"Well," the uncle said, "it is about atoning. Forgiving. I hope, sincerely, that I have not offended you in any way."

They all were silent.

"And if I did," the uncle continued, "I beg your forgiveness."

The lawyer spoke. "I, too," he sighed, "hope that I have not offended anyone here. And if I did, I ask for your forgiveness."

The boy knew he should talk. He willed himself to speak, his heart beating fast, afraid of disappointing the seamstress, of not seeming manly enough in her eyes. "I hope I have not done anything to offend any of you." He quickly added, "Please forgive me if I have."

Silence followed.

Then, the seamstress began to speak. The boy was excited to hear her speak again. Again! Her gentle voice mesmerized him. "I understand. Me too. If I've done anything to offend any of you," she said, "I wish to atone."

Then there was silence.

Slowly, in the following hour, each took their new position in the pit, like soldiers returning to their shifts. The boy sat on the lid of the bucket as the night began. He could hear the family above eating and talking loudly. His thoughts traveled to his mother and father.

He remembered the disappointed look on his father's face when the boy had blamed him for not leaving his family. That look haunted him.

He remembered the day of atonement at the synagogue before the war began. Being clothed in white, heading to the synagogue. Everyone went, the synagogue had never been so busy.

Sitting on the bucket, the boy could almost hear the cantor's deep voice. The cantor stood at the elevated platform in the center, his voice resonating through the sacred space. The air was filled with a mixture of whispers and the rustling of prayer shawls, as the congregation swayed in collective prayer. The boy's family, dressed in their finest white garments, took their seats among the sea of worshippers.

The synagogue was full of light from its grand chandelier. They spent hours in the synagogue. At night, the light from the chandelier was bright, as if God himself was present. During the following morning, rays of sunlight filtered through stained glass windows, casting colorful patterns on the polished wooden floor. The boy's eyes were drawn to the intricate carvings adorning the ark that held the holy scrolls, artistry, craftsmanship and dedication of generations gone by.

The boy remembered how the cantor's voice rose and fell, carrying the ancient prayers that echoed in the hearts of the worshippers. The boy understood the prayers, although they were biblical, ancient, thanks to the diligent teachings of his father. As the haunting notes of the prayer filled the praying hall, the boy's mind could not help but wander to the meaning behind the words. The ethereal melody, paired with the weighty lyrics, held a significance that transcended language.

He recalled the translation: "All vows, obligations, oaths, and anathemas…we do repent. May they be deemed absolved, forgiven…"

These words, steeped in ancient Hebrew, carried a profound

significance for the boy. A collective plea for forgiveness and a desire to start anew. He understood that this was not just a day of personal repentance but a communal endeavor to release the burdens of unfulfilled promises and unkept vows. A day of reconciliation, a chance to wipe the slate clean, and a commitment to strive for a higher moral ground in the year to come. The weight of the ancient words lingered in his thoughts.

His thoughts turned dark.

He remembered the walk to the synagogue in the snow on that cursed day of moving into the temporary camp. The entire community was expelled from their houses.

In the grand synagogue, the pews were gone, everything was moved aside. "Move inside!" the soldiers shouted, but there was no more room. Thousands of people were crammed inside.

Babies were crying, sick people were leaning on their families, old people staring into space.

On the stage, on the holy of holies, stood the angel of death—people in the community had already nicknamed him. He had been the most murderous of all the Nazis. *The butcher.* He shouted commands, mocking the community. He shot his gun at the ceiling, scaring the crying babies.

The boy held his sister's hand.

Not far from where the boy stood, a man complained to the butcher about how crowded it was. The boy cringed, this man should have known better. The butcher was incensed. "Crowded? Crowded?" he shouted, "Well now it will be less crowded." He pointed his gun at the man—

The boy felt the shudder through his sister's hand. "Don't look!" he said, covering her face. But he saw. He saw the butcher shoot the man who complained. The two shots echoed in the synagogue. The man collapsed, blood spilling from his head like wine, his eyes staring into space, his mouth still moving for a few long seconds.

The soldiers quickly dragged his body outside.

Next to the boy stood his cousin. She was still alive then. His entire family was there, cousins, nephews, uncles, and his beloved grandparents. Forty-two of them. The entire family.

That same synagogue, once a symbol of prize, a bride shining in the glow of betrothal, a gathering place for the sacred Day of Atonement, the pinnacle of the community—was turned into a transit hall, from where people were sent to the camps, for hard labor—of which kind, no one knew. No one returned from there.

The uncle whispered, "Let us change positions."

The boy crawled from the bucket to the ground, lying down. What time was it? He laid there, trying not to think of his family, of the butcher, of the man gushing blood, or of his beautiful cousin whose dress was soiled with blood.

He tried to push the thought of revenge aside, but it kept reemerging as he drowsed in and out of hallucinated sleep. They changed positions again, and he was in the middle, between the lawyer and the uncle. They were speaking over his head.

What hour was it?

He heard them speak to each other. They rarely spoke. The boy became alert.

The uncle sounded torn. "I…" he cleared his throat. "I…" he spoke again.

The boy turned his face in the darkness to his uncle. What was his uncle trying to say? Was it about his wife, taken to the trains? About his daughter? The boy waited. Finally, the uncle spoke.

Finally, the uncle spoke.

"This day," the uncle said slowly, speaking not only to the lawyer, but to the seamstress, "is to stress the importance of our word."

He paused, his words echoed in the pit. "We don't have much in this world. But our word, our vow, is priceless."

Then the lawyer pleaded, "Go on."

The uncle smiled. The boy could hear it in his voice. "I don't know much about this holiday, quite frankly. What I do know is that we need to apologize to the Creator for us having broken our promises… Any lie we made, any harm we've done, even the smallest, is against the promise we pledge to God each year, to be and do our best."

The boy shifted uncomfortably. There was no room for his feet in the middle position, as the bucket was placed in the center.

The uncle continued. "Even under duress or in times of stress, we are expected to do good. Because we promised to. Our word is important." He sighed. "Sometimes, that is all we have."

The boy thought of his grandmother. He hesitated, but then said, "Grandma said—grandma said that even our words aren't ours."

There was silence. The boy feared he had interrupted.

"Go on," said the lawyer.

The boy swallowed. The lawyer rarely spoke to him.

"She said," the boy said slowly, "that nothing is ours but one thing. We may think we have fortune, or wit, or good looks, but it's never ours; all of it is temporary."

The boy paused, seeing his grandmother before his eyes, her radiant version, the one before the war, before the baby grandchildren were taken to the trains in that cursed transport with her husband.

He continued. "She said the only thing we have forever is what we give to others. What we give to others out of a pure heart can never be taken away from us."

The uncle's voice broke. "Mother. That sounds exactly like her."

Silence ensued.

The boy noticed this was the first time the uncle had said anything of his mother—the boy's grandmother—or, in fact, of anyone in the family. The uncle had a clear policy of speaking nothing about the people 'out there.' The boy understood very well that speaking of the family could raise demons. Anger. Despair.

The uncle tried to avoid that at any cost.

Therefore the boy was surprised when yet again the uncle whispered, his voice barely audible, "She told me, 'You need to be the reason someone believes in the goodness of people.'"

Silence.

Then the seamstress spoke. "I wish I'd met her. Perhaps I will someday."

The uncle hurried to change the subject, his voice practical. "Do you know the list of confessions?"

The lawyer coughed quietly. "You mean…'the twenty-four?'"

"Yes."

The boy remembered this prayer vaguely. He had gone to the synagogue each year, and listened as the cantor chanted out loud. But could someone have actually *memorized* all the confessions by heart?

"Well," the lawyer said, "I think it goes… 'We have been guilty. We have betrayed others. We have stolen…'"

The boy listened carefully. He could not help but think of the heinous soldiers, led by their madman, their hateful fuhrer and the cruel butcher. *They* have been guilty. *They* have been betrayed. *They* have stolen…!

"'…We have spoken falsely,'" the lawyer continued, "'We have caused perversion. We have caused others to do evil…'"

The boy felt a sudden rage building up inside of him. This list the lawyer recited brought up the memories he had seen during the last few years of the war, events he preferred to forget.

The image of the butcher was seared behind his eyes, his pure bloodlust and sickening joy in taking human life. The boy could not shake the sound of gunshots shattering the air, the way human bodies went limp, contorting in strange ways before smacking the ground, like shoes tossed aside.

"'We have had evil hearts,'" continued the lawyer. "'We have been violent…'"

The boy could not take it. Pure hatred boiled to the surface, the look on his sister's eyes as they marched in the snow to the ghetto, the whip that hit his back, he could still feel where the whip hit him, leaving a mark to remain there for weeks. He sat up, agitated. "Why should we recite these?"

Silence fell.

"It's them," he whispered, trying not to shout, "It's *them* who should atone!"

The uncle whispered, "No one is totally free of transgressions. Papa—your grandpa—used to say, 'Before you judge someone else, stop and think of your own wrongdoings…'"

"But," the boy insisted, "you can't possibly compare—"

"I do not," said the uncle. He paused for a long moment. "I do not. But I can compare myself to myself; I can compare the person I would like to be, to the person I am. And for that difference, I can willfully atone."

The boy shook his head vehemently. He embraced his knees to his chest, burying his face in his torn trousers.

The uncle spoke to the lawyer, "Continue."

"'We have become desensitized to dishonesty,'" the lawyer continued with the list. "'We have given bad advice. We have disappointed others. We have been contemptuous. We have rebelled. We have enraged others.'"

The boy saw his cousin before his eyes. If he was a true man, he should have taken the bullets that claimed her life.

The voice of the lawyer continued, taking the blame on them, not admitting they were victims at all; forgetting. Forgiving—crimes, killing, taking innocent young lives. The boy felt fire within him, his rage building, exploding.

"...We have turned away from other people's suffering," continued the lawyers. "We have fallen victim to our impulses. We have committed offenses. We afflicted others. We have been stiff-necked. We have been wicked. We have been immoral. We have erred. We have misled others.'" He sighed and concluded. "'We have misled ourselves.'"

As silence filled the pit, the boy felt his ravenous appetite. At this time of day usually he would be eating the last bite that he had kept—the bite to last him to the night. But there was no bite, only hunger. The hefty meal the night before was forgotten as if it had never existed—an entire potato, half a slice of bread, gone and vanished.

He placed a hand on his protruding ribs, then slid it down to clutch the cave that his stomach had become. Bitterness bubbled up inside of him, rising to his throat.

Some time later the uncle whispered, "The purpose of this is not, if I am correct, to wallow in guilt. It is to purify us so that we can serve better. So that we can be used by God in a better way. So that we can become a 'light unto the nations.'"

The boy said nothing. All he thought was that now, in this pitch-black pit, starving, the farthest thing he could think of was being a 'light' unto anyone.

It was then that his uncle moaned—ever so quietly. The boy was too distracted to notice what was happening to his uncle.

Most days in the hiding pit were alarmingly the same. Unusual days, like fasting on Day of Atonement, were rare and far between.

The boy's innermost thoughts always drew back to his family; to his friends; to the hope for life, and the constant fear of death.

One late evening the maid was not her cheerful self.

Upon handing the meal to the four of them, the maid whispered, "They found two bodies in the river."

This piece of news grabbed their attention.

"They had most likely been hiding with some family," she said. "No one knows which family, or what happened. But their... throats were slit." She sighed. "People say the family who was hiding them became scared."

In the darkness that followed, the boy tried to think about anything but slit throats, bodies floating in the river.

He tried to keep himself busy with math and geometry, as well as trying to remember historical dates and facts, rehearsing his old orchestra concerts, and thinking of the future.

But death was more alluring.

As was despair.

As was revenge.

Once in a while a positive memory would come to mind, like a torch of light in the darkness. How his grandmother used to take him along on her various errands: visiting the orphanage, visiting the poor, visiting the hospital. He was always being dragged around as a kid. His grandma would tell him, "You don't know how fortunate you are until you lose it all. We must never turn a blind eye to human suffering, do you understand?"

Images of his grandmother flickered before him. Quickly his thoughts immediately turned sour. Remembering how desperate his grandmother had been after all the family's wealth was taken away...after the house was taken... after they were crammed into a tiny apartment with about forty people in the segregated enclosure. Then, when her husband was taken to the trains in that first transport, after she chose to hide, he refused to hide, how he refused to give away the young children, how he chose to go with them to the trains. How she became a broken person.

How she seemed to just wait for her turn.

The boy began feeling that all-too-familiar sensation of guilt. Guilt at being alive—alive at least for the time being.

His thoughts turned to how he had tried to escape the segregated ghetto, which had become a big jail. After much deliberation and effort, he managed to find a place between buildings; a climb on a gutter could lead down to the street outside the ghetto. It was doable.

He convinced his mother and sister to come with him. They agreed. His father however, did not want to leave, choosing to remain with the grandparents who were unable to escape.

The boy, his mother, and sister escaped and stayed in the other part of the city, waiting for his father to join them so that they could flee the city, through forests, at night.

The boy sighed. *If only. He could have saved his sister; his mother.*

His mother was so unhappy away from his father. She cried all the time. Eventually, she chose to return—return to the claws of the ghetto with the soldiers ruling their lives, taking the boy's sister along with her.

The boy could not remain away from the three of them. A day later, he, too, returned to the ghetto, earning a few more precious weeks with his family before the end came. The boy recalled returning to the ghetto, upset with his father for not having escaped—it was because of his foolish father that the boy's mother and sister had to return. He faced his father, upset, provoking his foolish father. "Dad! Why didn't you escape and join your family?"

His father looked at him, his eyes full of silence, of disappointment; as if the education his father had given the boy had failed. He adjusted his glasses. His father murmured, "Which family, son? What will become of your grandparents, my parents?"

The boy swallowed hard, evading his father's piercing sad eyes. He knew his father was right. His grandparents were in their seventies, unable to do everything that escaping entailed.

Now, in the darkened pit, his father's voice kept torturing him, "Which family, son? What will become of your grandparents, my parents?"

His father had strength of character.

Unlike him. His father stuck with his parents, courageously facing whatever came.

He felt the guilt rising, filling his chest, overwhelming him with pain.

He swallowed hard. He turned from the wall to his uncle, who was laying in the middle of the pit, next to the seamstress. "Uncle?"

His uncle moved. "What?" he asked, with obvious anger. Something was bothering him.

"Give me another exercise, please," the boy whispered. "A more difficult one." To himself he added, 'So difficult, it could last for hours, and days, and years. Let it last forever, Uncle…because I just cannot bear it—the guilt… I just cannot bear it…"

His uncle was not cooperating, sighing.

The boy thought that something had happened to his uncle. His uncle became tired, distracted, complaining. Sighing heavily. His hand suddenly clutched the boy's left shoulder. The boy's left shoulder hurt from the uncle's fingers. "I have to tell you something."

The boy's breath stopped. His uncle—his anchor, his solid ground, the architect of the pit, the one remainder—what did he want to say? And why were his fingers pinching the left boy's shoulder? Why could he hear pain in his uncle's voice? Why did his uncle's breath come with the foul odor of death itself?

Chapter 58: Light

Paris, 1970

Age 42

I

Paris summoned the scientist again that year. His uncle was diagnosed with an acute case of lung cancer.

The doctors said it was the final-stage lung cancer; that the uncle had only a few months left to live.

The scientist did not accept the diagnosis. He sought out the best cancer specialists in America. "Money is not an issue," he muttered on expensive international calls from Paris. "I'm sending you the medical reports and x-rays by express air mail."

But the phone calls that followed in response were not optimistic. They could do nothing for his uncle: bringing the uncle to America would not save him. It was too late.

Sitting near his uncle's bed in the Parisian hospital, the scientist forced a smile. The uncle's wife stood on the other side of the bed, holding his hand.

The scientist's leg shook, the way he always did when he was nervous.

"Shhh…" the uncle said. He was hooked up to various life support machines.

The uncle turned his head to his wife and said, wheezing, "I—need a minute—with my nephew…"

"I will be in the hallway," the wife said. She squeezed her

husband's hand gently, and left the room.

The uncle sighed heavily, then inhaled deeply, about to say something important.

The scientist leaned forward, eager to hear his uncle's wisdom. His uncle had been speaking so reticently, preferring silence over speech. Yet now it seemed he wished to say something important.

The uncle whispered, "How is the business?"

It was so typical of his uncle to ask about that of all things. The scientist chuckled. "Fine. Good." He added. "Great, actually."

"And that factory in Israel?"

"Very good."

"How—many—workers?"

"Four hundred and fifty now."

"So many families," the uncle whispered. "Very impressive."

They sat there in silence.

The scientist wanted to say so much to his beloved uncle. He wanted to say, "Thank you," and "Don't leave me!" and "What will I do without you?"

He did not want to sadden his uncle. He had tried to put on a brave show, to pretend that there was hope his uncle would heal. But, looking at his emaciated, frail body, the scientist knew there was only one direction this was headed.

He was overwhelmed by emotions. His uncle, his only kin, his only blood relation, his only link to his entire family whose bodies lay in unmarked graves.

He was sorry for himself. Sorry that the old mama left him.

And he was lamenting his crumbling marriage, now in the final stages of divorce. He could no longer hide it from his children, and that pained him the most. He and his wife had put on a merry show for years, all for the sake of his children. But now the curtain was falling on this ill-fated marriage, and he felt he was nothing but a failure, in the most important field that ever mattered to him—more than science and more than a million medals and honors—he was failing at *family*.

The uncle breathed deeply.

The scientist leaned in again. He wanted to hold his uncle's hand, but he did not dare. He did not want to hurt his uncle's feelings by implying his uncle was weak.

As he watched his uncle breathing heavily, his thoughts turned to his children—how would they survive without their mythical great uncle, the teacher of math and sciences, the one who could tell them a few more words about the war when their own father remained mute about the subject?

What would his children have, no uncle, no married parents, no proper home? Failure. Failure. Failure.

His eldest daughter, now in university, encouraged him: "Dad, it's better for you and mom to be happy separately than miserable together."

But the scientist's son was only thirteen. *How would he cope?* The scientist knew he had failed miserably. Miserably.

"Shhh…" the uncle said.

The scientist could not hold it any longer. Ever since the old mama died, ever since the divorce procedures began, he was a wreck. And now the cancer was devouring his uncle, eating at the flesh of his adoptive father, killing the voice of reason, strength, and courage.

He buried his face in his uncle's hand. The weak, feeble hand that once was so strong. The hand that had once protected him was now looking so pale, ashy, and cold.

And here they were, both of them silent. With so much he wanted to tell his uncle, so much that he wanted to hear—and they were not speaking. Or, worse, speaking about the business of all things, rather than about what would be. Rather than about how the scientist would survive. Rather than about their relationship, their friendship, their bond forged in fire, their love that grew strong when their family turned to ashes around them.

The uncle breathed heavily. "You know…" he whispered.

The scientist perched his ear to the uncle's feebly moving mouth.

"You—know… I am…so proud—of—you…"

The scientist bit his lip. He screwed his eyes shut, trying not to cry. "You are?" he asked.

"Of course…. You've done—very—well…. My sister… your mother, she would have—been—so proud of you…"

The scientist tried etching the words on his heart, lest he forget.

"Do you—remember," the uncle whispered, "when you were—a child… and you—memorized… all the capitals of Europe?"

"Yes…I remember."

"She used—to grin, your mother… She shined… You were—her greatest—pride."

The scientist bit his lips so hard he hurt himself. He held tightly onto his uncle's hand. He glanced out into the hallway, embarrassed to be such a wreck. He grabbed his uncle's hand, refusing to believe he was dying.

The scientist was still a boy, and they were still in the pit, and living without the uncle would be dangerous. Bearing his heart, he begged his uncle. "Please don't leave me."

"You'll… be—fine… Take care of my wife…"

The scientist nodded in agreement, "Of course, Uncle."

They sat there in silence.

The uncle breathed heavily. "And don't… be… so hard—on—yourself…"

The scientist was unsure what the uncle meant.

"…Your marriage—you've done—your best. Now…carry on. I know what—it is like to—lose a wife…. But there is always…a new day dawning, you hear me?"

The Jewish cemetery of Paris saw the scientist again that year. He was torn between two graves, and God had stolen his anchors, releasing him to drown in an abyss of depression, grief, and sorrow that he would not know how to cope with. In the past, in such a crisis, he would pick up the phone and call the old mama, or the uncle. He would fly out for a long heart-to-heart conversation, at the end of which he would leave, his vision cleared, his conviction strong.

His success—the factories—meant nothing to him. His children were almost like strangers to him—they knew nothing of who he truly was. He did not dare tell them of his past. He did not want to relive it, nor did he want to pain them.

Now he had no one to call, no one to fly out to, no one to save him from the spiraling depression, which was threatening to take the meager comfort he had managed to find in his life after the war, and threatening to take his life, too.

II

The scientist did not know that despair was to give birth to breakthrough—not in his science, but in the science of the heart.

Yet, when he was through the emotional winter, he could see no silver lining. His loved ones had died, the old mama, the uncle, and he was now divorced.

Divorced. A diploma of failure etched like a tattoo on his ringless finger. The stripe of skin on his ring finger, where the ring once stood unmoved, was now wincing in the sun, shaking in the wind, pale and obvious, a stripe of shame, like an armband on a sleeve during the war years.

He found it difficult to concentrate on his work. He had two factories on two sides of the planet, nearly two thousand people working for him, and yet, he found no reason for being.

He had no one to consult with, to confide in, to love. His beloved uncle was gone. His beloved old mama was gone. His wife was gone from his life.

His 13-year-old son stayed with him. But the scientist found it difficult to speak of things more profound than his son's homework. Over the years the scientist had learned that, in order to be a proper father, he must not speak of emotions. He had learned from his wife not to mention the war; not to "scare the children." He learned that he was not good with the children.

And so they never really spoke. And now he feared his son was a stranger to him; an American child, who knew nothing of his father's past.

His two daughters, now both in universities, told the scientist not to be so harsh with himself. But he heard, instead, 'Stop complaining, Dad.'

As the years went by, he began fearing that his children would never really know him. Not unless he would one day learn to speak of what had happened to him; not unless he would learn how to express pain. He allowed himself to tear up with his uncle, or with his old mama—never with the children.

He was afraid to show not only weakness, but also joy. He was always afraid to feel joy, fearing it was only momentary.

Emotion was a dirty word.

Now, divorce had exacerbated the loneliness he had always felt before. He had never felt so lonely. He hoped for a miracle. Apart from his children, he saw no reason for living.

The weight of grief hung heavily over him, a suffocating presence that seemed to dim the very air around him.

He did not know the same forces in nature that wrought beauty from adversity would also forge purpose in him.

He was about to find out.

Chapter 59: Darkness

Poland, 1944

Age 16

"I have to tell you something," the uncle whispered to the boy. The boy noticed his uncle's speech was too slurred. Almost as if he were drunk.

The boy's breath stopped. His uncle—his anchor, his solid ground, the architect of the pit, the one remainder of his family—what did he want to say? And why were his fingers piercing now into the boy's shoulder? Why was there agony in his uncle's voice? Why did the uncle's breath smell so badly?

What was his uncle trying to say?

"Uncle, what is it?"

His uncle groaned. "Never mind."

"Uncle!" the boy insisted.

His uncle breathed heavily.

The boy never—ever—heard his uncle complaining.

The uncle was usually very reserved. Stoic. He never complained. But in recent days, long before the fasting, and long after it, he would let out a painful sigh. What was on his mind?

The uncle's grip on the pit was slowly loosening. Before, his word was the word of God—he was the one talking to the maid, he was the one who made the rules: switching positions every couple of hours, the division of food, no intimacy between the lawyer and his wife, the minute of light upon division of the food—life.

Yet now his behavior has become erratic. One time he let them sit for what felt like hours in the same position. The boy was on the bucket then, it could have not been only two hours. It was maybe five or six hours—his body ached from sitting.

Finally the lawyer whispered to him, "Shouldn't we change already?" to which the uncle answered hurriedly, absentmindedly, "Yes, yes, let's… change positions."

The boy lay there waiting for his uncle to speak. But his uncle said nothing, his hand still gripping the boy's shoulder tightly.

The boy pondered, worried. Recently the uncle, who was always such a gentleman with the maid, calling her "Madam," always displaying utter gratitude, peppering his speech with "Thank you," and "please," was nowadays sour, disengaged, almost aloof.

Was his uncle sick?

Did his uncle lose hope?

His uncle moaned. "Let's switch positions."

They all switched positions again, although it had not been two hours yet. The boy, now in the middle between the uncle and the lawyer, leaned to his uncle's ear. "Uncle? Is everything alright?"

His uncle made a sound which both sounded like an affirming yes, and at the same time did nothing but to affirm the boy that nothing was alright.

At night the maid brought them food. Two potatoes.

The seamstress divided the potatoes into four parts in the light of the oil lamp.

The boy chose his half of a potato. Then the uncle reached a shaking hand for his half.

It was cold, winter, and snowy outside and yet the boy saw that his uncle's forehead was dripping with sweat.

It was about a minute later, after they had turned the oil lamp off, that the uncle suddenly, violently, moaned.

The lawyer sounded upset. "What is it? Speak!"

The uncle's voice sounded broken. "I…" he began. "I," his voice defeated. "I think I may need help."

Chapter 60: Light

Paris, 1970

Age 42

For months the scientist was burning in despair. Following the death of his uncle, the old mama, and his divorce, he could see nothing good coming from this hell he called his life.

It was strange, at first. As odd as it seemed to him, the scientist had to admit to himself that the divorce actually allowed him to improve his relationships with his children.

He was getting to *see* them.

He met with his eldest daughter at her university in Israel. He frequented his middle daughter at her dormitory in Philadelphia. He began going on walks with his son, learning to listen, learning to converse, and learning to be an active father. It was not too late, he discovered.

His son, still in school, lived with him in Philadelphia. Yet the scientist had multiple trips abroad for the company. More often than not, the son joined his father on his many business trips.

The high school administration did not like it, but the scientist did not care. His son's grades were still high; he easily caught up with all the schoolwork he missed each time. Now it was their time together, on his trips.

He bought the records his son listened to. And although the music was unappealing, to say the least, he listened to it repeatedly. He read the lyrics on the jacket, and asked his secretary to help him decipher the strange English, featuring words he had never heard, *groovy, far out, funky, boogie, bummer, jive.*

He began calling his son "Dude" and asked to "chill out" together. When his son gave him an attitude, the scientist *kept on truckin'*

Slowly, the son began looking forward to walks with his dad, to trips with him. They began speaking of sports and books.

They went to movies, and watched *Jaws* together, and then *Rocky.* Although the scientist was embarrassingly frightened, he did not leave in the middle. He did, however, close his eyes more than once.

He spent a lot of time with his son, as well as with his daughters. When his ex-wife was vacationing during Passover, he invited his daughters to join him and his son in Philadelphia. He spent two days in the kitchen, on his own, reading from recipe books, and cooking an entire Passover meal.

"Dad," his daughter exclaimed, "I wasn't even aware you knew how to cook."

"Neither did I," he admitted. "But it's sort of like chemistry, like putting adhesives together," he remarked.

His children smiled at him. Their father looked at his broken family and sighed. "I'm so happy we're together." Then, at the end of the Passover Eve, he said, "This year enslaved, next year free, this year here, next year in Jerusalem."

It was evident, as they sat by the Passover elaborate dinner, that the scientist had lost much, but also gained much. He had lost his marriage, but gained his children. He lost his uncle, but gained a new family, finding friends in his own three babies. He lost his old mama, but he became an old mama, of sorts. He found it in himself.

He also remembered his early childhood, and how his mother and father would try to bond with him and his sister. His parents would dance around the parlor with his sister, humming tunes. Meanwhile, his parents would indulge him in his favorite activities—such as building structures out of blocks.

The scientist was happy to know that he was now responsible for making amazing memories with his children.

From the murky waters of spiraling into depression after losing his dear ones, came buds of lotus in the dark water. From the forest fires of his loneliness, came a renewed spring of personal growth, with new, deep roots. From the pressure and suffocation exerted deep within the crevices of his soul, new formations appeared, the hardness birthing brilliance, the suffocation yielding strength, the rough turning into diamonds.

At the end of the Passover meal his son asked, "Dad, can we ask you a question?"

"Sure." the scientist said, although he became not so sure by the second.

"Can you tell us about the war?"

His son stared at him. The sisters glared at their little brother—he was fourteen already, he should have known better.

The scientist choked up. He quickly became teary-eyed, his face pale.

The eldest daughter brought him a glass of water. "Forget it Dad. Drink."

The scientist tried drinking some water, the coolness refusing to slide down his burning throat.

How could he unravel the threads of his past, open that Pandora box? How could he broach the subject without instilling anxiety and fear in their innocent hearts? Was it fair to burden them with the weight of his sorrow, especially when their young lives were already marked by the aftermath of their parents' divorce?

The memories, clouded with guilt and shame, were locked within him, a vault guarding the unspeakable horrors. The fear of misunderstandings haunted him, the fear that their tender minds might not grasp the enormity of the darkness he had faced. He had spent decades striving for normalcy—why should he now expose them to his past, to lay bare the language of a history that defied articulation?

Wasn't it wrong, focusing on the past instead of the present, instead of planning for the future?

How could he breach the wall of silence? How could he share

with them his darkness without casting shadows on their young innocence? The specter of survivor guilt loomed large, whispering that their young hearts need not bear the burden of his survival.

The fear of being misinterpreted gripped him, of being judged. A fear that his narrative might be lost in the translation between generations, leaving them with fragments of a story that defied comprehension.

All these years, the desire to cultivate a sense of normalcy for his children brought him to the constant realization that the past must be buried.

He grappled with what it would do not only to them, but for himself, too: the toll that revisiting those memories might exact. He was no longer married, and, although his former wife never wanted to hear anything about the war, he still felt that he had someone there. Now, he questioned whether he could bear the emotional weight alone.

He sipped water again, his hand shaking.

His middle daughter put her hand on his. "It is okay, Dad."

He wanted to. He wanted to, so badly. But he was afraid that once he had opened his mouth, he could never stop. And the nightmares, he was afraid that the nightmares, now kept somewhat at bay, coming only every couple of weeks, would return, haunting him each and every night.

"One day," he said quietly, and then added, "I promise."

The years passed. His eldest daughter moved to Israel and he visited her often. He traveled with his son, now sixteen, while overseeing an expansion of the factory, building a second plant in Israel.

His daughter, who was studying for her PhD in Israel, called him. "Dad, I'd like the two of you to join me for a large dinner this Friday."

"But," her father protested, "we won't know anyone there…"

"I'll introduce everyone to you, Dad."

"But…your brother will feel uncomfortable!"

"Dad, he'll be fine, and so will you. There'll be many interesting people there. Besides, I already said you two will come, so it would be rude to cancel."

He did not know that this one meal was about to change his life.

Chapter 61: Darkness

Poland, 1944

Age 16

The lawyer waited in the darkness. The boy, too, waited for the uncle to speak.

The uncle's words from a minute earlier echoed in the pit,, floating in the still cold air. "I think I may need help."

Yet the uncle did not elaborate.

The lawyer's voice sounded softer. "What help do you need?"

The uncle sighed. "My tooth hurts." He exhaled heavily from his nose, his mouth shut tightly.

The lawyer said, "Let me see." In the darkness, his hand reached for the corner where he always carefully placed the oil lamp near the bucket.

"No," the uncle said, "we need to spare the oil."

"Nonsense," the lawyer said.

The boy felt grateful for the lawyer.

The lawyer lit the oil lamp. "Open your mouth," he commanded.

The boy leaned forward.

"Good," the lawyer encouraged. To see better, he needed the uncle to tilt his head slightly to the right, so the light from the lamp allowed him to examine the damage. He gently touched the uncle's jaw, tilting it to the right—

"Ugh," the uncle moaned as the lawyer's hand touched his jaw.

"I'm sorry—" the lawyer hurried to say, examining the mouth.

"No, no," the uncle spoke. "It is fine," he said and opened his mouth widely, moaning as he did.

The lawyer brought his arm down, the lamp casting different shadows above them, behind each of them. He gulped and slowly turned the knob of the lamp, the light dimming and dimming, the last tiny column of smoke rising and disappearing in the complete darkness. He did not say anything. None of them did.

The boy felt helpless. *What should they do?*

That night, the lawyer said, "Madam?"

The maid looked at him, surprised.

The uncle shook his head and closed his eyes, putting his hand on the lawyer, trying to stop him—

But the lawyer persisted. "We need help. We need a dentist."

"A what?" the maid said loudly.

"A dentist," the lawyer said and looked at the maid, then at the uncle, who was forcing a smile between groans. "I'm alright."

"He is not," the lawyer said.

The maid, exasperated, spoke with a high pitch. "How am I to get you a… dentist?"

"Or a doctor—"

"You are out of your mind! Who can I trust nowadays—" she said, her voice becoming a wail, her eyes tearing. "This is a—this is a—"

She did not complete her sentence.

Everyone remained silent.

The uncle waved his hand dismissively, yet it floated in the air like a drunkard's hand, feebly landing on his lap. "I'm fine, fine!"

The maid sighed heavily. "Let me see what I can do."

In the darkness that followed, no one spoke. The boy began praying. He never prayed: not when his family was taken to the ghetto, not during the gunfire at the grand synagogue. The boy could never pray to a god who let bloodthirsty soldiers scour the ghetto like hunters, rewarded by their commander, the butcher, treating his family like vermin in hiding.

He did not pray on that cursed snowy day when the world was blanketed and instead of returning to join the march to the train station, he dared to run away, darting towards the city outskirts as gunshots rang out and he sprinted through the forest, day and night, seeking refuge up the hill in that small, almost forgotten cabin.

The boy could not—would not—pray to this pitiful, powerless, cruel, mocking god.

Until now.

The boy clasped his hands together, unwillingly praying to the God who had forsaken him, forsaken his family, forsaken his people. "Please, God, get us a doctor."

The hours passed excruciatingly slowly.

When, the following night, they heard the secret knock on the door that gave them the answer they already knew deep down. No doctor could come and save the uncle's life.

II

After hours that seemed like days of waiting for the maid to return with a doctor, a dentist, or a savior, they heard the secret knock.

The lawyer lifted the floorboards.

The boy's heart sank as he saw no one but the maid and her husband, both kneeling down and staring at them. "This is preposterous," the maid's husband said, shaking his head, his face pale, his eyes glaring, scared, haunted.

The uncle was suddenly woken alive. "I'm fine!" he grunted.

Yet the boy could see the uncle was not fine; in fact, he suddenly noticed in the light that entered the pit, that the uncle's face was swollen—his right side looked as if he was hiding a giant potato in the corner of his jaw.

The maid looked at the uncle helplessly, then at her husband, then at the uncle, then again at her husband, frantically turning from one to another.

The boy had never seen her like that.

The lawyer said, "We must help him."

The maid's husband said, "*You* help him, we cannot." He grabbed his wife by the arm, forcing her to stand up. She followed up, confused, then whispered meekly, "I'll take the bucket."

The lawyer gave her the bucket, and took the empty bucket and the bowl of potatoes and leek. Surprisingly, she then handed him another bowl. "Soup," she said apologetically. "Maybe it will help—"

The uncle's words were nearly indecipherable. "Thank you!" he said, and his hand motioned to the lawyer to close the floorboards already.

The maid stood up, but, to everyone's surprise, her husband kneeled back down. He looked at the lawyer, his eyes haunted. "You have to understand us."

The seamstress suddenly said, "We do. I do." She gestured with her chin upwards toward the other room. "You must protect them."

"Not only the children! You too!" the husband said, a strange tinge of desperation in his voice. "All of our lives—" he struggled to complete the sentence and for a moment the words died in his throat. "I am not sorry for standing against my wife, or for changing my mind. We are in this together now; each of us…as important as the next."

The uncle repeated slowly, feebly, gesturing with his hand, motioning for the lawyer to lower the floorboards already. It was as if he had not heard the husband at all.

The husband looked at the reclining uncle. He winced looking at him. "I… I will… don't lose hope."

The seamstress said, "A dentist's kit."

"What?"

She spoke again quietly. "A kit. Dentist's kit."

"Maybe," the husband said, his voice feeble, barely heard, unwilling to commit, scared of the shifting sands to which he was leading ten souls, gambling on their lives.

"Thank you," the seamstress said, and in a unique act reached her fingers, her hand clasping his hand. "Thank you!"

The husband remained there impassively, his face frozen, unchanged, bewildered, as the floorboards slowly came down, like a theater curtain falling on the last act of a tragedy in which everyone meets the same fate.

In the darkness that followed the lawyer reached for the lamp.

The boy took the soup and the spoon, and gently, like a caring mother, tried to convince the uncle to drink the soup. "Uncle, please. The soup will be good for you."

The uncle shook his head, unwilling, moaning and groaning.

The boy tried to force him. "Uncle, please—"

"I'm alright!" the uncle exclaimed, his agitated movement pushing and spilling the soup on the boy's pants.

The boy put the empty bowl with the remaining soup in the corner, near the lamp and lay next to the uncle.

Everyone lay there, silently. It had been hours since they

changed places. The boy wondered, even if they would get a dentist's kit, would the seamstress be able to do what needed to be done?

He kept hoping for the swelling to cease on its own, for the uncle to shake off his fatigue and repeated groans, and sit up, rejuvenated, calming everyone, putting the sun back in the center of the galaxy, and returning all the stars to their course.

Night turned to day. The only sound in the pit were the punctuated groans of the usually stoic, brave uncle.

"Uncle, are you alright?" the boy asked, as helpless as he had felt since his father's refusal to leave the enclosure.

"My eyes."

"Your eyes?"

"My eyes," the uncle moaned, his speech slurred. "Swollen. I have—a terrible—headache."

Then came the knock. The boy had prepared for it, hoped for it, prayed for it. Yet when it came he jumped, as if he had not heard it daily for months. He had waited for this moment, but as the lawyer lifted the floorboards, the boy dreaded what was to come.

Chapter 62: Light

Israel, 1977

Age 49

I

The scientist's daughter invited her father and her brother to attend a Friday meal at a family in Tel Aviv. The scientist could not cancel, although he wanted to.

The daughter asked her brother to sit next to her, but there was no chair in that corner of the long table. "Sit there, Dad," she said and pointed at a free chair.

The scientist sat down politely, trying to brush off the veneer of awkwardness he felt in Israel, where everyone seemed so confident, so strong, so very Israeli. He did not feel that he belonged, and did not enjoy sitting at the other side away from his children.

The dining room was adorned with warm, golden candlelight, casting a cozy glow over the long, white tablecloth. The family hosting the dinner, close friends of his daughter, exuded a genuine warmth. The fragrant aroma of a home-cooked meal lingered in the air. *Home.*

As they settled into their seats, silence followed. The air in the room seemed to shimmer with a gentle anticipation as the hostess, a woman of grace and quiet strength, approached the beautifully adorned Shabbat table. She carried a sense of reverence with her. A pair of elegant candlesticks were cradled in her hands. They were heirlooms passed down through generations, each bearing the scars of time like badges of honor.

As she delicately lit a match, the smell of sulfur greeted them. The flickering flame started its dance on the first candle. Then she lit the second candle, lighting up the room even more. The soft glow from the candles cast a warm radiance over the faces gathered around the table, creating an intimate haven where time seemed to stand still.

The hostess closed her eyes, her hands hovering above the flames in three gentle circles, creating a sacred space between the earthly and the divine. Bringing her palms above her closed eyes, she recited the age-old blessing in an unheard whisper. She intoned, her lips moving quietly, carrying the weight of a thousand whispered prayers. The candles warmed her face as she completed the sacred ritual.

The room seemed to hold its breath as the final blessing left her lips. The hostess opened her eyes, "May we have Sabbath of Peace, Shabbat Shalom."

"Shabbat Shalom," everyone answered.

"Shabbat Shalom," the scientist murmured.

As her husband began the blessing for the wine and for the bread, the scientist felt he was transported back to a world he thought had vanished forever. The sulfuric aroma of the matches, the baked Sabbath bread, and the red wine, all mixing in the air, triggered a cascade of memories that wove through the fabric of his consciousness, connecting him to a time and place long before the war, when he was but a child, when life felt safe.

His mind drifted to Poland, where the fragrance of freshly baked bread wafted through the air and the laughter of family echoed in the large apartment with the many photographs on the wall. His old home. It was a time before the war, a time when his mother had prepared for the Sabbath, her hands expertly shaped the dough into loaves, the warmth of the kitchen embracing him as he and his little sister helped her in the kitchen.

The dining table was adorned with traditional dishes, the laughter that bubbled like a brook, and the warmth of his mother's gaze on him, her son, her pride. The blessings became a conduit to a world that he had tried to forget, for it brought too much pain, remembering the ending of it all, the ending of his mother, the ending of happiness.

He shut his eyes, listening to the prayer, as a symphony of nostalgia embraced him like a long-lost friend. It whispered tales of resilience, of a family that faced adversity with unwavering strength, of a father who refused to leave simply because he wanted to stick to his parents and not betray them.

The glow of candles guided him through the corridors of memory, illuminating the faces of those who had once shared the warmth of Shabbat candles and the aroma of home-cooked meals.

He opened his eyes, and saw from across the table, at the far end, his daughter smiling at him. He smiled back at her, then at his son.

Soon they began singing old songs. It was a moment of unity, a time-honored tradition that connected them to their roots, a soulful resonance of generations past.

He remembered the songs. They never sang these with his former wife. Neither with his uncle—it was too painful. The old mama—they never properly celebrated the Sabbath. But here, it felt like his old home, mixed in modern settings, with a television in the living room and a fridge that needed no ice. But it was not much different from his childhood home.

The lyrics he remembered from days gone by. When he was a boy, he sang them, not knowing what they meant. Now a sense of sanctity echoed in the words, the sentences, the stories of welcoming the Sabbath, of honoring the wife of valor, of opening up the table for the angels to join.

The family and guests, now a chorus of voices harmonized, not with perfect precision of pitch, but with a perfect precision of heart. The songs were etched into his soul, and as they were sung again, they brought a sense of longing that he had not felt in years, and new tears came into his already wet eyes.

In the ebb and flow of the music, the songs became a living testament to the resilience of the human spirit. He was swept away with awe. What moved him the most was not the songs themselves, but the fact that they were still sung.

"Excuse me," he heard a voice next to him, jolting him out of the memories. These were her first words to him. "Excuse me, are you okay?"

II

He was so engrossed in the memories the songs of Sabbath stirred in him, that he did not notice everyone had already begun eating.

"Excuse me," the lady seated next to him asked. "Are you okay?"

He looked at the stranger, still overwhelmed by the memories. "Yes, yes," he answered.

She smiled and looked at her plate.

Seated at the bustling dinner table, the scientist found himself drawn to the polite lady next to him.

He realized his cheeks were wet, and hurried to wipe the remnants of tears in order to make himself more presentable. On the other side of the table, in the area where he now noticed mostly younger people, he saw his daughter and son engaged in lively conversation with another young man.

He glanced at the woman sitting on his right again. She extended a friendly hand, introducing herself. "I'm a librarian, I understand you are an author."

"An author!" he scoffed, afraid he would be found out as an impostor. "I wrote a scientific book, and some essays, but not an—"

"What is the book about?"

"It is about a measuring technique I helped develop, a way to gauge how stress is accumulated on surfaces." He saw she was not intrigued, and he added, "physics and chemistry."

She smiled. *Was she just being polite?*

He wanted to engage in more conversation with her.

Someone asked him to pass the salad.

As he passed the bowl, he couldn't stop worrying that the librarian thought him a bore.

He suddenly remembered the old mama, and the way she used to listen to him rambling about scientific developments. He missed her terribly at that moment.

Thinking of the old mama suddenly made her real, as if she was standing behind him, whispering into his ear. "Son-of-mine, *talk* to her!"

He found himself stammering. "It really is about revealing the heart of materials," he said.

She turned to him. "The heart of materials?"

"Yes, it is a journey where science and art intertwine. It's called photostress—photo being art, stress being science. Imagine, if you will, steel, glass, ceramics, and other materials, each holding secrets that beg to be unveiled."

"And you revealed their secrets?" she asked with a twinkle of mirth in her eyes.

"They revealed their secrets," he said, strangely enjoying the conversation.

"And they revealed them to you?"

"I listened," he said.

"Oh. Not a common quality."

He shrugged, not knowing what to say. He turned to his comfort zone, speaking of science. "This technique has allowed scientists to cast a spotlight on the materials, subjecting them to the whims of stress and pressure. Photostress revealed the vulnerabilities of materials, showing the weak spots."

"The weak spots?"

"Where a material can break." He looked at her earrings, dangle earrings, hanging down below the earlobe, featuring a gemstone. "Your earrings, for example. You probably want durable earrings that won't break."

"Of course."

"Yet, if the designer—by the way, beautiful earrings—wanted to make them more durable, he would—"

"She would…?"

"Of course, *she would* add more volume to them. However, that will add weight, and you don't want heavy earrings."

"I hate it when they drag my earlobe," she said.

"Right," he agreed, finding it hard to concentrate, stunned by her smile.

"Adding more volume is unwise in this case, as it adds weight. The trick is to find out only the weak spot, probably at the curve of the piece, or at the connection to the hook, or maybe at the end, where it is heaviest, where it holds the gemstone."

She looked at him strangely. "Is this where PhotoStress comes into the picture?"

He looked back at her, surprised. "Yes! Precisely!"

As the conversation unfolded, he found it easy to converse with her. She listened intently, asking intelligent, surprising questions. Finally he said, "Enough about me. Tell me about you."

"I'm a librarian. I love the power of stories to change lives." She grinned, her eyes crinkling at the corners.

Over the course of the meal, she talked of her family with gratitude—her parents, how they immigrated to Israel, how she loves her nephews and nieces.

Was she his age, or younger? Was she married? Divorced?

He looked at her left hand and saw no ring.

They spoke and spoke. Her genuine curiosity shone through as she probed deeper, asking insightful questions that prompted the scientist to articulate the complexities of his work in a way that felt fresh, after giving the same hundreds of lectures and presentations about his electronics and inventions.

"I've always wondered about the intersection of science and art," she mused, a thoughtful expression on her face. "I think it is always in these intersections that real innovations happen."

"Exactly," he exclaimed, "it's a delicate dance between empirical evidence and artistic exploration."

As the evening progressed, the conversation naturally evolved in and out of the scientific realm. She shared snippets of her favorite literature, drawing connections between the worlds of life and storytelling. The scientist found himself captivated not only by her intellect but also by the passion that infused her words.

In the midst of their dialogue, the scientist, typically grave about the seriousness of his work, found himself recounting a humorous incident from the lab, involving a language barrier and a mistranslated instruction.

The librarian's laughter, genuine and infectious, reverberated through the dining room. He felt giddy.

"You're not just a scientist; you're a storyteller too," she chuckled. "It's refreshing to see that even in the world of electron entanglement, there's room for a good laugh."

The scientist nodded appreciatively. "Humor is a universal language."

As people began leaving, the scientist did not want the evening to end.

Finally, the librarian had to leave.

The scientist stood up and took her hand. "It was really a pleasure conversing with you."

"No, it was all mine," she said, with something like expectation in her eyes.

He did not want her to leave. "Drive safely," he tried to continue the conversation clumsily. "The drivers today…"

She nodded, a smile on her face, and she hugged the hostess. Her exit made the room colder.

"Dad!" his son suddenly said to him, glaring.

Chapter 63: Darkness

Poland, 1944

Age 16

I

The lawyer opened the floorboards. It was bright outside, midday. The maid beamed. She whispered, "The babies are asleep. My eldest," she said proudly, "got a hold of this." She handed a leather booklet to the lawyer.

The lawyer opened it. The boy saw a dozen tools inside. The seamstress crouched over and her nimble fingers traced the contours of the worn leather binding.

As the boy gazed upon the array of tools nestled within the kit, he drew back. These were surgeon's tools. Knives, scissors, a hammer; the muted glow of polished steel shone in the all-too-bright light that came from the outside.

A roll of gauze fabric was tucked in a dedicated puckett, as a pair of forceps lay with jaws agape, ready to extract. Next to the forceps, a series of probes and picks awaited their turn. The boy saw the pointed tips, the handles, worn smooth by years of use; a mirror, its surface reflecting the boy's eager expression, captured his attention. It was a small, circular mirror. The boy's mind buzzed with fear.

The seamstress's fingers stalled. She looked at the maid and nodded, but the boy noticed some slowness to her nod.

The maid heard movement of one of the children in the other room. She glanced back at the lawyer and at the seamstress. "God be with you," she said and got up off her knees with an audible high pitch exhale of worry.

The lawyer thanked her and closed the floorboards.

Back in the darkness, he lit the oil lamp.

The seamstress seemed pale in the dim light of the lamp. She looked at the tools in the toolkit as if they were hieroglyphics, a riddle she could not solve. She looked at her husband, and, swallowing hard, shook her head negatively, looking down.

The lawyer pushed air out loudly. He wetted his lips. He asked the uncle, "Open your mouth."

The uncle opened his mouth. The lawyer held the lamp and drew back. He turned to the boy.

The boy saw the lawyer's expression, the oil lamp illuminating his face ominously. "You will need to do this. I cannot take… responsibility."

The uncle, whose eyes were shut, opened one of his eyes and blinked, his brow contorted. He looked at his nephew. "If I could, I would do it myself…"

The boy gulped.

The uncle stared at him like a cyclops. "Could… you?"

The boy nodded. He felt his heart beating fast.

The uncle slurred, "Just have a look, please…!"

The lawyer held the oil lamp up, touching the floorboard ceiling. The boy kneeled to the lawyer.

The uncle opened his mouth widely and moaned, holding his hand to his cheek, the pain having radiated from his jaw upwards. "My ear!" he cried.

"It is going to be alright," the boy said with a strange tone, as if his mother was speaking from inside him. His mother—who spent days by his side when he had a fever, switching wet towels on his forehead, putting his feet in a boiling water bucket, massaging his fingers.

The uncle barely opened his mouth. "Uncle, wider, please."

The uncle nodded and then pulled his head back, his mouth

gaping at the ceiling, in agony reserved for horror paintings by Goya.

The boy looked at the mouth and drew back.

He looked at the tools in the kit. His hands trembled. There were so many tools in there he didn't know where to start. He picked one up.

He gently tapped on the teeth in the back of the mouth. Seeing his uncle's response, he understood it was the big molar in the back, the wisdom tooth.

The boy knew it was not only his uncle's mouth that was in his hands; but his uncle's life.

II

The uncle who was stoic usually, moved uncomfortably. His mouth was swollen, puffed and red, with pink-white areas near the teeth at the back.

The lawyer whispered, "That is the wisdom tooth."

"This one?" the boy pointed at the rotten tooth.

The lawyer and the boy's heads bumped. The lawyer sounded agitated as he saw what tooth the boy was pointing at. "No, behind it."

The boy saw the molehill at the back, and a tiny white bone peeking from it.

The lawyer said, "You should take that one out, the wisdom tooth."

The boy was alarmed. He thought the rotten tooth should be taken out. It was already sticking higher than the others, with red gums all around it. "I think I should take this one out."

The lawyer said nothing.

The boy tried to look at him, gaining the lawyer's approval. But the lawyer seemed strangely fearful. His wife sat there, clasping her hands.

If he did this procedure, would he possibly kill his uncle?

Why were the lawyer and his wife unwilling to do this themselves? They were the only adults in the pit. He was just a boy.

His uncle moaned, and the boy tried calming himself down.

He began pushing the probe on the rotten tooth, hoping to see it moving, as he recalled with his little sister who used to push her tongue against a wobbly tooth in her mouth, showing him how it was about to fall.

But the uncle's tooth was not wobbly at all—and when the boy pressed on the gum under it, the uncle let out a tortured, agonizing, animalistic sound, and pus came out, blood gushing from the mere press. The boy had barely touched it!

The boy's body began repulsing, protesting against him, his tummy churning, a strange wave rolling up his chest, up his throat. He wanted to vomit.

He saw his uncle's one eye, full of liquid, tears, looking at him, at his direction, shining in the light of the oil lamp above.

"It will be alright," he heard himself say. His mother always said it, even when the boy used to sweat and hallucinate, his body feeble and hot. "It will be alright."

The boy said it again, repeating it like a prayer—not so much for the uncle, but for himself. He neared the mouth again. He tried not to gag as he stared at the swollen, throbbing mass. Meeting his uncle's gaze, his one eye wide open and watery, his brow contorting rapidly, the boy realized just how much pain he was in.

The boy held the probe tool. He touched the swollen gums and his uncle moved slightly, the boy suddenly wanting to gag as he saw a fountain of pus coming out of where he pressed, the pus then turning red. Blood.

It was excruciating to watch. Ungodly suffering. The boy was in a position he could never imagine, to inflict pain in someone he cared for, for their own good. *If he didn't do something his uncle could die.*

The boy's hand holding the tool trembled even harder as he prepared himself, taking a deep breath. *He had to do it.*

He tried gauging what to do. The probing tool would not do. He had to grab it, grab that brown tooth, much like his grandfather grabbed a nail with a nail puller or a pry bar.

In the toolkit he saw a tool consisting of two handles connected at one end by a joint, with a pair of pointed and curved blades at the opposite end.

He took it and looked up at the lawyer above him. The lawyer nodded approvingly.

Encouraged, the boy repeated again, "It will be alright, uncle."

His hand shook as he took the beak-like forceps.

The uncle had closed his mouth.

"Open," the boy said, strange authority in his voice.

The uncle opened his mouth widely, obediently, his facial expression again like the paintings of hell, agony and misery exemplified.

The boy reached with the forceps to the mouth, and tried placing it on the rotten tooth, but it kept sliding, full of pus and blood around it. A pool of blood collected drowning the gums, and his uncle's palpitating tongue shone in the light, moving like an ensnared snail.

The boy tried gripping, grasping that tooth, but the uncle let out a long wail, a sound the boy would have never imagined could ever come out of his calm, exacting, collected uncle.

The boy noticed his own fingers became slippery—was it sweat? Saliva? He saw blood on his fingers. The blood pooled in the uncle's mote-like area between the teeth and the side of the mouth alarmed him. "Uncle, listen to me. You need to wash your mouth with water and spit it out into the bucket."

The uncle, incredibly obedient, sat up. His dizziness subsequently dropped his heavy head on the lawyer's shoulder.

The boy put the bloody forceps in the kit. He had done nothing yet. He noticed his hand was shaking.

The seamstress poured water into the enamel cup, and gave the bucket to the uncle.

The uncle gargled the water and spat a slimy, bloody spit that ended with a trail of saliva dripping from his mouth. The boy wanted to tell him to drink again, but thought that if he waited much longer, his uncle might pass out. "Lay down, head back!" the boy commanded.

He took the forceps in his hand. "Open your mouth."

The mouth gaped at him.

The gums were swollen, but less flooded in dark red. Pink gums showed themselves, like peaks of mountains. The boy wiped his fingers on his coat, only to feel the seamstress's hand shoving him some gauze from the kit.

He cleaned his hand and grabbed the forceps, a better, firmer hold of it. He neared the tooth, placed the forceps on the tooth and pressed.

An animalistic sound came from the uncle, a harrowing grawl, as the boy tried gripping the tooth, the uncle resisted, his face moving, his head turning from side to side, like a drunk.

The boy knew this would not work. He needed the lawyer and the seamstress to assist him. "Hold his head!" he commanded the surprised lawyer.

The lawyer seemed useless, unable to do much with his arm held up high with the lamp, the other feebly placed on the uncle's sweaty hair.

At the same time, above them near the bed, the maid was kneeling on the floor, praying. Her toddler son who had wobbled to the bedroom thought his mother was playing a game, wanting him to come.

The toddler son heard a scream coming from under the bed. The maid's eyes shut wide open, looking at her son's bewildered face. "Mamma, who is under the bed?

Chapter 64: Light

Israel, 1977

Age 49

The Sabbath meal ended, and the fascinating librarian left. The scientist followed her with his gaze as she exited the door. The dining room felt colder.

"Dad!" his son startled him.

"What?"

"Go after her!"

"What?"

"Go and invite her for a date."

"Are you crazy?" the scientist hissed, embarrassed by his inappropriate son. How could his son be so blunt?

"Did you get her number?" the son asked.

The scientist glared at him and blushed, trying to silence his son with his glare.

The son looked away in disappointment. "I would have asked for her number."

Later, in the car, heading to the hotel, the son watched through the window, silent.

"Did you enjoy the dinner?"

"Yeah."

"What did you like about it?"

The son shrugged.

The scientist wanted to connect with his son. "I don't think I should have asked for her number," he said, incredulously.

His son ignored him, as teenagers so naturally do, with an embedded, innate ability to torture their parents.

"Should I have?" the scientist asked, his eyes fixed on the road.

His son said, "Yeah!"

"I don't think she was interested," the scientist said.

"Dad, she was totally hooked on you."

"Hooked on me? No, she was not."

"Dad, she totally digs you. I saw her."

He scoffed, a jumble of words spitting from his mouth. "No—she—I," words coughed from his mouth, "why—ridiculous!"

The son said nothing.

The scientist fixed his eyes on the road. "You think she did?"

"Absolutely. I think you should call that family and find out her phone number."

"Phone number! I don't do this kind of stuff! I'm…I don't do this kind of stuff!"

"Yeah? So how did you meet Mom?"

"Well," the scientist searched for words, "that was a different era…"

"Right…"

The following day, Shabbat, the scientist dropped his son at the home of a new friend his son had made. His daughter was busy with friends, and the scientist was lonely. He missed his work, but it was a Saturday. He felt he had no one to call. Caged in the hotel room, he recalled the conversation with the librarian. Was she just being polite? Or genuinely interested?

Usually, conversations were laborious for him. Yet with her, they were easy; he even found himself funny. Her eyes haunted him.

He picked up the phone to call his daughter, but then hung up. He was approaching his 50th birthday, but was still behaving like a boy. Did she want him to call? Would she be rude?

Trapped within the confines of the hotel room on that Saturday afternoon, the scientist found himself in contemplative silence. The memory of the previous night's dinner lingered, and his thoughts were a stormy sea of self-doubt.

The librarian's image occupied his mind, her laughter echoing in his ears. The scientist, known for his analytical prowess, suddenly felt disarmed in the face of his own emotions.

He picked up the phone, fingers hovering over the dial, contemplating the act. An uneasiness settled in his stomach, an unusual sensation for someone who spent his days deciphering complex equations and making complex business calls involving millions of dollars.

What if he misread the signals? What if she found his call intrusive or worse, absurd?

Should he call his daughter, asking for the hostesses' number, just so that he would embarrass himself—before his daughter, before the hostess, before the librarian?

A myriad of fears crept into his thoughts. The fear of making a fool of himself, of intruding into her life uninvited. His mind conjured scenarios where she would dismiss his advance, leaving him to grapple, bruised.

"I'm too old for this," he muttered to himself, contemplating his nearing 50th birthday. The scientist who could unravel secrets of the cosmos, who had by now owned dozens of patents under his name, suddenly found himself entangled in the complexities of the chemistry of human interaction—or imaginary chemistry. The idea of asking for her number seemed alien, a task more daunting than any scientific challenge he had ever encountered.

Images of his son's disappointment flashed before him, a stark reminder that perhaps he wasn't living up to the expectations of those who looked up to him. With a heavy sigh, he placed the receiver back on the hook, deciding to wait for a clearer sign.

He tried pulling out his notebook to do some calculations, preliminary sketches of new electronic sensors he was now developing. Yet all he could think about was the electricity he had between the librarian who kept laughing and smiling, listening intently, nodding her head with a twinkle in her eyes.

In that hotel room, he remained trapped, suspended between the desire for companionship and the fear of rejection, wrestling with the complexities of emotions he rarely allowed himself to confront.

Working himself up to having the courage to call his daughter was like heating a large cauldron. It took hours. He lifted the phone more times than he would dare to admit. Finally, when evening came, just before he was supposed to leave to pick up his son, he lifted the receiver and dialed.

Chapter 65: Darkness

Poland, 1944

Age 16

I

The maid looked at her son terrified. The groans from the pit were clearly audible. She grabbed her son violently in her arms and while hurrying to the kitchen, she began to speak loudly, trying to drown the noises from the bedroom which door she was now closing. Her son glanced behind at the bedroom's bed still confused as the door shut closed. The maid exclaimed, "Now-now, let's play a game of helping Mamma make dinner!"

In the bedroom, below the bed, the boy attempted to subdue his unruly uncle. Immediately upon impact with the tool, the swollen mass began gushing pus and blood. It smelled horrible, like an animal's corpse was rotting in his uncle's mouth. Still, the boy persevered, digging harder into the abscess gums. His uncle desperately cried out, squirming and shaking so much that the boy almost could not continue. He had to finish quickly. "Hold him!" he begged the lawyer.

Seeing that the lawyer and his wife would not suffice, the boy placed his forearm on his uncle's forehead and pressed hard, holding him down. Finally, he got a grip on the tooth itself, holding his breath, he pulled on it, the pink gums filled with small rivers of dark red. He tried ripping the tooth out with all his might.

It came out! The boy rejoiced, only to discover that it wasn't all of it. It was only half of it. The tooth crumbled under the force of the forceps, splintering into two. The root was still in.

He heard himself saying, "Almost done. You will be alright."

The uncle, his mouth still open and bloody, gestured to the boy to continue, grabbing the boy's hand and pulling it to the mouth violently.

The boy looked at the half tooth, deeply rooted. He had to puncture the gum to get the other half out.

He took another tool, with a narrow blade-like ending, a tiny sharp spatula that shone in the light of the lamp as he grabbed it. He placed his forearm again on the uncle's forehead and began slicing, digging, cutting, puncturing, as the blood started gushing violently, bright red spreading into a large pool while the uncle groaned.

The boy hoped he had dug enough. He put the bloody blade aside and grabbed the forceps again, trying to get a grip of the deep root of the tooth poking like an island in a bloody sea.

The uncle let out a sob-like, deep exhale that sounded worse than any scream.

The boy tried gripping the tooth, and pulled, but it was still held firmly—he had never realized how deeply the teeth were rooted in the mouth. He then recalled his own teeth, as a young boy, and the teeth of his sister, with their long portion of the tooth that extended below the gumline and anchored the tooth in the jawbone. This was not a frontal tooth, it was a molar, and the boy recalled two long horn-like roots at its base.

This meant he would have to go deeper in the uncle's mouth.

"Almost done," he said in a voice that convinced no one, as he reached again for the blade-like tool, this time deciding it was too small. The small kit had a larger, mean-looking knife, a periosteal molt. The boy took it and prayed.

He thought of having his uncle spit, drink, but he was afraid he was running out of time. "Hold on, uncle," he said, and he began pushing the molt blade, following the side of the broken tooth deeply into jaw. He pierced the knife deeper, from the back side of the tooth near the palpitating tongue. The uncle shook violently.

He dug as much as he could, as each movement he made generated more of the red substance leaking as he cut through the gums.

His uncle's body shook with agitation.

Had he dug deep enough?

He wanted to cry, wanted to stop, wanted to run away—but instead he took the forceps, determined to continue.. This tooth had to come out now. "Hold on, Uncle, hold on."

He gripped the slippery tooth amidst the shiny red ruins, digging both sides of the beak-like grips from both directions deeply into the gums, the uncle shook violently, his legs jumping. The seamstress held his legs, sitting on him.

The uncle gasped, inhaling sharply as the boy clutched the tooth and tried pulling the tooth, only to discover the grip slipped.

The thrust threw him away and he had to catch his breath. He looked at the lawyer, hoping for the lawyer to try instead of him, but the lawyer just looked at him passively. "Again!"

He nodded to himself as he positioned himself on the body of his uncle, forcing the bloody mouth open, his uncle nearly drowning in blood and pus. The boy gripped the tooth—his arch enemy—and instead of trying to pull on it, he began trying to jolt it back and forth. The uncle whimpered, delirious with pain.

The lawyer said, "Good, good."

The boy kept pushing the stubborn broken tooth from side to side, wiggling it, his uncle's body arching violently. He pressed back on his uncle's forehead, and kept rapidly jolting the tooth, quaking it in quick successions, until he felt a strange lack of resistance.

He brought the forceps up to the lamp and saw the entire root shining, while the top was rotten brown, the roots were white, covered with some blood but nevertheless white, shining, long. *He had the tooth!*

He began exhaling, half laughing half crying.

His uncle seemed as if he had passed out.

The lawyer, still holding the lamp, said, "Quick, clean him off."

The boy leaned on the uncle. "Sit up, spit, Uncle."

The seamstress helped with the water and bucket. The boy's hands shook as he brought the enamel cup to the uncle's mouth.

The uncle was barely cooperating, his eyes half-shut. The boy was worried for him.

He helped his uncle spit thick blood into the bucket. He tried to give his uncle water but his uncle fell back, moaning.

"Gauze," the lawyer said.

The boy took all the gauze from the kit, and told the uncle, "Open your mouth!"

The uncle wailed, not understanding it was over. He opened his mouth to the heavens, crying. The boy put the gauze on the red throbbing well, and gently closed his uncle's jaw. "We are done, Uncle, we are done. We are done."

The tooth was out. The uncle lay there, his chest rising and falling, gauze turned red sticking from between his lips.

The boy shivered.

"Lie down," the seamstress said.

The boy lay down in the side, his uncle spread in the middle like a breathing, moaning corpse.

The boy heard water in the bucket as he heard the seamstress was washing the forceps and other tools, wiping them, and placing them neatly in the kit.

The lawyer spoke to the uncle as if the uncle was dead. "Alive?"

The uncle grunted.

The boy noticed his clothes were soaked in sweat, and he shivered.

The lawyer turned the knob of the oil lamp, and the light disappeared.

In the darkness, the seamstress, now sitting on the bucket, reached for the boy's leg.

In what seemed like an attempt to console him, she searched

for his hand. She stroked his hand and then patted his hand, squeezing it, gripping it as if to say, 'you did well.'

The boy did not want for the hand to go away, and when it disappeared a moment later, the boy imagined the hand was holding him, staying.

His uncle's sighs, loud exhales, punctuated the silence, like a metronome, at a steady pace.

The boy squeezed his eyes, tightly closing them. He bit his lips. Tears dropped on his cheeks. *Please, God make him feel better.*

An hour later the lawyer asked the uncle again, "Alive?"

Muffled words came through. "Much, much better," the uncle announced through his gauze-filled mouth.

The boy, exhausted, thanked God.

They did not switch places.

The boy lay against his uncle. He held his uncle's coat. It was as if by holding onto his uncle's coat he was begging his uncle to come out of it.

His uncle's sighs, still audible, became slower, less frequent.

The boy drowsed into sleep.

Hours later the floorboards opened. He saw his uncle was not sitting up, and he, too, remained lying next to him.

The maid looked worriedly at the lawyer and his wife. The seamstress said, "The storm is behind us."

The maid glowed. "I prayed!"

They exchanged buckets and then there was darkness again.

Sleep came and went, punctuated only by often sighs from the uncle.

The boy felt his father's hand on his forehead. His father said, "Thank you."

When did his father join them in the pit?

"Thank you," the uncle said again.

The boy smiled in the darkness.

Every couple of hours they lit the lamp to inspect how the mouth was looking. Slowly, the swelling went down. The uncle began feeling better.

Three days later the uncle slowly chewed on a slice of bread, sitting upright, his face back to its original size, as if his tooth was never infected.

Days passed. They were back to their usual routine, changing places every two hours. Even math equations were being discussed again.

It had been nine months since they had gone into hiding, and the maid finally began to bring good news. The occupying army was suffering greatly from Allied assaults. "The Eastern Front kept being hit," she said, "or at least that's what people have whispered to me in the market…"

The boy noticed the uncle's face changing. "Madam, please, could you possibly get us a newspaper?"

The maid glared. "No way! Already I feel people watching what I buy and making their calculations, wondering why my daughters also come to the market to buy things… 'Isn't it strange?' they say! I can't…"

The uncle nodded.

The maid continued, "People know me and my husband can't read. Why should I now buy a newspaper? For my daughters? Why would they need to read a newspaper?"

The uncle nodded. "You're right."

The maid sighed as she drew the bucket out and handed the uncle the clean one. She frowned. "Let me see what I can do."

Three days later, when the maid peered at them upon the rising floorboards, she had a big grin. "I bought fish, and guess what they wrapped it in!"

She handed them two sheets of newspaper.

The uncle smiled. "You are one of a kind, Madam!"

The maid grinned and said loudly so that her husband could hear in the kitchen. "Now-now, don't let my husband hear you or he'll get jealous!" She turned to the seamstress. "When you first came to our home, you said you were a seamstress, right?"

The boy saw the seamstress's face suddenly light up. "Yes, madam. I was—I am!"

"I am sorry to ask but my eldest tore a couple buttons off her dress yesterday and I was never good with needles…"

"Of course. Give it to me!"

The maid handed the dress and sewing kit to the seamstress.

The uncle and the lawyer held the stinking wrinkled newspaper sheet in their hands as if it was the holy scrolls.

They were not even interested in the bowl of food that the boy was eyeing, with potatoes, a piece of bread and a shiny slice of fish—real fish!

The uncle folded and cut the page in three sections. "We'll each read a section, read from both sides. Memorize as best you can. Then we'll turn the lamp off and retell what we read."

The boy received the piece of newspaper and struggled to read the letters in the light of the oil lamp. The sight of the seamstress, her figure illuminated softly by the lamp, distracted him. She deftly handled the spool of thread, cutting it with precise, graceful movements. The gentle way in which she held the thread piece between her fingers enamored him. Her sight enveloped him, causing the words on the newspaper to blur. He became blind to everything except her small, innocent action of licking the thread tip and penetrating it through the needle hole. He gulped.

The uncle hit his paper. "I knew it."

"What is it?" The lawyer asked.

"Keep reading!" his uncle commanded.

That night the uncle took the liberty of using the oil lamp just a little longer than usual. Each of them read a section of the newspaper that came with the fish the maid bought in the market.

The paper was three weeks old, yet it was still news—they haven't read the news in nine months.

The boy read the yellowed paper columns. He was disappointed not to read anything about the occupying army losing. Instead, it was only becoming stronger, building more forts, realigning more troops, getting a better hold of the entire continent.

When they turned the light off, each repeated what they read. The boy told of the fortifications, strategic adjustments, Force Redistribution and Operational Reorientation in the Eastern Front.

"Great!" the uncle smiled.

"What is great?" the boy asked.

The lawyer said, "It's all over. You can hear it between the lines."

"Between the lines?" the boy asked.

The lawyer smiled. "Realignment? That means defeat."

The uncle's chimed in, his voice in the darkness betraying a sweet smile. "And fortification means that they are suffering damages."

The boy badly wanted to believe them; they were older and wiser. And yet, he had heard optimistic forecasts like these for the past five years, ever since the war broke out. Each time—after every such prediction—things had only gotten worse.

He wanted to tell them that. But he chose not to. Why should he ruin their good mood? This was a rare occasion, hearing the lawyer and the uncle excited about something.

When the seamstress spoke, her sweet voice was intoxicating. He rarely heard her speak—a little on the Day of Atonement, a word here and there with her husband. But now she was describing which ministers met with the führer, of the führer's pride of the nation, and of the importance of supporting the front in this 'war-economy.'

The boy listened not to her words, but to her cadence, her softness, her literary prowess. It occurred to him then how difficult it had been for him in the silence, nearly succumbing to his rage and fear for himself and his family. What must it be like for her, never speaking, only the physical presence of her husband at her side protecting her from that horrid abyss? To survive, it seemed she spent most of her time pretending not to exist at all.

As the seamstress pored over the article, the boy felt a deep sense of shame well in him. He had focused on her beauty and his desire instead of acknowledging the person sharing the pit with him.

Then the two men conversed. Recently they had begun arguing. It was petty things, small disagreements, but they always made the boy tense. The pit had no room for fighting. If they become loud, they might get caught. Or, worse, the maid and her husband might decide it was unsafe to keep the loud four hiders under their floor.

The boy mustered courage and whispered, "Shhh."

His uncle lowered his voice, whispering adamantly to the lawyer about the Eastern Front, about the nearby river, the bridges. The lawyer argued about fortifications and the strategic hill they were on.

Suddenly the uncle stiffened. "Hush now!" the uncle said, in a way the boy thought was quite disrespectful to the lawyer.

But then the boy realized what the uncle was saying.

They heard a strange sound in the distance.

The sound grew louder, roaring. There was no doubt about what it was.

Chapter 66: Light

Israel, 1977

Age 49

The scientist finally mustered the courage to call his daughter and asked if she could help him get the librarian's phone number.

Within the same evening, he had the phone number written down on a piece of paper. He held the piece of paper as if it were gold.

The scientist and librarian spoke briefly on the phone and agreed on an "early dinner." He would pick her up from the library at five.

On the evening of their first official outing, the anticipation of their rendezvous lent an air of excitement to his day in the labs of the Israeli factory.

As the clock hand edged closer to their agreed-upon time, the scientist left early.

He parked his car near the library entrance.

As he stepped out of the car, he checked his reflection in the car window and adjusted his tie with a thoughtful expression.

The familiar scent of old books and the subtle hum of intellectual pursuits greeted him as he entered the library.

Just as the librarian was about to close for the day, she caught sight of the scientist waiting by the entrance. A smile tugged at the corners of her lips as she gracefully made her way toward him. Her attire blended sophistication with a touch of whimsy, a dress with a jacket, with fashionable big hoop earrings that were all the rage for young girls. She certainly felt like one.

"Good evening," the scientist greeted, a warmth in his eyes as he extended his hand.

"Good evening," she responded, and kissed him on the cheek. He felt bad for not having flowers—his silly son convinced him otherwise—but the tie which his son opposed was where the scientist drew the line.

They strolled towards the car, engaging in light banter that seamlessly wove together laughter and deep conversation. She recalled his stories from the dinner, and commented about them, as if no days had passed since then.

He opened the car door for her. She noted that and beamed.

As they settled into the car, the engine hummed to life, and the evening unfolded like the turning pages of a captivating novel.

He had made reservations at a restaurant, which she knew was serious and proper. "Can I offer an alternative?"

He turned to her.

"Eyes on the road," she laughed.

"What alternative?" he asked, stressed. Did she not like the restaurant?

"The sun is setting in an hour. Let's go to the beach, there are many cafes there, no need to make a reservation."

He felt as if his life was going off course—and he liked it. "Very well. Direct me." He pointed to a booklet of the maps of Israel.

"I don't need that," she said, "turn right."

The journey was adorned with laughter, exchanged anecdotes, and the occasional shared reflection on the magic of libraries and the knowledge they held. The car carried them through the city streets.

The car rolled smoothly along the coastal road, the rhythmic sound of the waves growing louder as the scientist and the librarian approached the enchanting beachside café in Tel Aviv.

Choosing a table right by the water's edge, the scientist pulled out a chair for the librarian, who took a moment to absorb the serene ambiance. The evening breeze carried the scent of saltwater, intertwining with the inviting aroma of freshly brewed coffee from the café. The rhythmic ebb and flow of the waves provided a natural soundtrack to their magical evening.

As the waiter approached with menus, a friendly smile played on his lips. The scientist enjoyed seeing the cordiality and friendliness that the librarian exhibited to the waiter.

With their orders placed, they settled in, the anticipation of the sunset casting a warm glow on their faces.

Engaging in a delightful conversation that seamlessly wove together their shared interests, they found themselves immersed in a harmonious exchange. Laughter echoed in the air, creating an atmosphere of shared joy and mutual understanding.

As the sun began its descent, casting hues of orange and pink across the horizon, the scientist and the librarian shifted their attention to the breathtaking view. The rosy sky, ablaze with color, mirrored the warmth that had blossomed between them. The quiet acknowledgment of the beauty around them spoke volumes, grounding the magical atmosphere of the evening.

They did not speak, but words were not needed.

Later, she leaned into him, and the scientist thought she wanted to kiss him. But instead, she loosened his tie. "We're in Tel Aviv, not New York," she winked at him.

He felt embarrassed and turned red. He should have known, he should have listened to his son.

After dinner, they walked on the beach. He saw her taking her shoes off, and hurried to take his shoes off as well. His expensive trousers were getting wet from the waves, which usually would have stressed him out. But now he did not care.

Amidst the splendor of the sunset, they took a leisurely stroll along the water's edge, the soft sand beneath their feet inviting them to share dreams and reflections. She wrapped her hand in his. His heart beat fast.

They ambled along the shoreline, the waves tickling their feet, flooding and retracting, ebbing and flowing. Finding a secluded spot on the beach, the scientist and the librarian gazed up at the stars that had emerged in the darkened sky.

He did not know he could feel this way at this age. It was like he was a boy again.

The scientist, his eyes reflecting the shimmering constellations, said, "I'm happy I chose to come to that Shabbat dinner."

"Me too," she said.

As the night unfolded, the scientist was reluctant to end the magical evening, and they decided to part ways with a promise to explore more chapters of their story. The car carried them back, and he dropped her off by her apartment building. He envied her neighbors.

The echoes of her laughter and the promise of another enchanting encounter lingered with him as he boarded on the airplane the following day.

Was there something there, between the two of them? He suddenly wanted to go back to Israel, just as he had left.

CHAPTER 67: DARKNESS

POLAND, 1944

AGE 16

I

The sound was distant at first, but grew louder by the second. It was a distinct throaty roar, like a motorcycle or an automobile, only much, much louder.

The boy suddenly said, "Airplane?"

"Hush," the uncle said. The unmistakable sound of the distinctive sputter and growl grew louder and then began fading away.

They remained in silence, but the boy kept thinking he heard the echo still reverberating in his heart.

The uncle whispered, "British."

The lawyer asked, "How do you know?"

The boy wanted to know as well.

"Smooth, refined hum. It's the Spitfire. The Nazis have the Stuka or the Messerschmitt. Higher pitch."

The boy wondered about his uncle's knowledge in everything. He wanted to be just like his uncle.

The atmosphere changed in the pit.

They were optimistic.

The boy asked the uncle, "Uncle, why are some engines high

pitched and others lower pitched?" more than he wanted to know, he wanted to strike a conversation with his uncle. Now that his uncle was feeling better, he was friendlier.

The uncle went on to whisper about how early engineers designed the combustion engine, developing it over the years. In his words, the boy learned how humanity strove toward constant betterment of itself, people collaborating together for shared goals, goals so great they often took years to accomplish, even generations.

At night after they divided the food, they turned the lamp off.

Just as they were all finishing eating in the darkness, the lawyer said, "If I am not mistaken, the Holiday of Lights begins today."

The boy's heart stopped. *The Holiday of Lights!* It's been a year since he lit the candles with his family in the cramped apartment in the ghetto, praying for the war to end, standing next to his father and mother and sister and those who were not taken to the trains yet.

He thought of his family.. Sudden fear grasped him as he realized their faces were blurry, his memories difficult to pull and look at.

The uncle said, "The airplane earlier was a sign. We should light candles."

The boy felt a strange sadness mixed with a sliver of hope.

The uncle did not want to bother the maid and her husband with more unique requests. And in the pit they did not have a candelabrum. But they had the oil lamp. The uncle reached for the lamp. "This lamp will be our eight candles."

The boy felt excitement building in him.

The uncle asked the lawyer, "Do you want to recite the prayer?"

There was a long silence. Then, suddenly, the lawyer's voice changed its hue, a different color imbuing him as he chanted a quiet melody that made the hairs on the boy's neck stand. The lawyer sounded exactly like the boy's grandfather. "Blessed are You, God, Ruler of the universe…"

The uncle lit the oil lamp.

The lawyer continued with his song, "...who sanctified us with Your commandments and commanded us to kindle the lights of Hanukkah."

"Amen," said the uncle.

"Amen," said the boy.

"Amen," said the seamstress.

They all stared at each other, and then, slowly, their eyes fixed on the lamp.

The light was precious.

It was the thick of winter, snow was piling outside. The boy knew in some camps far in the East, his family was working, performing hard labor. He thought of his mother's gentle fingers, of his sister, of his father. Of the nephews. *Were they all warm enough?*

Did they have adequate dwellings?

Were they safe?

He somehow feared the answers.

Staring at the bewitching flame which he had grown to take for granted for a minute each night, the boy thought back to the days before the war. Every year, in the midst of winter, his grandmother would take him to visit the village she grew up in, Vishay. He was very young. All he could remember was the glory of the candelabra in the window of each house. As they walked through the small town, they saw candelabras lit everywhere.

The uncle slowly turned the knob of the oil lamp off, as the small flicker of light dimmed red before turning into ash gray and then melting into the darkness around them.

The memory of his grandmother holding his hand and pointing at the windows with their various candelabra, pained him. His grandmother—whose never ending strength seemed to vanish, like a flame extinguished, when the fingers of war began collecting the family.

She would mumble to herself, "The babies. The babies," shaking her head, covering her mouth with her weak, wrinkly hands, her eyes wide open, with disbelief at the catastrophe that befell them.

"This light," the uncle said in the darkness, jerking the boy out of his haunted thoughts, "reminds us of the commandment to be a light unto the nations."

"Command," the lawyer corrected, "not commandment."

"Well, I say commandment," replied the uncle in defiance.

The boy suddenly became stiff. *Were they arguing? Again?*

There was an unspoken rule that arguing was not allowed in the pit, and this argument over a single word felt trivial.

"Well," the lawyer said tensely, "where does it say it is a commandment?"

The boy wished he would stop, but the lawyer continued, his voice amused. "Is it one of the Ten Commandments? The eleventh commandment?"

The uncle sounded terse. "I don't care where it says it or it doesn't say it. All I know is that our family always preached for being…" his voice broke, "…a light unto the nations."

The boy knew the lawyer must avoid responding at all cost—his uncle's voice hinted of raw emotions, and that was when people were most dangerous.

Then came the lawyer's voice. Like a crash of fast moving trains, the boy could see it all happening before him, helpless to stop it, like trying to capture a precious glass in midair, slipping from a hand, falling slowly, twirling in space before violently meeting the floor, shattering loudly to countless pieces; the lawyer chuckled. "Whatever you say, but it is *not* a commandment."

II

The boy watched it all unfolding before him. The uncle vs. the lawyer. Two egos batting. The uncle had spoken a minute earlier with raw emotions, "I don't care where it says it or it doesn't say it. All I know is that our family always preached for being…a light unto the nations."

Then came the lawyer's voice, train crash, smashing glass, one match to spark an explosion. "Whatever you say, it is not a commandment."

The boy gasped. He had to stop the arguing or else it would escalate. *Could they not see they were all stuck together, for better or worse?*

No one could storm out of the pit! They depended on the calmness of his uncle, on the reason of the lawyer. Their lives depended on the tone of conversations being limited to whispers, on cooperation, on friendship.

The uncle responded with irritation, speaking all too loudly, "I said—"

"I think—" the boy interjected, nearly shouting.

In the darkness, he felt everyone looking at him.

He froze, not knowing what to say, how to put an end to the stupidity of the two men. Years earlier, when the war broke out, his mother said to his sister in the kitchen, "It is men who brought us another Great War. A war of thugs. Of immature bullies."

The boy panted heavily. "I think," he said again, not wanting any of them to continue arguing, the air so thick, he could cut it with a knife. Could they not see they were being stupid? Only a moment earlier they had such a special moment, lighting the make-believe candelabrum.

But now each man was sitting on opposite sides of the pit, not lying down as usual, and there was something in this opposing seating that brought the smell of territory, as if trying to convince not only one another, but also winning the admiration of the boy and the seamstress.

The boy knew he had to say *something* or else this argument might lead to a real fight. His uncle sounded more emotional than the boy could ever recall, and the lawyer seemed stupidly ignorant of the precarious situation he was getting them all into, and the uncle was not about to retreat.

Another second passed. *Think fast!* What should he say? Recently there had been quite many sparks of arguments in the pit, but the boy had never been as concerned as now. And he knew that asking them to quiet down never worked, only for a minute, and that their arguing could become a fire from which they would all get burned.

Could they not see that their lives depended on this precarious balance of peace?

He thought of his grandmother, of walking with her in the village of her childhood, of seeing the candles in each window.

Palms sweating, he said, "It is the holiday," he gulped trying to earn more time. "And Grandmother would take me to Vishay."

The uncle hummed in agreement.

"And she would point at all the windows," he saw his grandmother before the war, strong, mighty, a beacon of light, a tower of fortitude. "And she said, as one small candle may light a thousand, so can one person…"

His voice died.

He knew he had lost it, that any second the lawyer and the uncle were to pick the fight. Then, he heard the voice, as if it was an angel.

"It is thanks to your grandmother that we are here."

The uncle sounded pleased. "My mother is….was…is…"

The uncle paused, looking for a suitable description, a compliment to his mother, a suitable adjective. He found none.

The seamstress spoke again, seeming to complete his sentence. "… A Light onto the Nations?"

The uncle smiled. "Yes. That is a good description. A light onto the nations."

The seamstress sounded unsure. "Is it like 'Cast your bread upon the waters…'?"

"Sort of," said the uncle. "Light unto the nations does not

speak of any gain in return, no promise of tenfold. It's just a commandment. Or a command, a precept."

"Right," said the lawyer, "a precept."

The boy, who had not breathed in a long minute, finally exhaled. "A precept." It was as if his very grandmother was with them, in the pit, holding his very hand.

Chapter 68: Light

Israel, 1977

Age 49

After meeting the librarian, the year that followed was marked by frequent flights, as the scientist, fueled by an insatiable desire to be near her, found himself crossing continents with increasing regularity. The thrill of arrival, the anticipation of seeing her, and the warmth of shared conversations became the highlights of his journeys.

The international phone bill skyrocketed, a small price to pay for the comfort he found in hearing her voice during business trips or quiet evenings at home with his teenage son.

In Philadelphia, the apartment the scientist got following the divorce, a place that had little soul, began transforming under the librarian's hands. Whenever she visited, she made sure to infuse plants, art, and fabrics, making the clinic-like modern apartment feel like home.

The scientist's daughters were initially skeptical of the new woman. But after seeing their father with her, they, too, became her friends. Soon they became avid supporters of their father's newfound happiness. They observed the way he smiled, the spark in his eyes when he spoke of her, and the subtle changes that love had wrought upon him. Their initial reservations gave way to genuine happiness for their father, as they witnessed the transformative power of love.

His teenage son, always attuned to his father's moods, observed the positive change with a mix of curiosity and note-taking. He learned from his dad how to respect a woman, how to love a woman, how to make a woman laugh, be heard, and be known.

The son had never seen his father so content, so genuinely happy. The once-formidable scientist, known for his analytical mind and dedication to research, now found joy in the simple pleasures of shared laughter, quiet walks, and the companionship of the woman who had captured his heart.

"Dad, I think you should marry her."

The scientist laughed, studying his son's face.

"Just saying," his son said.

By the second year of their friendship, the scientist was inviting the librarian to various business trips, always booking an additional room for her.

The librarian really wanted to go and see places from the scientist's childhood. But he did not want to go to Poland and was terrified of anything that was close to Germany.

Seeing the disappointment in her eyes, he decided to take her to Paris.

He asked his former wife to have their son for one week, during which he took the librarian to Paris. He eagerly introduced her to the landmarks of his post-war years. They strolled through the historic streets, and climbed the Eiffel Tower stairs.

He took her for a picnic in the Luxembourg Gardens. He took her to lunch with the aging moneychanger. They visited the scientist's uncle's second wife. The librarian saw him with different eyes, speaking French, feeling at home.

Finally, on the last day in Paris, he took her to explore the city's museums, and she saw a side of him she never knew: an artist, dressed in business attire, a poet with a lab coat. He enchanted her.

The librarian, in turn, opened the scientist's eyes to the beauty of her homeland. Together with his son, the three of them traveled up and down the Holy Land.

They walked the cobblestone streets of Jerusalem and deposited their wishes written on tiny pieces of paper at the Wailing Wall. In the forests on the outskirts of Jerusalem, they meandered through whispering pines, the scent of frankincense carried by the breeze.

It was summer, and the older sister wanted to spend a week with her little brother. After the four of them had breakfast in Tel Aviv, the scientist and the librarian went exploring the country.

Underneath a silvery desert sky, they embarked on a moonlit camel trek through the vastness of the Negev. The dunes whispered ancient secrets as they traversed the sandy expanse, the rhythmic footsteps of their desert companions blending with the soft murmur of the night.

At the edge of the Ramon Crater, the two of them found themselves wrapped in blankets under a celestial canopy, lost in the cosmic ballet of stars that adorned the desert firmament.

They coated themselves in the mineral-rich Dead Sea mud, their bodies buoyant in the magical waters that held the secrets of timeless rejuvenation. The scientist felt at the peak of his happiness there at the lowest point on Earth.

In Safed's mystical corners, they stumbled upon a hidden gathering of Sufi dervishes, swirling in ecstatic dance beneath the ancient arches. The air vibrated with the mystical energy of the dance, transporting them to a realm where time seemed to lose its grip.

They climbed Mount Carmel in the blazing sun, overlooking the sea, the fragrance of blooming flowers mingling with the delicate notes of the exotic sea breeze. They found a cave and hid in it from the sun. The hidden alcove became a sanctuary of tranquility, a secret garden where they found a small hidden creek.

Aboard a quaint sailboat, they sailed the tranquil waters of the Sea of Galilee at sunset. The colors of the sky reflected in rippling water, the boat gliding through the water like a vessel of dreams set adrift in the golden hour.

In the Galilee, they submerged in the therapeutic waters and indulged in a day in the ancient Roman baths. The healing waters became a source of rejuvenation, their bodies immersed together. He held her hand in the hot water.

They visited colorful markets and met even more colorful people. Through her eyes, the scientist saw a different Holy Land, one beating with beauty and love, a harmony between all people that he had never read about in the news before.

The daughters and son began embracing her as a cherished member of the family. Their shared moments became treasured memories, from lively family dinners to heartfelt conversations that spanned hours into the night. Next to her, the scientist was easier to be around. She made him smoother around the edges, more care free, less anxious. The scientist, once accustomed to solitude, now found joy in the lively chatter and warm presence that filled his home.

And so, two years after their serendipitous meeting on a Sabbath eve, the scientist, after receiving the blessing and encouragement of his children, proposed to the librarian.

The librarian and scientist stood beneath a canopy in Jerusalem, surrounded by the ancient stones that bore witness to their journey.

The scientist's children, now not just witnesses but active participants in their shared narrative, held the pillars of the canopy.

The scientist promised his heart to the librarian, vowing to love and cherish her for the rest of his life.

The scientist crushed the glass beneath his foot and they were officially married.

Everyone's good wishes mirrored the genuine happiness radiating from the scientist's face.

In that moment, the scientist knew that he had learned how to love and be vulnerable again. He knew that this was the woman that he'd spend the rest of his life with.

The librarian moved to live with him in Philadelphia, but they frequented Israel often.

Everything seemed to be miraculously well. He was truly happy, for the first time in his life.

Until that phone call.

CHAPTER 69: DARKNESS

POLAND, 1944

AGE 16

I

Winter continued in full force. Thick snow piled up around the cabin. Each day the husband made sure that the opening of the small air pipe outside near the doghouse was not blocked by snow.

One night, just as they were finishing eating their meager meal in the darkness, the lawyer sighed. "One year."

Everyone knew what he meant. Twelve whole months passed since they had entered the pit.

The boy, wanting some attention and warmth, whispered jokingly, "I don't suppose we're going to celebrate that, right?"

He expected a chuckle; an acknowledgement of his wit, any sign of tenderness. It has been so lonely at times with these strangers, including his reticent often-cold uncle.

"I think we should," said the uncle.

The lawyer snorted, "I'm not going to celebrate—"

The boy tensed, knowing an argument was brewing. He was therefore thankful when the seamstress interjected to her husband, "I think we should."

She spoke so rarely, that her voice casted a spell whenever exercised. Silence followed. She continued, "We should not take for granted the fact that we're here; that we're alive."

In the darkness, the boy heard her shuffling her hand most likely putting it on her husband's shoulder, or, wrapping her hand in his. Her voice was mesmerizing. "I think we should celebrate it. We have food. We have air to breathe. We have our lives. There's much to celebrate."

The boy pondered her words. It was indeed as if an angel spoke. He loved her. He would be there for her if anything would happen to her husband—that lawyer who did not appreciate his wife enough, who did not show her the tenderness that she deserved—tenderness that the boy could surely give her.

Dangerous warmth spread in his body.

The seamstress whispered. "I am thankful for having survived this year." She continued. "I'm grateful for having all this food."

Silence.

She then added, with a lilt of amusement in her voice, "I don't think I will ever want to eat potatoes again in my life!"

They all laughed quietly.

She added, air in her voice. "I'm grateful for this wonderful family hiding us."

"I am grateful," she spoke as if in a prayer, "for your good mother having shown such kindness to our hostess, and for this goodness to save us now."

They were silent. The boy could sense the uncle was appreciative of her comment. So was he.

"I am grateful," she said, a whimsical inflection in her voice, "for your odd math lessons!"

Everyone laughed.

She continued, "Though I understand none of it, all of your sines and tangents, I still am thankful to hear human voices around me…"

She had tears in her eyes.

"I am grateful," the boy said suddenly, surprising everyone, "for having the two of you here." He swallowed, his heart beating fast. "My uncle would have been too boring for me to be stuck alone with him for a whole year."

The uncle retorted with a smile. "You'd be too boring yourself! No math lesson tomorrow!"

They laughed.

The boy could not stop the sense of elation in his heart. *How long has it been since they laughed?*

They were in dire need of laughter, of life.

"I am grateful," said the lawyer, "for you helping us leave the ghetto, and leading us through the forest on the day of the…" His voice broke. "… last transport. We may very well owe our lives to you."

"I am grateful," the uncle hurried to say, "for you having hid me in your apartment after I escaped the butcher."

Silence followed.

The uncle spoke again to the lawyer. "I am grateful for your gold coins, sustaining us here. Without it, the madam could not have gotten us the food, the lamp, the oil. Thank you."

Silence.

The boy said, "I am grateful for that too."

"It's nothing," whispered the lawyer, barely audible.

The boy wanted the conversation to continue, but it died out.

Some time later the uncle whispered, "Positions," and they all went back to their positions. The boy, on the bucket, felt that although they were trapped they were somehow also free. Free, and safe. A year in hiding. His lot could have been worse.

He was hoping that by spring they would be released; that he could celebrate Passover with his reunited family, and tell them of all that transpired in hiding, of the meager food, the math lessons, of the dog outside, of the darkness and the oil lamp.

Hours passed, they changed positions. Like a slow dance, like the slowest rat race, like migrating birds through the seasons.

Nights became days. Days—nights.

Snow melted outside.

Birds began chirping.

And in the pit, the four people kept rotating positions in an everlasting, neverending, circle of captivity.

II

Outside the pit, life continued

Drops of water oozed through the outer wall of the pit as the snow outside melted.

One day the lawyer spoke as they divided the food. "If I'm not mistaken, Passover starts tomorrow at sundown."

The uncle smiled. "Incredible. Passover… The holiday of freedom from slavery… Don't you find that apt?"

The past few weeks were encouraging. The newspapers, which the maid brought, detailed more and more "realignments" on the Eastern Front. The occupying army was apparently retreating. Soon, the uncle argued, their region would also be liberated by the Communists.

The boy was not as hopeful. And now that Passover had arrived, almost without notice, his hopes sank. The crushing reality that it had been over a year, some fourteen or fifteen months, sank into him. Unable to help himself he despaired for the future. Would he spend the rest of his life in hiding, his youth squandered, his body growing into a hunched man who had never seen the world, who would never travel, could never invent innovation, could never kiss a girl?

The uncle was elated. "We should not let this holiday pass us over!"

The boy wondered why they had not celebrated it the previous year. They had already been in the hiding pit by then, had they not?

As if hearing his question, the uncle whispered. "Last year we were all still adjusting to our situation. But now, we must celebrate it."

The lawyer sighed heavily. "You know what that means, right? No bread at all."

"We could manage," said the uncle, "but only if all of us agree."

The boy swallowed hard. The little bread they did receive was their greatest treat. Even a tiny slice of bread melted so deliciously in his mouth. It had texture, it had richness… Unlike potatoes, it felt *man made*. The ground, baked wheat melted in your mouth. *It was the best.*

Passover, the boy knew very well, would mean eight whole days of refraining from bread *altogether*.

The boy felt his uncle's hand on his shoulder. He knew what that meant. He could not let his uncle down, not now, not when his gloomy uncle sounded cheerful.

"I agree," he sighed.

"Good," the uncle said.

The lawyer sighed heavily. "I'm in too."

His wife murmured, "Me too."

The following day the boy sensed a unique atmosphere in the pit. Passover.

He recalled his grandfather presiding over Passover Eve. The table was always set with the finest of tablecloths, the finest of dishes, saved for this once-a-year occasion. They drank wine merrily, four whole cups! And the songs were enchanting and long. They would recline according to the customs. It would be a long time after midnight that he would hear his grandfather concluding the odyssey of the evening. "This year we are here, next year—in Jerusalem! This year we are slaves, next year—free people!"

After the house grew quiet in the evening, they heard the familiar knock, and received the two potatoes. When the floorboards closed, they turned the oil lamp on. This time, however, the uncle did not hurry to turn it off.

The seamstress rarely spoke. But now she did. "This decision, to celebrate the holiday, our Easter, is the smallest—*dignity*—that we can offer ourselves here."

The boy agreed. He felt somehow as if his identity was sharpened. A sense of belonging to something greater than himself: to a kin, to a People, to a nation.

The lawyer pushed aside the bucket to the corner, where the lamp usually was placed safely. He reclined on his arm. "We cannot sit tonight."

The boy knew the requirement for Passover Eve was not to sit on chairs, but to recline. Each year his grandfather would recite, 'This special evening we shall not sit, but recline…'

The boy quipped, "We've been practicing it all year!"

They laughed quietly. The boy felt happy for making them laugh.

They all reclined clumsily, their legs tucked behind each other's torso, as they created a makeshift square. The soft glow of the oil lamp flickered, casting shadows on the one bowl of two potatoes.

"Wait," the seamstress said and reached her hand behind the bucket, took out one of the old pieces of newspaper, straightened it with her hand, then placed it below the bowl.

The boy's eyes bulged. It looked like a tablecloth!

The uncle nodded in appreciation, then looked at the lawyer expectedly. They all did. It was as if the lawyer was their rabbi.

The lawyer looked at the uncle. "No wine."

The uncle said, "We'll do with what we have."

The lawyer cleared his throat. "Thou shalt Sanctify." he reached to the water pitcher. His wife handed him the enamel cup. He poured the water carefully, delicately, as if it was wine. He held the cup high.

"Blessed are You, Lord our God, Ruler of the Universe, who creates the fruit of the vine."

"Amen," the uncle said.

"Amen," the boy answered sheepishly.

The seamstress whispered, "Amen," encouraging her husband.

They passed the cup of water around.

The uncle was the last to drink. He stirred the cup, shaking it gently and drank. "Agh! Nothing like Cabernet Sauvignon!"

The boy enjoyed seeing his uncle elated, almost tipsy-looking. In every Passover Eve the elders were obliged to drink the four cups, by the end of the evening all of the elders were usually drunk, slurring words, and more jovial than ever—while the young ones would usually fall asleep on cushions and pillows by the table, the meal lasting into the wee hours of the night.

They poured the second 'wine' cup. The lawyer smiled. "You will get tipsy tonight."

The uncle retorted, "You will have to carry me home."

Although they peppered the rituals with jokes and humor, there was an unspoken understanding of the significance behind the rituals. As they partook in the retelling of the Passover story, their words carried the weight of generations, connecting them to a shared history, transcending their current situation.

Then they began singing. Quietly, in a whisper. The boy, being the youngest, sang the four questions, the same questions asked for centuries: "Why is this night different from all other nights?"

The lawyer recited. "Pharaoh was probed to decree the release of the Israelites from their shackles, Exodus of the Israelites, from bondage to liberty, as Moses demanded, 'Let my people go.'"

"Well recited," said the uncle. He kept the lamp going.

The seamstress nodded, closing her eyes. She thought of the collective memories of people who had endured centuries of persecution. The retelling of Exodus became a lifeline, connecting them to a heritage bigger than their predicament.

The boy noticed a tear coming down her cheek.

They drank the third cup. The lawyer, staring into the boy's eyes, said, "In every generation, one must see oneself as if they personally came out of Egypt."

The boy listened intently. He had heard it so many times, yet it somehow felt fresh, relevant. Passover wasn't just a recitation of ancient events; they were now in bondage. They were awaiting their own Exodus.

They sipped from the fourth cup of "wine", and although the joke of the water being the finest of wines already grew old, they nevertheless repeated it as the cup was passed around.

As the makeshift *Seder* meal progressed, they began singing "Dayenu." The boy's heart skipped a beat. "Dayenu" was his favorite Passover song, a melody that had always filled their home with joy and laughter.

They sang quietly, their voices barely above whispers to avoid detection. The familiar tune brought tears to the boy's eyes. The song, a staple of Passover, recounted the many miracles and blessings bestowed upon the Israelites during their exodus from Egypt. Each verse ended with the refrain "Dayenu," meaning "it would have been enough," expressing gratitude for each divine gift.

"If He had brought us out from Egypt, and had not carried out judgments against them—it would have been enough, Dayenu!" the lawyer whispered, his voice trembling with emotion.

The seamstress joined in, her voice soft but steady. "If He had split the sea for us, and had not taken us through it on dry land— it would have been enough, Dayenu!"

For the boy, singing "Dayenu" was bittersweet. The words spoke of a freedom he could barely remember and a hope that seemed almost out of reach. But in that pit, surrounded by these strangers that had, after a year, become a wartime family, the song also became a testament to their resilience. If their forebears had endured and triumphed, perhaps they could too.

As they finished the last verse, the uncle's eyes shone with unshed tears. He placed a gentle hand on the boy's shoulder. "No matter where we are, as long as we remember who we are, we are free in spirit."

The uncle extinguished the lamp. But their songs continued. Their whispered tunes were a delicate rebellion against the brutal war above, a silent anthem of defiance.

Late at night the lawyer concluded the ceremony. "The four cups correspond to the four promises of redemption: 'I will bring you out from under the yoke of the Egyptians, I will free you from being slaves to them, I will redeem you with an outstretched arm, and I will take you as my own people.'" Then, the lawyer recited, and the uncle joined in unison. "This year we are here, next year— in Jerusalem! This year we are slaves, next year—free people!"

III

"One year, three months," said the lawyer.

Nobody said anything. The boy felt exasperated.

He was already 16 years old. Another year in the darkness.

The news was supposedly good. But they had been reading the same news for several months now. Realignment here and realignment there. But still, no liberation.

The boy dreamed of the day he could walk freely under the sun. He dreamed of talking out loud. Out loud! Without having to whisper all the time…

He dreamed of having *privacy*, without feeling the breath of others blowing on his neck. He dreamed of kissing a girl. He dreamed of fondling a girl. He dreamed of more than that.

One day, in the early morning, they began hearing something.

The boy said, "Do you all hear it?"

The uncle said, "Shhh…"

They heard distant thumps. The ground shook.

The boy had never heard the uncle speaking with such excitement, as if announcing the arrival of the Messiah. "Artillery," he whispered. "Cannons."

They were excited. *Could this mean…?*

Suddenly they heard a motor. A car? They had never heard a car coming to this rural area.

They heard the car coming to a halt, its motor stopping.

The car door slammed shut.

The dog barked.

Then came the sound of boots, unmistakable. Soldiers.

The boy felt the lawyer moving uncomfortably. Then he heard him pulling out the knife. A car, a real one, stopped near the cabin.

In such a rural place! Up the hill! A car!

The car door slammed shut. Then came the sound of boots, unmistakable. The soldiers shouted at the maid, their voices a harsh staccato.

The dog barked loudly.

They all held their breaths.

But then, the boots sounded walking away from the cabin.

The car left, its motor's sound disappearing down the hill.

The maid soon came into the room, holding her toddler son by the hand. "Now-now, don't worry, sweetheart, the soldiers were just asking for directions to the bridge, that's all!"

The boy was grateful to the maid for letting them know what was going on.

The lawyer put the knife back in its sheath.

But the artillery continued throughout the day, as well as the following day.

As spring turned to summer, each week the sounds of cannons and machine guns grew louder. Through the ground they could hear what was happening great distances away.

"They're getting nearer," said the uncle one day, "and we need a plan."

But the uncle said nothing.

One day the machine guns sounded closer than ever. The boy shook.

That evening, at dinner time, the boy heard loud knocks on the door. He heard men's voices above him. He froze. They all did.

Chapter 70: Light

Israel, 1977

Age 49

All seemed to be going well for the scientist and his new wife until they received a phone call one evening.

The scientist should have known better about picking up the phone. He had a bad feeling in his stomach when it rang.

The voice was of a woman, speaking English with a German accent.

He could recognize that accent so well—the accent of the butcher, of all the soldiers who shot freely into the audience at the synagogue, who used their whips to discipline the march from the enclosure to the camp, and then weeks later, the march back from the camp to the enclosure, these were the beasts that treated him and his family as if they were cattle.

The voice continued speaking on the other side. "I am an attorney from the Cologne District Court..."

He could not listen to her words. Why were they after him? What did they want from him? He had spent his entire lifetime escaping from the Nazis, escaping from the Germans, escaping from his past.

"Sir, can you hear me? Are you there?"

His voice was feeble. "Yes...?"

His wife walked to him, looking at his face. Who was he talking to? Why did he become so pale?

"We presume," the voice of the woman said, "that we have caught a Nazi criminal, and we understand from the records that you are one of the only survivors who managed to escape the ghetto in Grodno…"

That cold day, escaping, running, hearing the gunshots in the distance. Then, hearing from the neighbors who visited the maid that the soldiers have cleared up the ghetto as if there was dirt in it. Hearing that they were all taken to the trains. Back then, he still had some hope—hope that he might one day soon reunite with his family.

"Sir? Sir, can you hear me?"

Who have they caught?

The scientist felt dizzy, his lips dry.

And why was calling him? Why now? Why, when he finally escaped?

"Sir? Sir? Sir, can you still hear me?"

"What's his name?" the scientist asked, his voice hoarse.

His wife moved closer to him, hearing the voice on the phone.

The phone clattered on the floor as the scientist fainted. *The butcher.*

CHAPTER 71: DARKNESS

POLAND, 1944

AGE 16

I

The four people in the pit did not move.

The voices spoke in the local Polish dialect. It was neighbors. The boy recognized some of the voices. That old nosy neighbor, always butting into the maid's business, was the loudest. Also the man who once, during a party, sat on the bed and complained about the smell. And another neighbor who spoke loudly at the party months earlier.

"The Nazis keep retreating."

"The Russians are only a couple of days away."

"But the Nazis are burning everything behind. They leave nothing intact. Burning barns, churches, whole towns, just so the Russians will find no food."

"They shoot people when they retreat. Anyone seeming to collaborate with the Communists, or to celebrate the Nazis withdrawal."

"We must be clever."

The boy could make out some of what was said. "But here, the Nazis are strengthening the lines. They are recruiting everyone..."

A man spoke: "Some say it will be the last battle, for either the Communists or the Nazis."

"The Nazis know that if the Communists cross the river, they are doomed," the old neighbor exclaimed.

"They call this area 'strategic.'"

"That's why they're sending all the troops here."

The boy's eyes widened in the darkness. *All the troops? There?*

II

That night the maid whispered to them as she brought some potatoes and took the bucket away, "It's getting dangerous. We might not be able to open the floorboards every day."

The uncle nodded.

But the boy could see that his uncle, the invincible, the all-knowing, was now distressed. Concerned.

The maid gave them two pitchers with water. "I want you to have more water, too. In case…"

The uncle nodded with appreciation and took the pitchers.

Then they all heard some thumping sounds from the forest. The maid hurried to get up, and the uncle quickly placed the floorboards back in place.

They were surrounded.

Now truly there was no escape. The boy felt this was coming. At long last, the soldiers would find them. All this misery for nothing, the boy thought to himself. Every hope he ever had came to ruin.

They did not dare turn the oil lamp on.

On the hill, loud sounds of banging and hammering did not allow the pit dwellers to sleep.

The boy felt the pounding sounds in the ground matched his own heart. Rapid, relentless. *What was happening?*

The uncle said nothing.

No one dared speaking.

The following night, the maid did not knock on the floorboards.

It took 48 hours, and the stench in the pit was overwhelming.

As was the hunger.

Finally, the maid came.

"I'm sorry," she whispered and handed them a bowl with several potatoes. "It's too risky."

She kept looking at the kitchen door, her husband hurrying her.

"The Communists are getting closer, the Nazis are retreating from the East. But… They've cleared some trees right here and built an army tent, a giant one." she swallowed hard. "I'm not sure how long—how—I know nothing—" she said, and took the bucket reluctantly, looking helpless.

The boy never saw her like that.

From the kitchen, the husband glared at his wife to close the hiding pit already.

She left, and the uncle hurried to close the floorboards.

The boy felt trapped. The agonized face of the maid, her wide-eyed, messy hair, was etched in his mind.

Fear crept in his body, clutching his heart, numbing his fingers. He was starving, but seemingly did not want to eat.

"Uncle," he whispered. "What is the plan?"

"I am working on it."

The boy thought of running through the night to the river, swimming to the other side, then making a run towards the Communists—they were advancing, so the maid said.

The following morning the sounds of digging continued. Were they indeed building trenches? The boy heard hammering and loud machinery.

And machine guns.

The boy knew the Nazis would burn the cabin. He did not want to die burning. The logs from above could collapse on them, the entire cabin was a burning material. The Nazis would never retreat leaving anything intact. He heard many stories about them burning barns, churches, whole towns, just so the Russians would have nothing to strengthen them.

Then came the explosion.

Chapter 72: Light

Philadelphia, 1983

Age 55

I

His new wife turned on the light near the bed. She had woken up from his screams.

He rushed to apologize. "I'll…go…to the living room…"

He hurried to get out of bed.

She looked at him eagerly. He still did not tell her about the phone call—she had to guess. Shadows from his past were chasing him, and she needed to know what they were. She wanted to help him.

"No," she said, "stay here, why the living room? I'm here with you. Tell me about your dream."

The scientist was not so young any more. He had five long decades behind him. And he still could not talk. Not about that. "Go back to sleep!" he barked.

He went out to the living room. He turned the lights, poured himself cold water, collapsed onto the spacious sofa, and took a deep breath.

Since that phone call from the attorney in Germany, things had only become worse.

While in the past he used to have nightmares only every other week, now they came each and every night.

He drank some of the cold water.

He should call and tell the attorney that he would not testify; that he had buried the past behind him. The butcher must now be in his late sixties. *Let others testify.*

Every thought of him made the scientist's heart sink. He could still feel the grip of the butcher's hand, the way the butcher pointed his rifle around like a toy that he enjoyed pressing on.

He remembered clearly how the butcher stood by an excited crowd at the main street of the ghetto. One woman and two men had tried to escape the ghetto and were caught. According to the butcher, a bullet was too good for them. He wanted them to be hung, dying slowly in front of the entire community.

From the window of the small apartment in the enclosure, the scientist, then just a boy, watched as the butcher wrapped the noose around the two men's necks. When it came time to wrap the noose around the beautiful young woman's neck, she spit in his face.

"Du…Judenschlampe…"

The butcher smiled at her as he pulled out a handkerchief and wiped his face calmly.

Then he put the noose around her neck and came off the improvised platform made of the single bench. He kicked the bench powerfully. The two men and the woman hanging tried desperately to release themselves somehow, as their bodies continued spasming, their faces reddening. The boy saw the wide eyes of the young woman as she ran out of air, her feet still shaking. He could not look away from her as her body stilled, her eyes still watching him, frozen.

A hand gripped him and the scientist jumped up.

"I didn't mean to scare you," his wife mumbled. "I'm sorry."

"No, I'm sorry," he said, embarrassed by his reaction. His kind wife, the librarian who had given up her favorite occupation, as well as her birth country, was probably now regretting having married him. Him and his neurosis and nightmares and constant agitation.

She looked at him, pitying him.

He sighed. "I don't know what's happening to me."

She walked around the sofa and sat down next to him. Here was this successful man, with factories on two continents, the holder of awards for innovation and technology, and he was unable to sleep. She looked at him with her loving eyes. "I want to hear."

He got up, nearly jumping. He walked around the living room, "Oh it's nothing, nothing…believe me, it's nothing."

"Whatever it is, 'nothing' or not, I'm here," she said. "I want to hear."

He sighed, "Ever since that phone call…"

She nodded.

"…the thought of that man just won't go out of my head."

She looked at him, encouraging him to speak.

He shrugged his shoulders and then stiffened suddenly. "Don't you want to go to bed?"

She did not move. "'The thought of that man,' you were saying," she said, "'just won't go out' of your head…?"

He wet his lips. "I don't…I don't want to talk about it."

She clasped her hands together and whispered, "Can I at least…Can you at least hug me?"

He sank on the sofa with a sigh and embraced her. He felt his heart beating fast, and a difficulty to swallow.

He tried to ignore it. He did find comfort in her embrace. *She was probably tired*, he thought. She must be embarrassed by his behavior. He sighed. "Now, why won't you go back to bed?"

She smiled. "Because I want to be with you."

The previous nights she had also tried to get him to talk. Without success. He was stubborn. Impenetrable.

She even suggested, on one of the mornings as they were drinking their coffee, that he should see a "psychologist." He brushed that idea away, offended.

Her fingers now stroked his head. With her other arm she held him tightly.

He bit his lips. "You look at me," he said slowly, "and you see…what do you see?"

Before she was able to answer he said, "I look like a man to you. A grown up man. But I died…" his voice cracked. "I died in the war."

She was not fazed. "Obviously," she whispered, "there was a part of you that died. But there's also a part of you that didn't die; a part of you that is trying to speak to you now. And it's speaking to you in your dreams. I've read a book about it. And I'm here to…"

He got up. "I don't need any of this psychological crap from your stupid books!"

She was silent.

Regret immediately stung him..

He went to the front door and grabbed his coat. "I'm going for a walk."

"No, you're not," she said.

"What?" he looked at her, his eyes widening.

She remained impassive, on the sofa. He had been running from her enough; he had been running from himself for too long. She had resolved that she would not allow this to happen again.

"Come here," she commanded and gently patted the sofa with her hand. "Sit."

Like a reprimanded child, he shuffled closer.

"Come here, now," she said, and as he went closer to her, she reached for his hand, pulling him to the sofa, pushing his head onto her lap. "You said that a part of you died there. I hear you. Can you hear that I hear you?"

He nodded. His chin quivered.

This was the beginning of a journey that was to mark the following days. Each night when the scientist woke up screaming, his wife sat with him.

He wanted to do anything but talk. He was willing to cut himself, to shout at her, to ruin their marriage—to do anything but have to go *there*. To the pain he endured under the floorboards.

But he knew she would not let him escape from it any longer.

She was kind and loving, but at the same time she was assertive and firm.

"I'm listening," she'd whisper.

"Tell me," she'd murmur.

"I'm here," she'd reaffirm.

For the first time in his life, the scientist spoke about the pit. About the eternity of his early adolescence.

Then, after a few sentences, after offering her a glimpse, he would stop speaking.

The next time that he had a nightmare, she would, as if anticipating that moment, turn the light on, and ask, "Were you in the pit?"

"No," he shook his head. He was reluctant to speak. Not of *him*. Not of the butcher.

"Not at the pit?" she asked, trying to prompt him to speak.

He was embarrassed. "In the ghetto," he began saying.

She waited for a very long moment.

Her husband said nothing. His chin quivered. His lips shook. He did not dare look at her but instead stared at his fingers. She watched his thumb obsessively stroking the edge of the blanket.

She waited for him to keep talking.

He wanted her to call it off for the night, to admit she was tired. Why was she pretending to care? He knew that eventually she would be overwhelmed by his baggage, by the suitcase of hell he was carrying with him like an eternal vagabond.

She spoke softly. "You were in the ghetto?"

"In the ghetto there were a number of Gestapo officers. They were terrible, but their Commandant—"

He could not seem to complete the sentence. How could he find a proper word to describe the bloodthirsty butcher? How could he describe the joy and the glee that he recognized in the eyes of the Commandant as he saw his victims dying before him?

The thought of him made the scientist cold. He realized that he was sweating from the nightmare and that his pajamas were wet and cold.

"A number of Gestapo officers?" his wife asked, urging him to continue.

"Their commandant," he said, "was the worst. He brought terror wherever he went. He seemed to take special…" —how could he describe the delight the butcher took in causing suffering to innocent people?

The scientist could still see him so clearly with his smug smile and the joy that he seemed to draw from his position of power.

His uniform was always impeccably ironed. The buttons shone, the boots glowed black. His smug smile bespoke a fiendish pleasure in human suffering.

The officer's uniform, adorned with the swastika, an emblem of darkness, seemed to pulse with fear, casting an ominous glow upon the atrocities and the dark sins that unfolded under its auspices.

The twitch of his upper lip betrayed a sinister anticipation, a prelude to the sadistic game that awaited those unfortunate enough to cross his path.

The officer's fingers, stained with the blood of the innocent, caressed the trigger with an almost affectionate touch. It was a grotesque intimacy, a communion with death that sent shivers down the spines of those forced to witness the atrocities he committed. His grip on the gun was possessive, fingers coiled around the weapon like a lover's embrace. The firearm, an extension of his hand, seemed to hum with a perverse vitality, ready to spew forth death at his slightest whim.

The joyous readiness with which he would pull the trigger. A choreography of death that unfolded with the cold precision of a nightmare. The laughter that erupted from his lips after each shot.

His eyes, devoid of remorse, locked onto his victims, a predatory gaze that stripped away their humanity, nullifying their very existence. It was a gaze that dissected their souls, leaving them exposed and vulnerable to the unspeakable cruelty that awaited.

The wife put her hand on her husband's hand. "You can tell me."

The scientist wanted to tell her, but he could not.

The shadows grew nearer every day.

II

"No, no, please, no!" he screamed.

The scientist woke up again.

He was exhausted, disoriented.

His wife quickly turned the light on.

The scientist did not dare look at her. How many nights now has it been? Sleep became dangerous. Everything in his life had changed since that terrible phone call. Why did they reach him? Why did he answer?

"Tell me," she begged.

His pajama collar was wet from sweat. He felt useless, the agony of weeks without proper sleep had left a mark.

"Is it related to the phone call?" she asked.

He sighed, too tired to resist her repeated pleas. "The butcher—the commandant of the ghetto," he said.

"Yes?"

"He was chasing me."

She nodded. "He was chasing you?"

"In my dream. He grabbed…onto my coat…I tried to escape…I really tried…"

She looked at him. He saw pity in her eyes. He knew she had good intentions, but he hated being pitied.

"It's this phone call. I should never have answered it."

She had been waiting for him to tell her about the phone call.

"They caught him."

"The commandant?"

"Yes. He is going to be brought to trial. I don't want to go there."

She looked at him. "You were invited?"

"To testify."

She looked at him, urging him to speak. She placed her hand on his.

He inhaled deeply. He was so tired, but so afraid of going back to sleep.

"Enough," he whispered and screwed his eyes tightly. "I cannot bear it anymore."

"I know," she whispered. "I know."

"I cannot bear it!" he shouted, knowing he would scare her.

She was not scared.

"It's the fact they found him. And that I cannot go, but I also cannot not go."

She tightened her grip on his hand, her touch providing a small comfort in the midst of his torment. The bedroom felt suffocating, the weight of the past bearing down on him like an unrelenting force.

She spoke softly, her voice a gentle anchor in the storm of his thoughts. "Talk to me."

"I wish I could escape it. But I can't. Not even in my dreams," he replied, desperation clinging to his words.

She leaned in, her warm breath brushing against his ear. "You don't have to face it alone. We'll get through this together."

His eyes met hers, searching for reassurance. He found it there, a glimmer of hope amidst the darkness. For a moment, he let himself believe that maybe, just maybe, the nightmares could be conquered.

"Maybe you should consider testifying," she suggested, her voice measured. "It might bring closure—"

"Closure!" he scoffed. Sometimes he thought she was too naive.

"Yes. Not just for you, but for your family. And for all those who suffered."

He recoiled at the thought. The idea of revisiting the horrors of the past in a courtroom was almost as terrifying as the nightmares themselves.

"I can't," he muttered, shaking his head. "I can't go back there. It's too much."

She squeezed his hand, understanding etched in her eyes. "No one expects you to be a hero, but sometimes facing our fears is the only way to be free of them."

He took a deep breath, the air heavy with the weight of his decisions. "I just want it all to stop. The dreams, the memories…I want to be free of it."

She nodded, her support unwavering. "We'll find a way. You don't have to carry this burden alone."

As they sat in the dimly lit room, the echoes of the nightmare still reverberating in his thoughts, he clung to the glimmer of hope that maybe she was right.

The following morning his daughter called. It was evening in Israel, morning in Philadelphia.

"Dad, this attorney called. They want you to testify about the killing in the ghetto."

The scientist did not answer. He was besought—now they were chasing after his daughter too? *The nerve. The audacity!*

"Dad, you must testify."

It felt as if both his wife and his eldest daughter were now plotting against him.

"I don't have to do anything!" he said. "I will not let this dictate my life!" he exclaimed—knowing well that in the past few weeks, this had been dictating his life.

"Well, you have another year or even two before the court case. But they are gathering testimonies now—"

"I will not testify, I don't need this burden!"

"Okay, okay, Dad, relax. When are you coming to visit me in

Israel again?"

He had no idea what his daughter was planning for him.

Chapter 73: Darkness

POLAND, 1944

AGE 16

I

The explosion was so loud that the boy expected the floorboards to collapse on him.

What was it?

He tried protecting his head, his arms crossed above. *An earthquake?*

A series of loud thuds followed, shaking the cabin. *It did not sound like cannons—or, did it?*

The boy found it hard to breathe.

The smell of something burning. He wanted out.

"Uncle," he began. "We must leave!"

His uncle hissed at him, "No! Grow up already!"

The boy felt as if his uncle slapped him. *His damn uncle*—the boy had never liked him anyway—*this arrogant uncle*—who was now going to sacrifice his nephew's life because of his stubbornness and arrogance.

The boy wanted to cry. He wanted to scream, but instead he stared into the darkness, his eyes wide open, sensing the end.

His mother.

The sound of machine fire persisted.

His loving mother.

In the midst of all the noise and commotion outside, the boy knew he was bound to die.

He thought of his mother. Of that last morning. None of them knew that was the day the Nazis were clearing out the ghetto.

That day, he woke up, and his mother prepared two slices of bread for him, spreading it with the jam he had been able to smuggle from the worksite into the ghetto a few days earlier.

That morning his mother looked at him lovingly. She had always been somewhat strict, quite a disciplinarian. But that morning, before he left the disheveled ghetto apartment to go work for the Nazi worksite outside the enclosure, his mother had suddenly grabbed his face with both hands.

She had looked him in the eyes before she kissed him on the forehead. "I love you, you know that, right?"

The boy's memories were abruptly cut when his uncle suddenly put his hand on his knee. "Shhh…"

The boy realized he was moving his leg nervously, tapping the wall.

He swallowed hard. *He shouldn't think about that.* It made him nervous.

He had not thought of his mother for quite some time. He had somehow managed to fend off these thoughts, knowing that these kinds of thoughts could drive him mad. As long as there was hope for survival, he could brush these thoughts aside.

But now there was no more hope—he had seen it on the maid's face.

The maid did not come that night. Nor the following night. The stench of their excrement saturated the boy's lungs, reminding him that they were emptying themselves with no food left to fill them up again.

He heard the older sisters' voices who remained in the cabin. Outside, Nazi soldiers were shouting.

Hunger.

Stench.

Fear.

The maid finally knocked on the door. Had it been three days? Or more?

The maid took the bucket from the uncle.

The boy noticed her eldest daughter standing near the bedroom door.

The maid whispered, "They blew up the bridges, did you hear the explosions? Trying to stop the Communists from crossing when they come…"

She handed them a bowl of potatoes. Her eyes, full of fright, landed on them, "Don't lose hope."

The boy thought she looked terrified.

The uncle closed the floorboards above them.

Finally now the smell was better in the pit.

No one wanted to say anything. They divided the potatoes and ate silently. The boy saved an entire potato for later—who knew when the maid was to knock again?

II

The sounds of bullets and machine guns intensified. The four people in the pit kept hoping for the maid to come and tell them that the Communists had won.

But that day never dawned.

On the contrary, they heard more and more vehicles around the cabin. Shouting in German.

The maid had refrained from opening the pit.

They heard soldiers in the forest, building trenches, tents—*who knew?*

Then came the moment which the boy dreaded.

The sound of the cabin door being violently pounded on.

The sound of the husband opening the door and trying to speak calmly.

They heard shouting in German.

Then they heard much shuffling around the cabin, running steps, with soldiers shouting, "Schnell! Schnell!"

The maid came into the bedroom. "Now-now, it is okay baby, we need to leave! We need to leave! There will be a battle here, we are being told to leave!"

Then came more shuffling and shouting. Many steps thumping in the kitchen.

Soon their worst nightmare came true.

The steps disappeared into the distance.

No voices at all.

The boy's heart sank like a stone as the truth dawned upon him: the cabin was empty.

His mind whirled with questions, but there were no answers to be found in the empty silence of the cabin.

Outside, the sounds of battle raged on in the distance. All they could hear was the pop of machine guns and the occasional loud boom of cannons. And they could smell the flames emerging from the fire.

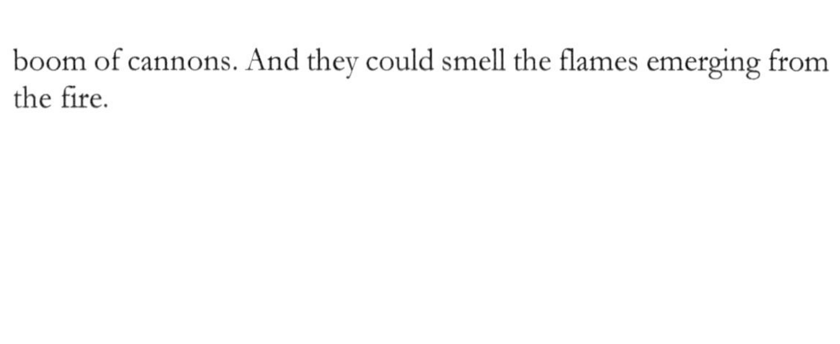

CHAPTER 74: LIGHT

ISRAEL, 1983

AGE 55

I

He did not want to ruin their Israel trip.

Up to that day, the trip had been a joy. He was happy to see his eldest daughter, now a doctor. His second daughter was still studying in Philadelphia. His son had begun college in New York.

Israel was a breath of fresh air. His wife always seemed so carefree when she was back in her home country.

The lightheartedness wound up the road on the outskirts of Jerusalem. His daughter drove.

"Where are we going?" he asked.

"You'll see," his daughter said.

He glanced back at his wife in the back seat, then at his daughter. "You know I don't like surprises."

The road was busy with cars. They turned onto the road and he saw the sign. 'Yad Vashem Holocaust Memorial Museum.'

"No, no, no."

"Dad, listen," his daughter hurried to say, "it's the Holocaust memorial day, there is a nice ceremony, many survivors are joined together, honored, it will do good for you—"

"I don't want to!" he said, and looked at his wife. "Did you take part in this?"

Before his wife could respond his daughter said, "Dad, let's just walk in, just for five minutes." Then she added the final blow. "To honor your family who perished."

He could not respond to this. His hand gripped the car door handle. He felt trapped.

The road wound up past many cypress trees.

He saw another sign from the window, its bold letters spelling out "Yad Vashem" against a backdrop of somber gray architecture. The entrance, flanked by solemn trees, appeared foreboding.

They parked the car. He did not want to step out.

"Dad, only five minutes," his daughter begged. "For the memory of the family."

He saw his wife looking at him. He did not want to seem weak to the woman he loves.

Stepping out of the vehicle, he felt the cold April wind filled with the scent of trees in the Jerusalem hills; olive trees, cypress trees, and the distant scent of citrus trees.

Near the parking lot, the entrance plaza, adorned with symbolic sculptures and commemorative plaques, led them toward the main building, a structure that seemed to echo the resilience and remembrance etched into its very foundation.

Then, suddenly, as if seeing a ghost, he started shaking his head incessantly. "No! No! I cannot go…"

The daughter looked at her father's wife helplessly.

The wife shrugged her shoulders.

His daughter said, "Dad, if you don't want to go in we won't force you…"

"I won't go!" he said.

"Alright," said his wife, "but we've come so far, and it's such a beautiful day. Why don't we take in some of the fresh air outside before we continue on?"

He nodded.

They went to a nearby bench and sat there in silence outside the museum.

It was a beautiful day. Spring. The trees near them led to a trail overlooking the Jerusalem Mountains. When the scientist had relaxed a little, knowing they would not force him inside, his wife said, "Let's take a short walk around these beautiful cypresses?"

He agreed. Trying to distract himself, he said, "Van Gogh painted cypresses beautifully."

"Yes," his wife said and took his hand in hers.

The three of them walked amidst the trees, on a small trail. Then they noticed some signs near the trees. The scientist read, "In Loving Memory of Oscar Schindler, Germany, Righteous Among the Nations."

He walked to another tree, his wife and daughter next to him. He read, "In Loving Memory of Father Rufino Nicacci, Italy, Righteous Among the Nations."

He walked further, another tree, another plaque. "In Loving Memory of Raoul Wallenberg, Sweden, Righteous Among the Nations."

He shook his head in disbelief.

He felt gratitude—there were many people who were courageous enough to lay their lives on the line to protect others. The title "Righteous Among the Nations" was official recognition by the State of Israel for those who had risked their lives to save Jews during the Holocaust. A commission headed by a justice of the Supreme Court examined and awarded the honorary title. It granted not only a medal and respect, but also honorary citizenship in Israel.

He thought of the maid and her husband. Over the years, he had sent them hundreds of letters, in each one, thanking them for being alive. The maid and her husband had already died, but he kept in touch with her five children and cemented a close bond between him and the eldest three daughters. He sent pictures of his children as they grew up. He sent money. When the husband died, he sent flowers. When the maid died, he flew to Poland to attend the funeral and spoke about her courage and cleverness.

But as he walked by these trees, each tree honoring a hero who had laid down their lives to save others in need, he suddenly felt a new purpose emerging in his heart.

II

The scientist had never been interrogated by Jews before.

The scientist's wearied gaze wandered across the faces of the committee members, each question deepening the ache within him. The room at the Holocaust Museum felt suffused with an air of solemnity, and the weight of memory pressed heavily on his shoulders.

"You realize, Doctor," the committee sat in front of him, "the The Holocaust Martyrs' and Heroes' Remembrance Authority in Israel carefully evaluates nominations for the title of "Righteous Among the Nations."

"I do."

"We understand that the maid and her husband were kind to you, that is not the question. But we must ascertain whether they actually saved your life, and whether that was at the risk of their own lives."

"Understood," he answered, fatigued. This was already the third hour of questioning.

He wanted to do it for the children of the maid and her husband. But the relentless questioning was draining his energy.

As the interrogation persisted, the committee delved further into the intricacies of the family's actions, their motives, and the risks they undertook.

"Can you provide a detailed account of the circumstances surrounding the rescue?"

"How did the family become aware of the Jews in need of assistance?"

"What specific actions did the rescuer take to save the lives of the people in the pit?"

"What motivated the family to help you?"

"Did they face any personal risks or challenges in providing assistance?

"How long did they hide you?"

The scientist's voice, once steady, began to falter. The

questions hung in the air, heavy with the passage of time and the burden of secrets held for decades. Each moment of concealment was a testament to the family's courage and the scientist's indebtedness.

"Did they receive any remuneration from you or the other survivors while they hid you?"

He answered honestly, thinking of the lawyer's gold coins given to the maid to buy food, or pay for the dog and the dog house. "From time to time, we gave her gold coins, to support the purchasing of food."

The sudden disapproval hung in the air. "You realize, Doctor, to have the title 'Righteous among the Nations,' we must prove that their motives were not financial?" The statement echoed in the room, casting shadows on the purity of the family's intentions.

The scientist, desperate to convey the truth, pleaded with the committee. "She was trying to feed the family, hers and us hiding there; she took the money to buy food." His words seemed to fall on deaf ears, a fragile defense against the skepticism that clouded the committee's judgment.

The room seemed to close in around him as the weight of his testimony lingered, leaving the scientist engulfed in a swirling jumble of memories and the relentless interrogation that sought to validate the family's sacrifices.

The committee's stern expressions betrayed no sign of empathy as they pressed on, firing each question with calculated blows to the scientist's already battered spirit.

The next question sliced through the air. "Did the family ever express any hesitation or regret in providing assistance?"

CHAPTER 75: DARKNESS

POLAND, 1944

AGE 16

I

In the pit, the boy tried hard not to think of the dangers outside. But somehow he knew the butcher was still searching for him.

He recalled the day he returned from labor in the construction site outside the ghetto. The baker's son was also with him that day.

He wished to forget how the sun dipped below the horizon, casting the desolate ghetto into an eerie twilight as they stood in line to go through the search to walk into the ghetto.

He could not erase the memory of that bitter cold day. A line of weary figures formed at the gate, waiting in silence. The boy stood behind the baker's son whose family—mother, father and older sister—remained at the very back of the line, moving their worried heads a little to the left each time the line progressed, as to keep eyes on their youngest child.

At the ghetto, soldiers executed their duties with precision. They rifled through meager possessions, their actions a silent proclamation of the harsh reality that governed the ghetto. A palpable tension gripped the air.

He recalled how he stiffened as he saw the butcher—the commandant—walking by to look at the inspection. Emerging from the gathering darkness, the butcher stepped forward, a looming silhouette against the fading light. His presence cast an unspoken dread, and the air became thick with the anticipation of his malevolent authority.

He remembered the butcher's single word. "Faster! Schneller!" the butcher shouted at the soldiers, looking at the long line outside the ghetto's gate, his chilling gaze piercing the boy's heart.

The boy noticed the baker's son hesitated to move forward.

The soldiers, now being inspected, shouted at the baker's son. He stepped forward, and they searched his body.

As they asked him to pull his shirt out of his trousers, the baker's son trembled.

They pointed the gun at the baker's son and shouted.

He pulled out his shirt, and a loaf of bread fell on the ground— he was trying to smuggle it into the ghetto.

The boy noticed the trembling hands as the baker's son raised his hands in the air.

The butcher walked closer to him. "Planning to bring this inside?" His question hung in the air like a guillotine waiting to fall.

The tense silence amplified the baker's son's reluctance to answer.

"Don't be afraid," the butcher's voice came surprisingly soft. Like a caring father. "Answer me."

The baker's son shook his head from side to side violently.

In unexpected benevolence, the butcher allowed the baker's son to pass. A fleeting wave of relief swept over the baker's son as he hastened into the ghetto—he lost the loaf of bread, but he gained his life.

The boy stepped forward, as he was next in line. He saw how the butcher reached to his gun as the baker's boy began walking away from the soldiers into the ghetto.

The gunshot shattered the stillness.

The baker's son crumpled to the ground.

The butcher walked, pleased, to the baker's son's body, surveying the aftermath with a sick satisfaction.

As the boy passed the examination and walked by, he felt the butcher's cold eyes on him. He kept walking, afraid the butcher would shoot him, too.

But the butcher did not—he waited for another opportunity. *Maybe the opportunity is coming now.*

The boy heard shouting in German from the outside. He shook in fear. Would he share the same fate as the baker's boy?

Over the year and four months that preceded, the boy had gotten used to the assuring voice of the maid and seeing her face every day.

He had gotten used to the sounds of the family above them.

Now they are all gone. The silence in the cabin made the boy uneasy. He was used to the toddler son babbling, the daughters discussing their days at school, the family dinners.

They could not hear the dog as well; the family must have taken him. No rattling of the chain, no barking at all. The boy wished he had been the dog himself. The life of a dog was more valuable than his.

To add to the distress, throughout that day he heard more and more motors, cars, and shouting.

None of them dared speak.

The air in the pit, heavy with unspoken dread, seemed to thicken with every passing hour. The day unfolded with loud sounds and vibrations of a battle closing on them. The relentless hum of motors, the harsh revving of engines, and the disconcerting shouting of commands reverberated throughout the shrinking pit.

The maid was no longer there to protect them, to speak to the soldiers, to spread pepper on the ground for the hunting dogs to be fooled by. There was nothing to protect them, no shield nor ruse, only thin floorboards and suffocating blankets separating between them and a battalion of Nazis above them.

They were surrounded.

The boy knew his end was coming. Soon, he knew, either the cabin would be hit by an artillery shell and set on fire, or the Nazis would burn it upon leaving, waiting with glee with their machine guns to see if any figure on flames was trying to escape.

The uncle said, "Our fate is together. Whatever happens to one of us will happen to us all."

Suddenly they heard the door of the cabin bursting open.

The boy nearly choked, trying not to make a sound, his tears flooding his throat.

They heard two soldiers above them. Maybe three.

The boy's eyes widened.

The lawyer pulled out his knife.

The boy heard the soldiers coming into the bedroom, their steps intent. *Someone must have told them.*

They must have tortured the maid and her husband. The daughters too.

The bed above them rattled. The soldier exclaimed, "It smells like Jews in here!"

CHAPTER 76: LIGHT

ISRAEL, 1983

AGE 55

It took a year for the Holocaust Museum to process the scientist's request, each time asking for more evidence, more statements, more questions.

The scientist was encouraged by his wife to "have patience."

A representative of the Israeli government from the Israeli Embassy in Poland went to visit each of the five children of the maid and her husband, now in their forties and fifties, to collect the testimonies.

A year later the scientist finally received the letter. "We are pleased to tell you that the award Righteous Among the Nations was granted." He was proud of himself. The multiple interrogations—recalling the painful memories—it was all worth it.

A ceremony was scheduled for a month later.

Over the years, since opening the Vishay plant in Israel, the scientist had many visitors to that land: businesspeople who wished to see the Israeli Vishay Intertechnology plant; fellow scientists, Wall Street investors.

When such an important person would come, the scientist made sure to be in Israel—and would personally meet the most important guests.

But never was the scientist as excited as when the plane from Poland landed in Israel, and a procession of the maid's five children, along with their spouses, eight children, and two grandchildren, made its way out of the arrival gate in the Tel Aviv airport.

"Welcome home," the scientist said, and proudly introduced his wife and three children. Many hugs and kisses were shared, and the Israeli consulate assisted in the luggage and the four taxis to the hotel.

In the two days that remained before the ceremony, the scientist and his wife, along with the children, took their Polish family around the country. The scientist drove one car, and each of his children drove another car.

And so the four cars traveled the roads of the Holy Land, taking the excited tourists to the various Christian holy sites. They visited Nazareth and Bethlehem. And they were baptized anew in the Jordan River.

The family was ecstatic, especially the grandchildren.

They also visited the Vishay factory in the desert. The maid's eldest daughter was surprised to see a few of the women scientists in the factory wearing a traditional Muslim hijab covering their hair.

Seeing her surprised look, the scientist said to her, "We provide work for everyone—Jews, Muslims, Christians. Equally." He wrapped his arm around the maid's eldest daughter. "I learned this 'policy' from some brave people when I was fifteen. You may have heard of them."

Unlike the previous visit to the Holocaust Museum, this time around the scientist walked in gladly, proudly. The four cars parked alongside many other cars belonging to various dignitaries.

The tree-planting and the following ceremony were planned for two hours later. But first, the scientist had prepared a surprise for the maid's children—especially for the three elder daughters.

Although it had been over four decades, the lawyer and his wife had never forgotten the grace of the maid and her family. The scientist had remained in contact with them over the years, visiting them every now and then in Atlanta, Georgia, where they had settled after the war. When the date of the ceremony was decided upon, the scientist invited the couple, now in their seventies, to fly to Israel for the ceremony.

The meeting was very emotional for the lawyer and his wife. The maid's three eldest daughters cried.

The scientist, witnessing this extraordinary gathering, could not contain the overwhelming surge of emotions that swelled within him. Tears welled up in his eyes, a testament to the strength of the connection forged by the saving of one's life at the risk of another's.

The reunion, though joyous, carried with it the bittersweet ache of missing pieces —the maid and her husband, and the scientist's late uncle, absent in physical form but vivid in the shared memories; and watching from above.

The scientist, usually composed and analytical, allowed the tears to flow freely, a cathartic release of the emotions that had built up over a lifetime of remembrance, agony, and gratitude.

After planting a tree in honor of their parents, the children and the large crowd went inside the museum's large auditorium, where the main ceremony began.

In front of journalists and representatives from various countries, the story of the maid and her husband was told.

Excerpts from the testimonies of the three survivors, as well as of the five children, were read out loud. At one poignant moment, the lady read an excerpt from the maid's middle daughter, about the night they found out they had to hide the four people in their home. The testimony told of how their mother spoke with more conviction than the middle daughter had ever seen her. "No, don't tell anyone. No, including the priest, including in confession."

The five children were invited to the stage and were bestowed with medals.

The scientist held his wife's hand tightly.

To conclude the ceremony, the rabbi of the museum began chanting the memorial prayer for the departed. As his voice echoed through the auditorium, the scientist felt transported to his childhood: the many days he had spent in the synagogue; the same synagogue from which the deportations took place, from which his parents and sister were taken. Where the butcher shot people mercilessly.

He began crying as the rabbi sang the prayer. The scientist's wife hugged him and he sobbed in her arms. Seeing this, the maid's eldest daughter came over and hugged him as well. She was soon joined by her siblings. The scientist's three children also joined in, followed by the elderly lawyer and his wife. As the rabbi recited the ancient prayer, the large group clung together, weeping.

When, three days later, the large family returned to Poland, the scientist knew there was one more thing he had to do.

CHAPTER 77: DARKNESS

POLAND, 1944

AGE 16

The Nazi soldier exclaimed, "It smells like Jews in here!"

"What's this smell?" said another, sniffing. "Disgusting. It smells better in the other room."

Fearing to breathe, underneath the floor, the four heard the soldier rising from the bed, his boots thumping on the floorboards as he walked to the other room.

They heard the soldiers toppling onto the children's beds in the adjacent room.

The uncle then did the unthinkable.

He gently lifted the heavy floorboards, blankets piled on top of them.

Some light entered the pit, and the boy could see the lawyer looking at the uncle with a baffled expression of terror. The boy was shocked as well.

But the uncle motioned to his mouth so they would be quiet, and lifted his head, trying to hear what the soldiers were saying.

"Man," said one of the soldiers, "it sure is going to be a rough one."

"Yes," said the other, "the commander said that we either win this one and keep the border, or…"

"Yes…"

"Can't wait for the other units to come already."

"Yes, I heard they even called for the special forces."

"Man, I'm exhausted. Going to take a nap."

"Me too."

Silence.

The uncle closed the floorboards quietly.

A few minutes later they heard snores coming from the other room.

"Come closer," the uncle whispered.

They all placed their heads in the center of the pit, their heads touching.

The uncle breathed in. "We've lasted up until now for a reason." His whispers were barely audible. "We didn't survive these seventeen months here in vain."

They all nodded. The boy felt his heart beating fast.

The uncle murmured, "Time is not on our side. Each hour we stay here makes us hungrier. We do have some water left, but soon we'll be losing our strength. Each hour also adds to the smell from the bucket."

They all nodded. The smell was becoming unbearable. Their instincts told them to walk away from that stench—but their other human instincts told them that danger—life-and-death danger—was looming outside the pit.

The uncle breathed heavily. "We were all hoping that by now we'd be free. I was hoping," he sighed again, "that we'd see the Nazis weakening. But they are not, and they are sending more units here. So time is not on our side."

The lawyer was nervous. "You already said that. What do you suggest?"

"I suggest," the uncle paused, "that we leave the pit. Tonight."

Chapter 78: Light

Israel, 1983

Age 55

His hands shook involuntarily as he stood on the courthouse steps, his gaze fixed on the looming entrance. Memories from the war clawed at his mind.

He did not want to go in. Not into the courthouse. Not to see the butcher from his nightmares again. "I can't," he stammered to his wife, his voice barely audible over the din of the bustling street. "I can't face him again."

His wife held his hand. "Take a deep breath." She squeezed his hand, her eyes conveying a mix of compassion and determination. "Deep breath."

He looked at her and forced himself to inhale. Their eyes locked, and the scientist drew in a shaky breath of the crisp European morning.

His wife smiled. "Good. It will be alright."

"Alright?" he managed a weak smile. "How can you be so sure?"

"Because we face this together. Always." She adjusted his collar. "I will be there, right by you."

After a long moment, he closed his eyes, and asked his parents for strength. Once, at the end of the war, they gave him the strength to do what was right. Now, too, he desperately needed their strength, their blessing. Eyes closed, he whispered a silent prayer, invoking the spirits of his parents. "Guide me, as you did then. To do what is right."

They walked inside. The hall was full, journalists and a curious audience. A Nazi criminal being caught and brought to trial was not an everyday event. As they entered, the noise of the street faded, replaced by the hushed tones of the courtroom. A sea of faces turned towards them—journalists, curious onlookers, all eager.

The litigator, extending a firm handshake, greeted them. "I did not think you would come. I'm glad you're here."

"She made me," the scientist smiled and pointed at his wife.

The litigator shook hands with her. "It was difficult for us to get your husband to come."

His wife, with a small smile, replied, "He needed a bit of convincing."

"This won't be easy." The litigator said, "We have long days ahead of us."

They were escorted to the first row. The scientist was introduced to two other men—two other survivors. Thirty thousand Jews had lived in the city—maybe a hundred at the most survived the war, but among those, many, like the scientist's uncle, had already perished. Seated in the front row, the scientist told them in Yiddish, pointing at the three of them together, "A small club."

They nodded, a somber acknowledgment of shared pain.

The litigator stood by them. "In the beginning the judge will enter and speak. Then they will let the accused in. We will hear the testimonies throughout the day, however long it may take. Only then will he be cross examined. The most important part is after your testimony, you will not be asked to the podium again, so give today all you have got."

They agreed.

Everyone rose. The room fell silent as all eyes turned towards the door behind the podium. The judge entered, bringing a hush over the courtroom. He sat, and the weight of the moment settled in.

The judge's voice cut through the quiet. He read out the proceedings in an authoritative tone that commanded everyone's attention. As the judge began to read out the proceedings, the weight of each word hung in the air.

The scientist, seated in the front row, felt the words wash over him like a cold tide. He sat there, drowning in memories, clutched by dread.

Finally the judge said, "Bring out the accused."

The scientist's breath caught in his throat, the air heavy with anticipation as the courtroom doors creaked open.

CHAPTER 79: DARKNESS

POLAND, 1944

AGE 16

I

They were all silent. They held their heads close to one another, whispering in the center of the pit.

The boy's nerves were overwhelming him. His heart was beating so fast he could barely concentrate on what was being said.

He could feel the panic within his entire body. His mind was filled with a tornado of dark thoughts about the various ways he was to die. Fire. Shots. Torture.

Maybe the lawyer was correct in having the knife. He had whispered once that he was to take his own life before the Nazis would get a hold of him.

And now the uncle was suggesting this preposterous plan: to leave the pit, all of them, together. At night.

The boy could barely utter the words, his mouth heavy, his lips stone like, his throat tight. "If we get caught? What do we…."

The boy felt his own breath loud in his ears. He knew very well what was in store for the three men, but he could not bear to imagine the fate of the seamstress. What would she have to face at the hands of these bloodthirsty soldiers resting in the other room?

"It's a risk we have to take," the uncle finally replied. "It's either we wait and stink and starve until they will open the floorboards and reveal us, or we take this leap of faith!"

No one said anything. The uncle knew he sounded crazy to them. "As long as we don't make any noise we won't wake the soldiers… They are exhausted. Once we get out of the cabin, we will head not to the river, but into the forest, making our way to the village through the trees. Hopefully we will find someone in the village to hide us."

"Hopefully," the boy said bitterly. "Have you forgotten who these neighbors are? They will gladly sell us for a sack of rice or sugar."

The lawyer said, "What if the soldiers catch us? What do we say?"

The boy noticed he was ignored.

The uncle said, "We will tell them we are escaping the Communists. That we hate them with all our guts. That we crossed the river from the Eastern Front, escaping the Russians."

The lawyer did not say anything. Finally he said, "They will tell. They will know. Why are we so thin? Why are we so pale?"

"If we speak with confidence and divert the conversation to how much we hate the Russians, maybe—"

The seamstress concluded. "We will have to try."

"Tonight," said the uncle.

No one spoke. The boy knew he had better enjoy his last few hours of life.

"Let's go over our plan one last time," the uncle whispered.

It was evening.

The cabin's door opened about an hour earlier, then was shut loudly.

Gunfire in the distance filled the air. The rat-at-at of the machine guns echoed in the pit.

The pit became so smelly from their waste that they were

sickened. They tried putting some earth on it, but it only helped so much. They had been there now for nearly two days without the bucket being emptied. They had long ago run out of food, out of water, and out of hope.

"We'll go out," the uncle whispered, "I will leave first.

"I will close the door to the bedroom. Then you will all come out. We will quietly exit through the window. We will run to the back forest and descend the hill to the village. There we will find an abandoned structure, a barn, or something like that. I will go and try and bribe someone to hide us."

The boy could barely listen. It sounded as if they were walking into the mouth of the lion.

The uncle entreated the lawyer, "Now repeat the story if we get caught."

The lawyer began, "We were occupied by the Communists three years ago, until the Nazis came. We hate the Russians. We love the führer. As the Nazis retreated, we tried to retreat with them, fearful of the Russians for having cooperated with the Nazis, giving them food and information. In recent weeks we escaped from the Russians as they came, raping and looting. We crossed the bridge two days ago, then it was blown. We want to go to Berlin."

The uncle said, "This is everyone's story. Even if we get caught, even if they torture us, we will not deviate from it. Promise?"

The lawyer said, "Promise."

The seamstress said, "I promise."

The boy gritted his teeth. "Promise."

The uncle said, "It's time." He reached his hand and the sound of suction followed as he opened the floorboards.

"Wait," the seamstress said.

The uncle said, "It's time." He reached his hand and the sound of suction followed as he opened the floorboards.

"Wait," the seamstress said. "We must pray."

The uncle seemed agitated. But it would be a bad omen to ignore the seamstress's plea.

"Quick," he whispered as he lowered the floorboards.

The pit was smelly and the boy was sickened. They had been there now for nearly two days without the bucket being emptied. They had long ago run out of food.

The boy could not concentrate, his only thought dedicated to the soldiers in the cabin above them. Throughout the previous hours soldiers came and went from the cabin, their voices confident. The boy knew they would shoot them on sight. All of a sudden he did not want to leave the pit.

"May it be Your will," the seamstress whispered, "O Lord our God, God of our ancestors, that You lead us toward peace, guide our footsteps toward peace, and make us reach our desired destination for life, gladness, and peace…"

The boy began tearing up. He had never felt as close to his death as he did now. In the distance they heard the constant noise of cannon fire and machine guns, into which they were about to step.

The seamstress continued whispering, "May You rescue us from the hand of every enemy, from every ambush along the way, and from all manner of punishments that assemble to come to earth… May Thou hearken unto the voice of our supplication. Amen."

"Amen," whispered the lawyer.

"Amen," whispered the uncle.

"Amen," murmured the boy.

The uncle did not wait. He lifted the floorboards.

There was a dim light outside, coming from the kitchen.

The uncle climbed out.

The boy held his breath as the uncle's steps creaked above. The boy thought the uncle should have been quieter.

The boy stopped hearing the footsteps of his uncle.

Suddenly he was afraid that his uncle might have escaped on his own, leaving them to fend for themselves, deserting them.

A long minute later he heard the clicking of the bedroom door.

They heard shuffles of the blankets, and the secret knock. The lawyer lifted the floorboards.

The uncle slid under the bed and lowered himself into the pit. He took the floorboards from the lawyer and lowered them down—for the last time.

The boy, the lawyer and his wife drew closer.

"There is one soldier sleeping in the other room," whispered the uncle. "Our room is clear," he said as he fumbled with his shoes in the darkness. "I closed the bedroom door. We'll leave again, I'll go first and hold the bedroom door's handle so if he wakes up and comes toward us, I can slam the door in his face." The uncle inhaled shakily.

The boy sensed he was nervous.

The uncle continued whispering, his words a rapid fire. "You must leave your knife here," he told the lawyer. "All of you take your shoes off, I don't want any squeaking. After I come out, while I'm holding the door, you," he told the lawyer, "will open the bedroom window, quietly. You'll go out to the yard first, then help your wife out. Then you," he said to the boy, "and finally I'll join you. Wait for me after you climb outside. Duck and put your shoes on, then I'll join you and we'll run to the woods."

They all nodded. The uncle warned them, "Even if we get caught—which we probably will—not deviating from our story, is that clear?"

They nodded again.

"All right," he said. "Shoes off."

The boy's fingers shook as he took his shoes off, wiggling his toes.

The uncle gave his shoes for the lawyer to hold.

He lifted the floorboards, and then climbed out, sliding slowly. He headed to the door.

The lawyer came out. Then the seamstress, the boy supporting her as she reached over. The boy bid farewell to the pit. And to his life.

Chapter 80: Light

Cologne, 1983

Age 55

The courtroom was full, silent, as through the courtroom doors a guard came, holding on to the accused.

The scientist thought they had the wrong man. He looked intently at the man—was this the butcher?

The scientist saw an old man, hunched, his eyes large, heavy wrinkles on his face. Was this the butcher, the "angel of death" who used to terrorize the entire ghetto, thousands of people? Was this the man with the meticulous uniforms, the shining boots, the hand embracing the ready revolver?

The man who had walked in and taken the seat near the attorney was a frightened old man. His eyes were staring with disbelief toward the judge.

Then the scientist noticed the old man's upper lip moving, agitated—the same tiny twitch of pleasure that the butcher had after shooting the baker's son.

The scientist stiffened. His wife, noticing his reaction, patted his hand. She forced him to look at her. He saw goodness in her eyes, and he nodded, reassured.

The judge called in the first survivor.

It was difficult for the scientist to hear the testimonies. But it was also liberating. Here there were two other people who had seen, who had been there. He did not remember them—the ghetto included nearly thirty thousand of them—but it did not matter that he did not know them personally; they were like brothers to him. Brothers to the horror that was their daily lives for two years, until the slow liquidation of the ghetto, ending in that day he managed to escape.

He glanced at the butcher repeatedly. At first it was difficult, he was afraid of the butcher looking back at him.

But as the hours passed, the scientist grew more comfortable being in the same hall with him.

The scientist could not stand the butcher's attorney. The attorney kept doubting the two survivors, interrogating them, expecting them to remember the dates, the exact time of day, and other trivial pieces of information—and when they could not recall, his tone indicated that their entire testimony was a fallacy.

His wife's hand remained in his hand the entire day. Even in the short breaks throughout the day, she never left his side.

Finally it was his turn to speak.

Chapter 81: Darkness

Poland, 1944

Age 16

The uncle held the bedroom door's handle.

The lawyer stood by the door, placing his and the uncle's shoes on the bed while he opened the bedroom window. Cold summer wind filled the room.

The boy followed the seamstress and stepped outside the pit holding his shoes. He glanced at the uncle, grabbing the bedroom door's handle. The uncle glared at him and turned to the window.

The boy saw the lawyer hesitate, not wanting to go outside. The boy looked back at his uncle, who motioned with his chin repeatedly for the boy to climb out the window.

The boy nodded. Their fate was already sealed. He lifted his leg over the window ledge, and felt dizzy as he reached his other leg, pushing himself over, he dropped quietly on the grass outside.

Seeing that the lawyer behind him was struggling, the boy placed his shoes on the grass and reached his hand to help the lawyer, all the while glancing over his shoulder—it wasn't dark enough. The deserted dog house, which the boy saw for the first time, was near the cabin's wall. The potato cellar was on the other side of the yard. The boy saw no soldiers.

Wind caressed his face, overwhelming him. He had forgotten what it felt like.

The lawyer landed with a thud on the grass. He reached his

hands to help his wife. The boy, too, helped her, and they lowered her quietly into the grass.

Inside the cabin, the uncle let go of the bedroom door and headed to the window when he realized the hiding pit was exposed under the bed—it could tell the exact story in an instant if they got caught. He leaned on the floor, his face contorting as he smelled the stench from inside the pit. He returned the floorboards to their exact place, and he placed the blanket and clothes on top of them.

Outside, the boy felt exposed by the cabin's wall. He peered through the window and was alarmed not to see his uncle anywhere.

Then the uncle's head emerged through the window seal, startling the boy. He climbed out. The boy offered to help him, but the uncle simply lowered himself from the window seal to the grass quietly.

The lawyer, pale and alarmed, handed the uncle his shoes. Then the boy realized he did not have his own shoes on. The boy was so dizzy; he almost fell down. He leaned against the cabin for support and put on his shoes.

The scent from the grass was overpowering, as was the air moving around him. He could not believe it. He was outside! He vowed to never take the small things for granted ever again. The uncle finished putting his shoes on, glaring at the boy.

The boy put the shoes on as quickly as he could, and stood up, trying to make the world stop spinning.

The uncle then looked to both sides and led them as they slowed down, running past the potato cellar into the woods, when they heard shouting.

"Stop!"

They halted in their tracks.

The soldier yelled at them. "Passwort!"

CHAPTER 82: LIGHT

COLOGNE, 1983

AGE 55

I

The courtroom was silent. He swore on the Bible and sat down. Everyone's eyes were fixed on the scientist, but his eyes were fixed on one person. His wife.

She looked at him lovingly, her kind eyes like soothing cold water to a body caught in hellish fire.

The litigator asked him technical, introductory questions. When he was born, where he grew up, how old he was when they were forced to move to the ghetto.

Then the litigator asked difficult, painful questions. What happened that night of the move to the ghetto; what exactly happened in the synagogue. Where was the man that was shot? Was the scientist certain it was the accused who shot him?

The litigator then asked him to describe the killing of his cousin. Painfully, the scientist spoke of the period in which they were taken from the ghetto to a temporary work camp on the outskirts of the city. Each morning they stood in the roll call, and sometimes a few lucky names were called.

"At one morning lineup I was especially intent on the names he was reading from a list. 'The following people,' he would announce, 'are not needed here. They are permitted to go back to the ghetto.'

One morning he read the name of a girl, and there was a pause, and nobody came forward. Then my cousin, sixteen-years-old, stepped out. It wasn't her name, but she had decided to take a chance. He looked at her, looked at the list, then took his revolver out of its holster, and shot her in the head—my beautiful cousin."

The litigator asked, "What did you do?"

"What could I have done? The shot rang out. Her body crumpled, and she was dragged away by one of the Jewish policemen. Like all the rest, I stood there staring, numbed."

His wife's face encouraged him.

The litigator said, "Later on the camp was dismantled and you returned to the ghetto for a limited time before the transport to Auschwitz. You were given hard labor to construct the Gestapo building outside the ghetto. One day, as you all returned to the ghetto, through the ghetto's gate, there was one person ahead of you in line. Tell us what happened then."

The scientist told of the baker's son, of the baker's son's relief as the butcher seemingly let him go—and how a second later the butcher shot him in the back and he dropped to the ground.

He told how the butcher walked over to him, pleased, looking back at the soldier with pride for his good aim, or for the way he "handled" the situation.

The scientist felt exhausted. His wife nodded at him, approving, feeding him with her eyes, offering strength with her calmness.

The day ended, to be continued the following day.

At night in their hotel bedroom, his wife held tightly to him. "You were a hero today."

He held her tightly. He had managed not to weep the entire day. But in her arms, now, his eyes filled with tired tears.

The following morning he continued with his testimony. He told of the noose and the hanging, he told of the sporadic killing in the synagogue. He spoke of how the butcher presided over the marches to the train tracks, where one transport after another, the dwindling community was taken to the "work camps."

Then the accused's attorney asked the scientist questions. The scientist answered calmly. Quietly. He did not let the attorney make him trip up.

The attorney saw how the scientist was not recalling—but describing what he was seeing then and there—as if he was still in 1941, 1942, 1943. He described everything with such detail, the attorney realized that asking the scientist questions became not an asset to the accused, but a liability.

"Your Honor," the attorney addressed the judge with a measured tone, "I have no further questions for this witness."

"Very well, we will go for a 30-minute recess and then continue with the accused's examination."

The scientist and his wife went to breathe fresh cold air outside.

It was over—his part was over.

They returned to the court. The judge entered. The guards brought in the old butcher.

The scientist watched as he took the stand, not knowing what to expect.

II

The scientist saw the butcher swearing over the Bible he would speak the truth and nothing but the truth.

"Nur die Wahrheit". "Only the truth."

His voice was raspy, quiet, diminutive.

Then his attorney began asking him questions. The old butcher began complaining about being assigned the difficult task of managing the ghetto—how he did not like it.

The scientist stiffened. This was far from the glee the butcher displayed in his role.

Then the butcher began lying. He never shot anyone. Other soldiers did—of their own volition—he was against it, absolutely against it. He never shot anyone.

When it came to the hanging in the ghetto, all three survivors described the same event vividly. He admitted to "having been there" and to having "unwillingly placed the noose" but that the hangman was the one to pull the bench, and that it was "terrifying to see."

The scientist shook his head in disbelief. He had expected the butcher to defend his actions, or at least to admit them. Instead, he wove lies—pitiful, ridiculous lies, putting on a sad face, as if he was wrongfully accused.

The scientist turned to his wife. He whispered, "I cannot stand this. He is lying without batting an eye."

His wife patted his hand.

He whispered, "I'm not going to waste our time sitting and listening to his lies. Life is too short for that."

His wife caressed his hand softly.

When the litigator finally took the stand and began cross examining him, the butcher played dumb. His lip twitched as the litigator mentioned shooting with a machine gun, killing at least ten people within the synagogue. That twitch, the scientist knew, was more truthful than the butcher's words, more than his pitiful puppy eyes.

The scientist kept listening to the lies, one after another. As the hours progressed, he already knew the butcher would say: "I didn't do it. I was not there. The others did it. I did it reluctantly."

The scientist grew impatient with every passing moment. He could be with his wife on a vacation, he could be visiting his children—he could be working on building something new, inventing a solution to a problem. Not wasting his time as if he was a prisoner in the camp on the outskirts of the city, locked within the gates, forced to stand in a roll call and witness the atrocities conducted before him.

He felt captive within the courthouse. The hours passed, and, case by case, the butcher rehashed the same sentences. "I didn't do it. I was not there. The others did it. I never shot anyone."

When the incident of the synagogue was brought before him, and the killing of over ten people with the machine gun, he said, "It was not me, it must have been one of the soldiers, I was not there."

As he spoke, a faint smile crept onto his lips, just for a moment, before he quickly masked it with a sorrowful expression. The scientist caught it—a flash of cold satisfaction.

The scientist stood up.

Chapter 83: Darkness

Poland, 1944

Age 16

They heard the voice barking the question again in German, "Was ist das passwort!"

The harsh command reverberated through the trees, sending shivers down the boy's spine. They had rehearsed their silence, a pact born of necessity in the face of imminent danger.

An eye-searingly bright flashlight illuminated their four thin figures.

"Hands up!" the soldier shouted.

They lifted their hands up in the air.

Pointing his rifle at them, the soldier whistled.

They did not dare to move.

The boy nearly wet his pants. It had been so long since a Nazi soldier had pointed a gun at him. All that he had escaped from was now running towards him at fall speed. *It was all lost,* he knew.

He kept holding his hands up, hoping for a miracle.

A moment later three soldiers emerged from the darkness behind the source of the blinding light.

The light neared him. The boy winced, afraid of being hit. He kept his hands in the air.

The soldier muttered to the others. "They might be spies; let's take them to the Main Command."

The boy's stomach churned as they were ushered by rifles urging them to walk forward, away from the woods, to the main trail, each step a march towards their end.

With soldiers pointing rifles at them, the four gaunt figures made their way into the headquarters tent a minute's walk away.

Chapter 84: Light

Cologne, 1983

Age 55

The scientist stood up. The entire courtroom fell silent. The butcher stared at him.

For a long moment their eyes met. The scientist felt bad for this liar. The scientist had spent the decades since the end of the war pursuing; seeking; chasing after the light. The butcher had spent the last decades hiding like a shadow in the dark.

The scientist turned to his wife. "Home," he said.

His wife stood up. A murmur hushed through the full courtroom. The scientist looked at the litigator and whispered. "Sorry."

The litigator, knowingly, said, "Thank you for coming."

The courtroom watched the scientist and his wife as they left, the scientist holding his wife's hand, not looking back, not supporting the ridiculous proceedings.

A long week passed before the litigator called him from the courtroom. "The verdict was announced."

The scientist said nothing.

"He will never leave jail. Seven life sentences."

The scientist hung the phone up. He was not glad, nor triumphant, but a feeling of relief spread across his body. His body relaxed, the guilt he had been carrying around for decades finally subsiding. The person who had caused his family so much pain was finally behind bars. This wouldn't bring them back but a chapter had been sealed, and he was glad to put it behind him.

Chapter 85: Darkness

Poland, 1945

Age 17

I

They marched through the main trail until they saw a large tent. *This was what was being constructed days before,* the boy realized.

As they were stepping toward it, more soldiers began surrounding them, looking curiously at the four figures. Some of them had no rifles, and seemed to have been on a break, now staring with interest at the fate of the four people who had popped out of hiding.

They stopped by the tent.

Two soldiers guarding the tent argued with the eager soldier who was the one to spot them. He seemed outraged, excited, proud.

The boy shuddered when suddenly hands were searching his body, squeezing his loins, thumping his body.

He saw the seamstress, to his alarm, searched by a soldier, disrespecting her, ignoring she was a woman.

They were pushed into the tent. An electric light hung from the tip of the tent. Behind a large desk sat a commander with insignias and medals on his uniform.

Tension crackled in the air like static electricity. The boy's pulse quickened as the commander's gaze bore into their souls.

"Commander," said the soldier proudly, "look at what I

found…!"

The commander looked at the figures—two men, a teenage boy, and a woman. "Who are you?" he barked.

They said nothing, as agreed upon.

"Do you not speak German?" The commander sighed. "Call the translator here!"

A soldier ran out to bring the translator.

Some soldiers peered into the tent, others even dared to stand inside—it was clear they all gathered to witness the spectacle.

The boy prayed. He wanted to live. It seemed like God must have a sick sense of humor to have them trapped in a pit's hole for a year and a half to then have them killed right after escaping.

A minute later a soldier came running in, followed by a translator who immediately saluted the commander.

The commander barked at the translator, "Who the hell are they and what are they doing here?"

The translator looked at them suspiciously and asked them in Polish, "Where are you from?"

The lawyer said, "We come from the other side of the river. We've been escaping the Communists."

The boy tried to keep his face blank. Unmoving. Innocent.

The translator explained to the commander.

"Lies!" barked the commander. "There are patrols all around the river bank. When and where did they cross?"

The translator continued.

"We crossed four days ago," said the lawyer, "and after we did, you blew up the bridges."

"Then we hid in a small barn by the river, some three kilometers from here."

After hearing the explanation, the commander yelled, "Three kilometers!"

He picked up the phone and began barking into it, yelling and cursing.

The translator kept his eyes on them. Skepticism was marked on his face. He could tell something was wrong with the man's story.

The boy felt the translator's eyes piercing him, stripping him. He feared the translator would have them take their pants down, and show their circumcised penises, proving they were Jews. Would they be taken out of the tent to be shot? Or would they be shot inside it?

The other soldiers kept looking at them, staring especially at the thin woman.

The commander finished yelling over the phone and slammed down the receiver.

The translator told him something. The commander motioned for him to hurry and ask them.

"Why is this boy so white?" the translator asked.

The lawyer quickly said, "Because he's scared to death!"

The sentence echoed in German.

The boy tried not to move or swallow too hard.

The commander leaned back, amused. "You really want us to believe that you came all the way from the other side of the river and no one caught or questioned you?"

After the translation, the lawyer responded. "We hate the Communists with our guts. We wanted to do whatever we could to get to the German side. And no, no one ever saw us."

The commander sighed. "Ask them if they have identification papers…"

It was then that the seamstress suddenly collapsed on the floor as they planned.

The lawyer said, "Quick, give her something to drink!"

The commander barked for someone to bring her coffee.

The lawyer said, "We're fatigued, we haven't escaped the communists in order to now be questioned like this by the Führer's beloved army!"

A soldier entered the tent running in from the outside, panting, yelling something.

The boy tried to look as apathetic as he could, but was certain they were discovered—probably their hiding place had been found. It could have been a footprint, or the smell. Maybe the Nazi soldiers were cold, and grabbed the blankets covering the pit for warmth. The pit kept them safe for a year and a half, but it could also tell all their secrets and lead them to their deaths.

John Kiss | 433

They were standing in the military tent when the soldier entered, panting, yelling something.

The boy knew their ruse was discovered.

The soldier yelled something to the commander, and the other soldiers began running out of the tent. The commander looked at the boy and the three people who could be spies. He motioned to the translator and whispered to him. Then he got up, took his rifle, and ran out of the tent.

The translator eyed them suspiciously and had a strange smile--a sadistic smile of taking joy in their misery. He motioned to two soldiers guarding the tent's entrance.

One soldier walked to the boy and pushed him with the rifle. "Schnell!"

The lawyer helped his wife up and carried her as they all walked out of the tent, following the translator, a soldier on each of their sides, pointing the rifles at them.

They were going to murder them outside, in the forest.

The boy walked eerily, quickly, stepping to his grave.

They kept walking down the trail. The boy reasoned that they wanted to slaughter them away from the tent, where the corpses won't attract the rats and wild animals.

They arrived at a small army shack, a wooden structure which seemed like a portable jail, with one narrow window and a lock on the door.

The translator said something to the soldiers, who remained by the shack, locking the door on the four spies.

Then the translator shouted at them, "You do not fool me! We'll deal with you later."

Chapter 86: Light

Israel, 1990

Age 62

The scientist's hair turned white. He still had some occasional nightmares, but the butcher had completely disappeared from them.

Something in the scientist had changed. People who knew him, colleagues, friends, said he seemed happier. More determined. More powerful.

He, too, knew something had changed in him.

Now in his late sixties, he tried to seize life with more zest than ever. What was it? What had changed him?

First, the public recognition of the family who saved him. Having brought them to Israel and honoring them as Righteous Among The Nations was a life-changing moment for him. A circle was closed.

Then, there was the court case. Seeing the butcher took much of the sting off from the terror that used to grip him.

He began feeling more capable of speaking about the past. Of sharing with his family. His relationships with his children improved. They were finally able to ask questions about his lost years. And he answered. Sometimes he spoke very slowly. Often with moist eyes. With spare words. With long pauses. But he *spoke*. He shared his story.

And so, his three children understood him better than ever.

They understood his insistence that they finish eating everything on their plates. They understood why he always looked nervous around big crowds of people. They understood why he hated guns and why, in the few times they had gone together to the movies, he would get up and wait for them outside, shrugging his shoulders whenever they asked him why he had left.

They understood the screaming they heard from their parents' bedroom, their dad waking up at night. They understood his tendency to take food with him everywhere. They understood why he always preferred the stairs. Why he hated small places, elevators, rooms without windows, underground shopping malls. They understood his haunted look.

They understood why, when there was a very loud sound, he always shivered or jumped, even if it was just the sound of an airplane. They understood why he could watch no crime shows on television with them, nor suspense series.

More importantly, they understood why he was often remote, unable to laugh much or enjoy many things. Now that he had finally begun speaking of his past, forty years later, he was slowly becoming a different man.

One Passover, with his wife holding his hand at the head of the long table, he told his children and their spouses some of what he'd been through. "This," he said at the end, his voice trembling, "is my liberty. You are my liberty."

They all got up to hug him. His daughters cried in his arms. Only a few years before, this would have been unthinkable.

With the aid and encouragement of his wife, the scientist began giving interviews about what had happened to him. He spoke of the guilt he had been experiencing ever since the war. "I'm afraid," he said slowly to one reporter, "that I will never be able to explain the guilt I carried, and still carry…"

The reporter asked, "What guilt?"

"Guilt, guilt… for not having died there myself. Why did I survive, and all of my family perish? Why did I not go and try to save them? Why did I betray them?"

But his wife knew, too, that the more he spoke about this 'guilt,' the better he felt, and the smaller this 'guilt' became.

There were many triumphs to come. Vishay Intertechnology was now expanding beyond his wildest dreams. They had founded six factories in the United States alone, and kept innovating. In Israel, he opened two more plants, and was supplying work for thousands of people. They bought electronics companies that had failed to innovate, and revitalized them using Vishay's latest technology. Vishay plants opened in Mexico, China, Malaysia, Taiwan and India, as well as France, the Czech Republic, Italy and Hungary. His company was now appearing in such lists as the Fortune 500. He felt satisfied. He was continuing his grandmother's legacy.

But nothing satisfied him more than a call to hurry to the hospital. In the past, he had many sad calls from hospitals, calls after which he held the hands of those whom he called family, before they faded before him.

This time, upon receiving the call from the hospital, he was elated.

Chapter 87: Darkness

Poland, 1945

Age 17

I

They were locked in the small shack down the trail. The translator had left them there with two soldiers.

The night was not cold. A small window revealed the stars. They sat, awaiting their trial in the morning, awaiting their execution.

The uncle stood, seeming to examine the window, leaning against the wall.

They did not dare speak.

They could smell the cigarettes of the soldiers who spoke quietly to one another outside.

The boy knew their story sounded too fabricated. He knew that the soldiers could easily deduce that they had been hiding just a few feet from them all along, in the cabin.

He felt helpless. He looked to his uncle for encouragement, but his uncle's eyes were glazed.

That night was the longest the boy had ever lived through. He knew that at any moment one of the soldiers could, just for fun, take his rifle and shoot them. Like the butcher did so often.

None of them slept that night under the watch of the soldiers. They did not speak either. They were each in their own world.

The boy thought of his violin. Of how that soldier had smashed it against the wall.

He thought of his grandmother, of how she had lost her will to live. He thought of his sister and his parents.

He thought of his beautiful cousin, who was shot before the family crumbled. Maybe she was the lucky one.

Soon I'll be joining you, he thought. *Soon we'll be together.*

Outside the night's sky was bright with stars. The boy tried not to cry, knowing he would not see stars again. He had been fantasizing about stars. About seeing the skies again.

It was as if the heavens themselves had opened their celestial curtains, revealing a performance made only for him.

He did not feel the angst of the lawyer and the uncle, nor was he enamored by the seamstress, nor did he think of his own life as the end was approaching.

His heart, once burdened by the weight of suffocating floorboards, now knew no bounds. Yes, he would be shot shortly, but for now he could soar like a comet across the star-strewn sky. All his thoughts of revenge, all his sorrows seemed to drown in the shimmering beauty of fireflies pinned to the heavens.

He remembered running through the woods, running from his fate, in the winter the year before the last. Now his fate finally caught up to him, but he was not scared. He saw the skies, and rather than wanting to see them a thousand more times, he was just grateful for the opportunity to gaze at them one more time.

Then the colors of the dark sky began shifting, like tea to which a drop of milk was poured, stirring the night sky, drowning the stars in lighter blue, taking away from their glimmer.

The boy's breath stopped as he saw it. A sunrise. The translator said they will see no sunrise. He remembered running through the woods fearing the light of day would expose him. But now he basked in the glow of the morning light, prepared for it to be the last thing he would see.

II

Then there was light. Seventeen long months he had not seen the sky. He marveled at how beautiful the sky was above the trees. The transition of colors. He felt the universe beckoning him to witness. *See! Behold!*

The boy stood agog.

He heard the soldiers moving about outside. He knew the end was coming, but for once he did not fear it.

The translator came. He looked at the lawyer again. "Tell me again that 'story' of yours!"

The lawyer got up and told him the story.

The translator looked at them, shaking his head in disapproval.

"The commander wants you sent to the directorate." He paused. "They'll execute you there most likely."

An anguishing hour later, three soldiers with rifles opened the shack. The translator did not come with them—he probably did not want his hands soiled with their blood.

They escorted them through the woods, walking from behind them.

The boy realized this was where they would do it. In the woods.

CHAPTER 88: LIGHT

ISRAEL, 1990

AGE 62

Nothing satisfied the scientist more than a call to hurry to the hospital. In the past, he had many sad calls from hospitals. This time, he was happy to receive the call. Ecstatic.

Upon entering the hospital room, he hurried to kiss his daughter, who was lying on the bed with her baby. The scientist glanced with a congratulatory smile at his son-in-law. Then his gaze fixed on the baby girl in his daughter's arms.

"Dad," his daughter whispered, "look at her!"

She carefully handed him the precious little bundle, a tiny baby with eyes tightly shut, snug in her blanket. Her tiny fingers, delicate little lips, and calm demeanor overwhelmed him.

The scientist's wife looked over his shoulder and rubbed him on his back.

He cradled the delicate newborn girl in his arms, a realization blossoming within him that transcended the boundaries of all his scientific achievements: he was now a grandfather. Others might not fathom the depth of his emotions. Others may not have understood what it meant for him.

As he gazed upon the tiny miracle, tears streamed down his weathered cheeks uncontrollably. His daughter, lying on the bed, initially smiled at the sight of her father's overwhelming happiness. However, concern flickered in her eyes as his sobs intensified, and his trembling became more pronounced. She exchanged a worried glance with her husband, unsure of the torrent of emotions overtaking her father.

The scientist's wife, perceiving the need for a moment away from the overwhelming scene, gently took the baby from his arms and placed her in her mother's embrace. With a tender touch, she took her husband and said to his daughter and son-in-law, "We'll just go to catch a breath of fresh air." She guided her overwhelmed husband outside.

They exited the hospital, seeking solace beneath the comforting shelter of a small clump of trees.

In the serenity of the hospital courtyard, the scientist, still overcome with emotion, mumbled, "There is something I haven't told you." His wife offered a warm smile, assuring him of her unwavering support.

Closing his eyes, the scientist's chin quivered, and tears welled up once more. "A few days before I arrived at the hiding place at the maid's cabin," he began, his voice laden with the weight of untold history, "my family sought refuge in the attic of our ghetto apartment."

His wife nodded, encouraging him to continue.

He continued, revealing a secret burden that had remained hidden for far too long. "We could not bring the babies with us," he confessed, recounting the heart-wrenching dilemma faced by his family during the dark days of persecution. "Babies and toddlers—they were a problem in hiding places. Their cries would betray the family's hiding place."

As he recounted the painful decisions made in the shadow of survival, the scientist sobbed uncontrollably. His wife enveloped him in her arms.

"My aunt, my mother's sister, had a baby, and so did my father's sister, and my father's sister-in-law, they each had a baby too. We did not know how long we'd have to hide. All the people who were found at the ghetto were rounded up to be sent to the camps. But we knew the three babies…We knew the babies could…"

The scientist's voice broke as a lump formed in his throat.

His wife embraced him.

"We knew the three babies could not stay with us," he confessed, his eyes wide open, frightened, haunted. "We wanted to hand them to someone, but my grandfather refused...He said..."

Gasping for air, he struggled to convey the weight of his grandfather's sacrifice. "He said, 'I'm not hiding. I will be staying with the babies.'"

The scientist began sobbing.

He cried and breathed heavily in her arms... "I will be staying! ...with the babies!"

His wife hugged him more tightly, crying herself.

"We were in the attic. We hid there for a day, hearing the soldiers entering the apartments throughout the building and in all the buildings in the ghetto. Taking people to the trains. We kept hiding. After two days, when we finally came out, grandpa was gone. With the babies..."

She cried with him.

A few minutes later, he wiped his tears, but they wouldn't stop pouring down his cheeks. "I've never told this story to anyone. I always felt so...ashamed, for not having gone with him..."

She squeezed his hand.

Two hours later they returned to the maternity ward. He embraced his daughter and her husband. "This granddaughter," he said, "is the greatest gift you could ever have given me."

As the years passed by, more such gifts appeared for the scientist. Another baby girl, and a baby boy, then another baby girl...His three children were all married and eventually blessed him with nine grandchildren.

This was better than all the accolades he had received.

It was better than the moment his company had gone public on the stock market.

It was better than when he had received France's Legion of Honor, and thought about his late old mama and how she would have loved to be there. He sensed her there. He looked at his wife, in the audience, and at his children and grandchildren. He felt not only the old mama, but also his uncle, the maid, her husband, and his own parents and grandparents…so many dearly departed who were *all* there, in his heart, with him.

There were also accolades around the world. In America, the President of the United States congratulated him at a large ceremony hosted by the Electronics Association in Washington.

The scientist stood there, in front of the large audience, and told a story into the microphone, the story of how, when he was a child, his grandmother had told him, "It's not what you have that is yours, but what you give. No one can ever take away from you what you have given."

He knew that message to be true. Over the years, opening more and more factories, buying out failing factories and saving them, he had helped thousands of people. His small resistors and other inventions were incorporated into more machinery than his mind could grasp. But it was how his inventions helped *people* that mattered to him the most.

One day, years later, his son, now running the company, asked for a meeting with his father.

His son was acting strange. He told his father, now in his seventies, about a large European company in a dire situation. It was nearly bankrupt. "The thing is," his son said, "that we can, if we buy it, save thousands of people from unemployment. We can use Vishay's knowledge to revitalize it. It's a no brainer."

The scientist looked at his son. "Where is it?"

His son hesitated, knowing his father's answer. "I will tell you, Dad, but you'll have to think it through. It's a good factory, Dad—worth saving."

"Where is it?" the scientist said, agitated.

"Germany."

Chapter 89: Darkness

Poland, 1945

Age 17

I

The boy, the uncle, the lawyer and his wife marched through the woods; the soldiers walked behind them.

The boy knew his back was exposed to them, and that soon enough they would shoot him. *This is where they would do it. In the woods.*

He kept looking around, ready to launch and run the moment he heard the rifle being cocked.

They marched for a long time.

It felt odd to walk again—walk on his own two feet. Erect. He remembered this forest from playing here during the summers. So much had transpired since then. A lifetime. The memories of running through this forest now seemed like a fairy tale. Him, running freely, playing with his sister.

The trail widened. In the far distance he could see the village. But as they turned the corner, he dreaded what would come next as he saw another large military tent with several soldiers standing about. Upon seeing them, the soldiers stood up at once.

One of the soldiers who had escorted them from the shack now walked to the guards guarding the large tent. The two other soldiers stayed with them, pointing their rifles at them.

A few minutes later the soldier returned with another officer.

The boy knew their lie was going to be discovered now.

The officer looked at the four. He asked the soldier quietly, "Are they Jews?"

"They say that they're Poles who ran away from the Russians, but they don't have their papers."

The officer shrugged his shoulders. "Tell them to piss off. It is a militarized zone. If we see any of them back here again, they're dead."

The officer turned and walked away back into the tent.

The soldier, somewhat stunned by the leniency the officer showed, said to the lawyer, "Go away! Go! If you come back again we'll kill you!"

The lawyer nodded, hurried to grab his wife's hand, and started quickly walking down the trail. The boy and the uncle walked fast behind them.

The boy kept expecting to hear the sound of the rifle shooting at them, and kept tense, ready to take cover on the ground.

But no sound came.

They walked on the main trail. In the horizon the village emerged. They said nothing. They were afraid to speak. The village drew near. The boy looked behind him. There were no soldiers following them. The boy's eyes widened. *Could this be real?*

II

In the final months of the war, the boy and his uncle, along with the lawyer and his wife, lived in the city of Grodno. The city was already liberated by the Russian Red Army. They rented two rooms in a shared apartment which previously was the ghetto.

No signs of the boy's family, though.

Each day, they listened intently to the radio, crackling with news of the war coming from all over Europe.

The boy walked aimlessly in the city, still trepidacious,, waiting for his family to arrive.

April arrived. The boy was on his way to the train station when he was suddenly enveloped in a hug.

Has the time finally come? Has his family finally found him?

He pulled back from the embrace and came face to face with the maid. She held his face in her hands as she exclaimed, "You're alive!" He felt his stomach drop momentarily in disappointment but hugged her tightly nonetheless. *This woman saved his life.*

After a tearful reunion, he ran back to the apartment to tell his uncle. They invited the maid and her family to celebrate Passover in the small rented apartment.

This time the four Jews served the food.

They toasted, celebrating Passover and Easter together, but above them hung the specter of the war, which still went on in Germany, as the Allies were closing on Berlin.

The radio remained a constant presence, its announcements a backdrop to their conversation. They heard reports of the Allies closing on Hitler, each news broadcast fueling their anticipation. The air was thick with a mix of anxiety and hope.

By the time May arrived, the tension had reached its peak. One morning, the radio burst forth with the momentous news: Germany had been defeated.

People poured into the streets, their faces alight with joy and relief. Spontaneous celebrations erupted, with Polish flags being waved and strangers embracing one another.

The boy visited the train station daily. *They should return any day now.* Surely his father was strong enough to survive the labor camps? His cousins?

Surely someone survived.

One day he saw, on the train platform, a gaunt man with a shaved head, glaring back at him.

The man was standing too close to the edge of the platform. He stared at the boy and finally said, in that guttural unmistakable old Yiddish pronunciation. "Amcha—Your-People?"

"Amcha—Your-People!" the boy answered and looked aside, he did not want to be associated with the madman. He noticed the man's arm had a weird tattoo, like cattle, branded with a number.

The man's eyes were bulging from their sockets. "Family?" he asked the boy.

The boy nodded. "My uncle. I am waiting for the rest."

"An uncle. You are lucky," the madman said and looked at the train tracks below. "I've no one left."

The boy was reluctant to engage with the gaunt, shaved man whose skeletal head and nearly transparent skin, along with the scary looking tattoo made him look alarmingly fragile.

But the man began speaking again. He mumbled strange things about a camp. "Gas," He said. "Out the chimney they went."

The boy turned and ran away from the gaunt man, from the unreal words spoken by the walking dead.

That night, when the boy returned to the apartment, he heard the lawyer saying that another one jumped to the tracks.

III

As the weeks passed it became evident no one would return. No one from his entire family; cousins, uncles, aunts, grandparents—no one returned.

With every walk to the train station his heart calcified, becoming stone.

Someone needed to take revenge. For his family. He was now 17. He could do it himself.

During the evening in the apartment the uncle noticed his nephew was thinking of something intently. After an hour of prodding, the boy finally asked, "Aren't you thinking of taking revenge? For our family? For your wife? For your daughter?"

The uncle was silent, gazing at the street below. "The best revenge is massive success. We will start anew. We will succeed, we will grow, we will prove to all our detractors that we are worthy of everything they tried to take from us."

The boy thought his uncle naive.

He needed a gun. He knew his uncle would not help, he would forbid him.

He needed money for a gun. A good gun.

Horrible stories began emerging, like the one he heard from the crazy man at the station. Gas chambers. Crematoriums. Mass graves for thousands of people in the forests.

None of it surprised him. The Germans were industrious at everything they did. The Germans who brought the end of his family.

Now was his time to take revenge.

Chapter 90: Light

Israel, 1998

Age 70

The scientist tossed in bed.

Over the years, his company had bought dozens of failing electronics and communication companies, saving them from foreclosure, from shutting down. With their expertise in cutting-edge technology, his company saved thousands of employees.

He could do it anywhere in the world. They now had plants in seventeen countries. He would do it anywhere. Anywhere—except in one country.

Sixty years earlier, the company was a manufacturer of radios that spread Nazi propaganda throughout Germany and Europe. It was a company that manufactured and sold parts for the army, for the Air Force. The name *Telefunken* was synonymous with the radio. It was synonymous with Hitler.

Telefunken was Hitler's baby, and it was a manufacturer of the affordable Volksempfänger, the radio that spread like wildfire after the Nazis rose to power. It was through this radio that the Nazis spread propaganda, hatred of all non-Aryans, and especially of Jews. *Telefunken* broadcasted lies about the blood-thirsty Jews, the enemies of the German people.

And now his son—his well-meaning, ignorant son, wanted Vishay to buy *Telefunken*.

The right thing to do was to let it die. It was one of the last remnants of Germany's dark history.

But would punishing the workers satisfy his hatred? Letting the company die would mean letting thousands of jobs die in the process. Jobs that so many innocent people clung onto…Should they bear the weight of their ancestors' wrongdoings?

The scientist lay restless in his bed, surrounded by the suffocating darkness that mirrored the turmoil within him. The buyout proposal, like an unwelcome specter, haunted his thoughts.

As the scientist grappled with his conflicting emotions, memories of the Holocaust clawed their way to the forefront of his mind. The faces of those he had lost, the echoes of pain and suffering. Could he reconcile his own history with the act of saving a company of 2,000 employees from foreclosure? This proposition seemed to dance on the graves of his dear ones who were murdered by the outstretched fingers of Hitler and his brainchild.

In the silence of his sleepless night, he glanced at his sleeping wife. What would she say? She would probably tell him to save this German failing company, to assist its employees, and to forget the past. She would say that a new generation had risen in Germany, that these youngsters should not pay for their ancestors' mistakes.

In the shadows of the night he was no longer sure of what was right. He felt the weight of familiar ghosts lingering in his mind. The memories, etched in the deepest recesses of his soul, whispered to him in the quiet hours, questioning the path he was considering, seeking revenge.

His parents, sister, and extended family—those who had perished at the hands of unspeakable atrocities—seemed to cast accusing gazes upon him. In the haunting stillness of the night, he grappled with the thought that by entertaining the notion of saving a German company with roots in Hitler's regime, he would be betraying the very essence of his lineage.

The imagined voices of his forebears echoed in his mind, their spectral whispers filled with the pain and suffering they endured.

He questioned whether they would understand, whether they would see the transformation the German company—and society—supposedly had undergone. The scientist knew that, in their eyes, this act could be perceived as a betrayal.

How could he align himself with Hitler's brainchild, manufacturers of the propaganda machine that wiped out his people, that killed millions? His family stood before him, pleading for justice and remembrance. Their faces, frozen in time, seemed to reproach him for even considering aligning himself with an entity that once played a role in their tragic demise. From the shadows of the night he slowly realized what he must do. He would not tell his son, nor his wife, for they would not understand.

He knew he must not tell anyone.

CHAPTER 91: DARKNESS

POLAND, 1945

AGE 17

I

His uncle was busy, trying to earn some money, and at the same time procure his nephew a tourist's visa to France. He was elated when he told the young man, "you'll go, and I will join as soon as I can."

The young man nodded. He was determined to buy a gun. He suddenly remembered his grandmother's secret places in her house. He did not want to go to the house his grandparents lived in. Yet, revenge was a fuel so strong; it gave him the courage to visit the past.

He went to their house. The young man stepped over the threshold of his grandparents' once-grand home, now a mere shell of its former self. The air was heavy with the scent of neglect, and dust motes danced in the dim light that filtered through broken windows. As he surveyed the empty rooms, a tide of desolation washed over him.

Here his grandmother told him bedtime stories.

There she tucked him into bed.

Here she patted his cheek with her loving hand, making him feel that he was her favorite grandchild.

Here she and his grandfather blessed over the Sabbath bread.

Everything was taken. All the furniture, all the silver cutlery.

The chandeliers. The stained glass lamps. The bookcase. Old prayer books in Hebrew were thrown on the floor, swollen with water, completely destroyed.

As he ventured deeper into the recesses of the house, the memories continued to unfold like pages in a torn storybook, each room holding its own tale of love, laughter, and ultimately, loss.

In the grand hallway, he paused where faded photographs once framed were now on the floor. He picked them up: a picture of his uncle and himself ice-skating and a large picture of the entire family, dozens of them.

He held the two photographs tight to his chest.

He walked to the parlor where the large dining room table once stood. Here, amidst the echoes of laughter and tears, he had found solace in the enduring bonds that made him know that he belonged—a feeling he never once stopped to ponder, to cherish.

In the kitchen, where the lingering aroma of freshly brewed soup and home-cooked meals once filled the air, he could almost hear the symphony of clinking pots and pans as his grandmother worked her magic. Secret family recipes that he would never be able to pass down, now a lost history.

In the aftermath of his family's demise, the living room stood as a solemn witness to the ravages of man. Once adorned with the regal presence of a grand shelved library, it now bore the weight of emptiness, the furniture gone, its floors littered with hundreds of discarded books.

Books. His grandparents' pride. They lay there, thrown violently, broken. Abandoned, akin to fallen soldiers left on the battlefield. Their once-proud spines, now broken and battered, fallen, scattered, without dignity or reverence.

He lowered himself to the piles of books, as if hit in the belly. Two years earlier he was used to seeing the sight of corpses on the streets of the ghetto. It was a sight he could not behold, not allow in; he raised a titanium wall around his psyche to enable himself to walk past them on the way from the forced labor outside the camp, back to the cramped apartment.

However, now, the sight of the books caught him unprepared. Seeing them so ill treated, made him shiver.

Tears came to his eyes as his fingers traced the weathered spines, each touch echoed memories of the books he read with his grandfather—and the forbidden books he read with his grandmother. Romantic Tolstoy, compassionate Louisa May Alcott, emotional Dickens, witty Austen, adventurous Mark Twain, nonsensical Lewis Carroll, grandiose Victor Hugo. Each of these volumes contained the worlds in which he escaped during his childhood, often not understanding the language or the nuances, however nevertheless enchanted with the imaginary worlds.

In the stillness of the room, the scent of aging parchment mingled with the stale air, a haunting reminder of the passage of time and the fragility of existence. There was a violence in the abandonment of shelfless books, a brutality that echoed the horrors witnessed beyond the confines of the room. Like the corpses strewn upon the streets of the ghetto, the books scarred by disregard, their pages torn and tattered, their expansive stories left untold.

For him, the sight of these desecrated volumes stirred a profound sense of mourning, a recognition of the profound injustice inflicted in these lost years.

The pain resonated with a visceral ache that settled deep within his soul. Each broken spine, each torn page, was a silent cry for revenge, a plea for restoration. Someone had to pay for the desecration of the books.

And for that, the young man needed money.

He stepped away from the heap of literary corpses, determined to find the money.

His footsteps echoed hollowly as he ventured quickly through the house.

Wandering through the rooms, he made his way, slowly, feeling haunted, through the house. His grandmother's laughter. Her many naïve lessons, believing in the goodness of men. Her haunted eyes toward the end.

He remembered his grandmother had several places in which she hid money. He was so often with her as a young boy. She did not want him to know where she hid the money, but he paid attention.

The first place, behind the wardrobe, had been found when the wardrobe was taken.

The second place, under the floor of the kitchen, had also been discovered. The tile was discarded near it, broken.

The third place, above the kitchen sink, much to the young man's surprise, remained untouched. He pulled out a brown envelope and thumbed through, counting the zloty. There was enough for a gun, surely.

He placed the money back in the brown envelope and thanked his grandmother.

He was about to run out of the house when he saw something lying on the floor.

II

The young man was about to run out of his grandparents' house when he saw something on the floor. Amidst the barren mess, a lone object caught his eye.

A prayer hat, discarded carelessly on the floor. It was a yarmulke cap, the very one his grandfather used to wear.

With a mixture of sadness and reverence, he reached down and held it, his fingers tracing the familiar contours. It seemed inconceivable that amidst the looting and pillaging, this small memento had been overlooked.

No one had bothered taking it.

He dusted it off gently. He folded it and placed it in the brown envelope, with the photographs he found and the money.

He left the house filled with memories behind him, not looking back.

Surprisingly, it didn't take long to find a revolver.

A man who heard his loud, street-side quandaries led him to his cellar, full of guns. He left with a revolver and an arsenal of dozens of bullets; he felt invincible.

Chapter 92: Light

Hamburg, 1999

Age 71

I

The scientist landed with his wife and his son at the Berlin airport.

The cold German wind found him like a hardhearted greeting, reinforcing his purpose.

They met two dignitaries who exchanged polite and formal words with them. The scientist shuddered as he heard German spoken between the two.

They entered a car, and were taken directly to the conference center where the purchase signing ceremony was to be conducted. Local German news was going to cover the acquisition of the German *Telefunken* by the American *Vishay*.

The scientist knew what he had to do. His hand gripped the car's seat belt tightly.

His son looked at him strangely. Recently, his son noticed his old dad was acting unusually. Maybe it was old age, now in his seventies, his father was unpredictable, emotionally driven. He wanted to charter a private jet. He said he did not want German security searching through his things.

The son noticed his father was breathing heavily.

He knew of his father's difficulty in coming to Germany. They spoke about it, his father not as business-oriented as he had taught his son.. Now there was an element of emotion he did not understand—he was not used to seeing his father so agitated. His father seemed like he was hiding something—what was it? What was his father planning?

Unease gnawed at the son's mind. He hoped his old man was not going to do something silly.

The scientist forced a smile and stared at his wife. She smiled back at him, squeezing his hand.

She, too, was worried about her husband. He would seem to converse and nod when he was speaking, but he was not present. Something was eating at him. He was planning something.

She saw him looking through the window and mumbling to himself. She knew his heart was heavy with the weight of generations past. She knew they were now on the soil of a country stained by the shadows of history, the country that claimed her husband's family.

The driver slowed down as they entered a large parking lot by a large conference center. Many cars were parked outside. A television crew was unloading large tripod stands and heavy cameras.

They got out of the car. The scientist saw his son following the two dignitaries into the conference center. "I need my suitcase," he said to the driver, pointing at the trunk.

The driver did not understand.

The scientist breathed heavily. "Ich. Brauche. Meinen. Koffer," he said in German—the venomous language dripping like poison on his lips.

His son hurried back to the car. "Dad, what's going on?"

The scientist looked at his worried wife and son. "Nothing, I just need my suitcase."

"Dad, later, when we'll go to the hotel."

His father never shouted at him, but now his voice rose in anger. "I need my suitcase!"

The driver handed him the suitcase.

The scientist grabbed it and began limping forward.

"Let me take that for you," his son said, reaching for the suitcase.

"No!" the scientist said.

The scientist's wife calmed his son, "It is fine, he is just excited."

But the son was unsure. He knew his father well. Something was amiss.

II

The scientist carried his suitcase, tightly gripping the handle. He walked behind his wife and his son, who walked into the conference center.

Germany.

At the large hall people were gathering, local cameramen were setting up. Many German dignitaries were there, collecting under the big "Telefunken" sign.

He saw the large sign and immediately recalled Hitler in all of the speeches he saw as a child, how his father dismissed Hitler as a lunatic. A lunatic who laughed as his family was shot and gassed. The logo *Telefunken* was on every official state recording, appearing on the very microphone into which Hitler gave his venomous speeches.

His wife looked back at him, noticing him shaking, visibly trembling. When he saw her looking at him, he forced an unnatural smile.

She walked to him. "Is everything okay?"

He nodded, not looking in her eyes.

He followed the dignitaries, taking them onto the stage. But he was not ready. He still needed to take it out.

"I need a minute," he said, and walked off.

In a locked room, he opened the suitcase, and found what he was looking for.

CHAPTER 93: DARKNESS

POLAND, 1945

AGE 17

The young man packed the revolver carefully inside clothes, putting it in the small valise the uncle bought for him.

His uncle suspected nothing. He walked with him to the train station in the early morning—the same train station to which no one from their family returned. "You are lucky to get a visa to France. In Paris, go to a synagogue, try to get yourself settled, see if you can register to high school or university. I will get my visa and I will join you," he said.

The young man nodded. He said nothing.

The uncle noticed something was strange in his nephew. "Is everything okay?"

The young man forced a smile. "Sure."

The young man boarded the train to France. He waved goodbye to his uncle.

But a few minutes later, when the train pulled into the next station, the young man got off. He bought a ticket in the opposite direction toward the German border.

He boarded the train. Looking through the window, his heart became as hard as glass.

His grandmother funded the trip. In his mind, his grandmother encouraged him to go and save the honor of the family. "The babies! The babies!" she cried.

The last stop: Danzig. A German city that Hitler took back from Poland. The young man was ready. He'd do it there. In the heart of those Germans—in the heart of those Nazis.

They deserve pain, he thought, each and every one of them.

They've brought it upon themselves.

He would restore pride to his family.

To his sister.

To his parents.

To his grandparents.

To the forty people in his family who had not survived.

With every hour of journey he thought of the trains taking his family, and the trains returning empty.

The train stopped. Final destination, Danzig.

Chapter 94: Light

Hamburg, 1999

Age 71

The scientist walked slowly back to the conference hall. In his pocket, he had it.

It gave him a strange feeling of peace.

He had it since 1945 and kept it a secret. Now was the time to use it.

And so, with each passing moment, he steeled himself against the tide of anguish and resentment, drawing strength from the unwavering conviction that guided his path.

The conference hall was already full of a hundred German employees and their families. As he entered the stage, a sign of relief appeared on his son's face.

The scientist sat down at the long table with German officials. He saw his wife sitting in the front row, looking at him. Did she know? Did she guess? Did she know this was to be his victory? The revenge of his family?

The *Telefunken* logo stood behind him as well as on the pile of papers on the table before him. *Telefunken. Telefunken. Telefunken.*

The ceremony began. A dignitary spoke into the microphone in German. How befitting—the Germans always loved to hear their own voices.

The German officials began, first signing the contract before sliding the agreement to him. Cameras flashed as the heavy document was presented to him.

He felt his pocket burning.

"Dad…?" his son said.

The scientist looked at the crowd, at the German dignitaries.

"Dad, you need to sign it now."

The scientist looked down at the contract and the pen in front of him.

He was there but also elsewhere.

He paused for a long moment. He had to do this. A wave of memories flooded him.

He reached for his pocket.

His wife, sitting in the front row, looked at him, worried. *Was he okay? He seemed…*

"Dad?" his son asked again. All the dignitaries were looking at him. There was silence in the conference hall.

The scientist's hand trembled as he reached into his pocket.

The scientist knew of the plans for the following weeks. His son and his team had inspected the company, the production models, and the operations. The company was behind on the global market. It was only natural that its sales had plummeted. But with a few tweaks here and there, by embedding Vishay's technology, the company could soon become healthier, more profitable. His thoughts came back to his parents. He wished they could be there. And not only them but also his little sister who never got to grow up—his sweet little sister to whom he never said he loved her, his sister with her bright wit and moral compass, his sister whose laughter made him forget what he was upset about.

Was she shot in the forest, naked, tossed onto a mountain of bodies dug in the ground? Or was she gassed, naked, unable to breathe one more breath into her young body, choking, gasping for air? Was she with their mother? Was she on her own? What were his sister's last thoughts? Did she think of him?

"Dad!" his son shouted.

Chapter 95: Darkness

Danzig, 1945

Age 17

As the train ground to a halt in Danzig the young man awkwardly collected his valise, stuffing it under his arm and hurriedly made his way to the carriage door.

Disembarking brought a wave of sound as he entered the cavernous space. Making his way to the station exit, the echoing staccato of German words conjured the young man's fears of soldiers hunting him through the crowd. He quickly searched around him and confirmed it was just a delusion of a panicking mind. The young man focused on his task.

The crowd surged around him oblivious to his thoughts filled with murderous intention. He pushed forward.

Walking out of the station near a narrow river he noted his surroundings. The houses, built in a quaint German architectural style, were almost unblemished. It felt idyllic, as though untouched by the destruction unleashed in the war.. This place had rested peacefully while his family was slaughtered—while they sent their own sons and husbands to kill.

Finding an alley, he pressed against a building and opened his valise.

His heart was cold as ice as he reached in and loaded the gun. Full, six cartridges.

This would do.

He locked the revolver and put it in his pocket, then covered it with his coat.

Walking out of the alley and into the street, he asked an old lady where the city center was. She pointed, and he walked in that direction.

Finally, he arrived at a large square.

The square was filled with women, a few elders on a bench, and children playing.

He had hoped there would be more men.

It doesn't matter, he thought. It was these women's husbands. These children's fathers. These old people's sons.

He knew what they had done.

None of these people deserved to live, have a future when his family's future was taken away.

He put his hand on his revolver. It was cold.

His hand shook as he slid the gun out of his pocket.

"Don't do it, son," a familiar voice spoke to him in his head.

"Mama?" he asked, amazed, looking around, trying to find the voice.

"Yes, baby. Don't do it."

The young man was irritated. "Mama, I know what I'm doing."

"No, you don't. This isn't right. Where is the son I raised? "

The young man's hand trembled on the gun's handle. "Mama, I'm doing this for you!"

"Not for me, son."

"But, Mama, I must. Can't you see that I must?"

He turned around, looking at the families in the city square. He heard his mother's voice again.

"Baby, I love you so much. Do you remember how I kissed you that morning?"

"I do, Mama, I can't forget it…"

"Now take your hand off this hateful thing. Doing this will solve nothing."

"But, Mama—"

"Look at me, baby."

"I can't see you, Mama!"

"Yes you can. Do you see the woman there, playing with her child? I'm her. Do you see that older woman, there, on the bench? I'm her."

"Mama… Mama…"

"You can cry, baby… It's alright. I'm here…"

"Mama…"

"I'm right here, right here…."

II

In Danzig, the young man rose to his feet, valise clutched tightly in his hand.

Overwhelmed with anguish and regret, he went to the river and took out the revolver, emptying the bullets before throwing it into the water. He felt as though a tremendous weight had been lifted from his shoulders.

He walked toward the train station and headed to the ticket booth.

The woman behind the window asked, "Where to?"

"The City of Light," he said.

"I beg your pardon?" the woman asked.

He smiled for the first time in a long, long while. "Paris, France."

"There is an overnight train leaving in four hours."

"One ticket, please."

He was no longer a boy. He was seventeen—a young man.

As he waited on the platform holding closely to his valise. The war had sculpted him from a boy into a young man, chiseling away all innocence.

The young man stood alone on the platform, in the fading glow of twilight. Soon he would be there, in Paris, the city that had beckoned him like a siren.

III

Night descended like a velvet curtain, enveloping the station as the young man prepared for the nocturnal odyssey ahead, a journey that would take him past Poland, Czechoslovakia, Austria, Switzerland, and westward to distant France.

With a heavy heart, he fully accepted the bitter truth: his family would never return. The specter of waiting was replaced by a steely resolve to embrace the future on his own.

Did he hear something? A rumble of a train approaching, or was it just his imagination?

Chapter 96: Light

HAMBURG, 1999

AGE 71

His son shouted at him. "Dad!"

His hand shook as he reached into his pocket, finding it. He pulled it out. Since 1945, he had been carrying it, afraid to look at it, afraid the memories would flood him.

But now it was the moment.

His son's mouth opened as his father pulled out an old brown envelope.

The scientist, his fingers shaking, pulled out a small skull-cap. He put the envelope down and fingered the edges of the round white yarmulke cap in his fingers.

Had he been back in 1943, when German-occupied Grodno was already "Jew-free," he could have put this on, and walked the streets, counting the seconds until he would be shot.

Now he was in Germany. He slowly put the yarmulke on his head, like a gentle blessing, a palm of his grandfather's hand.

A murmur passed through the crowd.

It was this yarmulke that he carried with him all these years. He had chosen, back in 1945, when he threw the revolver into the river in Danzig, not to take revenge but instead to honor the memory of his parents.

Now, amidst the clamor of celebration, his eyes saw not the dignitaries, cameras, nor even his eager son and his worried wife.

His eyes saw *them*: the faces of those he had lost, the silent witnesses to a momentous occasion they would never see. In the quiet recesses of his heart, he carried their memory, a testament to the resilience of the family.

The crowd beheld him. He began reciting the old Hebrew prayer: "May it be Your will, O Lord our God, God of our ancestors, that You lead us toward peace, guide our footsteps toward peace, and make us reach our desired destination for life, gladness, and peace…"

The scientist's son looked at him, stunned. His father was not observant and rarely wore yarmulkes, nor did he pray, let alone in public.

As the scientist prayed, he looked at his wife sitting in the first row, trying to control her tears. "O Lord, may Thou hearken unto the voice of our supplication. Amen. "

A deep silence fell in the audience. With trembling hands, he reached for the pen.

In that fleeting moment, as he poised to sign his name upon the contract, he knew he was guided by the light of his ancestors' resilience.

A calm peace flooded him as he chose yet again the enduring power of hope in the face of darkness.

He breathed in and glanced at the audience. Here he was, wearing his grandfather's yarmulke. He thought back to the war, escaping the ghetto, fearing being recognized as a Jew as he fled the city to the forest. Yet here he was now, in the open, wearing his grandfather's yarmulke in front of a hundred German employees and their families. He whispered under his breath as he signed. "This is for you, Grandpa, Grandma… Mama, Papa…"

With his signature complete, suddenly, someone began clapping, breaking the silence. Then another joined in, and soon everyone applauded loudly. Cameras flashed. The dignitary beside him extended his hand for a handshake. "Thank you," he said earnestly, "thank you for saving Telefunken."

The scientist did not know what to say. He nodded and turned to his son. "Now you do good for this company, you hear me?"

"I will, Dad."

CHAPTER 97: DARKNESS

DANZIG, 1945

AGE 17

The distant noise grew louder. The thrum of approaching iron wheels heralded the arrival of his train.

His white knuckles gripped his valise. All he had inside were two tattered photographs, a small journal, a sufficient amount of zloty bills to last him in Paris for a few weeks, a scarf, a newspaper announcing the end of the war--a relic he wanted to keep forever; a few clothes, a piece of a shattered window from his grandparents' home, and a brown envelope containing his grandfather's precious yarmulke cap.

The train emerged, then slowed down and shuddered to a halt. The iron wheels grinding, screeching against the tracks like violins preparing for the grandest concerto.

Chapter 98: Light

Israel, 2011

Age 83

The German company *Telefunken* had now become a part of Vishay. It succeeded tremendously.

As the company grew, more people were hired. The old scientist was pleased to hear his son's reports. He knew Vishay was in good hands. It was healthier and stronger than ever.

But *he* was not.

Now in his eighties, the old scientist's body was tired.

One day he collapsed in the kitchen. His wife immediately called an ambulance. He was rushed to the hospital, unconscious.

In the hospital, the doctors examined him. Seeing the look in the doctors' eyes, his wife hurried to call his three children.

The doctors said he was in a coma.

The wife was incredulous—could they not see he was just in a deep sleep?

Chapter 99: Darkness

Danzig, 1945

Age 17

The young man took his valise and climbed on the train, wanting to leave the past behind, to forget that night escaping from the ghetto, two and a half years earlier, begging for shelter, to forget it all.

The young man climbed into the empty train wagon, his valise clutched tightly in his hand.

He claimed his seat in the empty night train, stowing his valise above and casting a lingering gaze through the window upon the platform's edge.

He heard the high-pitched screech of the whistle, signaling it was about to leave Poland, the young man's home. Paris was waiting.

Chapter 100: Light

In the hospital, the old scientist lay in a coma.

His wife hugged his children—*her* children.

She told them how he had collapsed.

Soon the grandchildren came, the entire family joined to be by his side. Hushed conversations. Doctors. Tests.

The wife held her old husband's hands. *She wasn't ready to let him go.* She whispered to him. "Wake up, please. For me."

But he did not wake. He breathed slowly, his chest gently rising and falling. Only his eyelids moved ever so slightly.

He was not there. He was floating somewhere, and violins were playing.

He was floating somewhere. Violins were playing.

Sun. Its rays warmed him, blinding him with its kindness.

Music.

People—so many people.

He saw below him a crowd collecting on a pier—a large platform. *Was it a train station?*

From above, he glanced over the people, surprised to find out that he actually recognized his mother's late aunt—and his grandfather's father! Did he not die when the boy was only three?

Next to them stood the kind milkman who used to give him candies. And the first grade teacher, who praised him in his mother's ears!

Faces he recognized from his childhood, from his adulthood, even from recent years; people who he thought had passed long ago. *What were they doing on this train platform?*

The morning sun rose above the station, casting a warm glow over the gathering crowd. Suddenly he felt a rush of anticipation coursing through him as he saw *her*.

It had been years since he'd last seen his grandmother. Memories flooded him, of her gentle touch, her comforting presence. And now, here she was—amidst the throng of people, her face radiant with delight.

DARKNESS

The young man sat in his seat as the train surged forward. *Train.*

Two years earlier the trains took his kin to one destination: death. His entire family had embarked on such journeys bound for their death. Now he was reborn, a phoenix rising from the ashes.

LIGHT

His grandmother! His heart skipped as he saw her, resplendent in her meticulously chosen attire, just as he remembered her from their visits to the soup kitchens and the homes of the elderly. She wore her pearls, gleaming in the morning light. It was as though time had stood still.

With a sense of disbelief mingled with joy, he watched her interact with those around her, her smile infectious as she exchanged pleasantries with old friends and acquaintances. "Soon, soon," she said and kissed old aunts and uncles. "Soon."

And then, as if sensing his presence, she turned towards the train tracks, her gaze locking onto the distance with an intense love that took his breath away. "He will be coming soon, I know," she whispered to the man beside her, her voice barely audible over the violins. But the boy heard every word, and his heart swelled with joy.

Who was she waiting for? And when was he to come?

The man next to her said, "I bought him these chocolate bonbons. Rubenzahls!"

The old scientist could not believe it! This man was none other than his grandfather! *So young, so strong! So tall and imposing!* He saw great pride in his young grandfather's eyes. "He had some good Vishay sense in him after all."

The violins played louder. The boy's orchestra teacher and friends from his childhood were all playing. Unlike decades earlier, they were now playing *harmoniously*, in perfect unison. The orchestra teacher seemed elated. One violin seat remained empty, and the boy saw his own old violin, as if it was never broken—it looked strong, sturdy, its neck intact, its lacquer varnish shining in the morning sun, its strings perfectly stretched: ready.

He longed to join the symphony of strings, yet an invisible barrier held him captive, kept him but as a mere spectator, forbidding him from partaking.

His gaze swept over the revelers until it alighted upon *her*. His mother.

DARKNESS

He suddenly stood as an urge tore through him—to feel the movement of freedom, to be one with it. With a deft hand, he unlatched the window, creaking the narrow shaft open allowing the cold wind to rush into the empty wagon.

He slid out his hand through the narrow window. The cold air whispered secrets against his skin, stirring his soul as it danced through his outstretched fingers. He closed his eyes and thanked his good fortune. He was alive. *He was alive!*

LIGHT

His sweet mother!

She had not aged a bit—on the contrary—she shimmered with the same radiance as when she was pregnant with his sister. Clad in her cherished dress—the soft green dress with crimson blossoms reserved for special occasions. *That dress!* A relic of bygone spring days from his childhood.

With graceful poise, his mother extended her hand amidst the bustling platform, offered to a dashing young man sporting spectacles.

Could it be? Could this be his father?

The old scientist noticed the twinkle in his father's eyes as he adjusted his eyeglasses, securing them upon his nose before clasping his young wife's hand.

Yes, it was indeed his father. His hair had not turned gray yet. Embracing his wife, they danced upon the platform. As they waltzed amidst the crowd, his father whispered softly to his beloved: "Soon."

"At last," his mother exclaimed, unleashing a cascade of laughter, long withheld in anticipation, her laughter bubbling forth with expectation long pent-up.

"Let us dance for him when he comes," his father declared, guiding their steps with sweeping fervor.

"Indeed we shall!" she proclaimed, twirling and spinning, her laughter ringing out in joyous abandon.

Emerging from behind his mother's billowing skirts, his little sister appeared, her ponytail bobbing with each lively step. No longer gaunt from the trials of war, but plump with happiness. "Mama, look! I dance just like you! Papa, will he dance with me when he arrives?"

How the boy had forgotten her infectious happiness! He wanted to grab and hug his sister, to enfold his sister in an embrace, but like a bird over endless sea, the boy could not land, flying solitarily, unable to descend.

Bright sun shone from above. On the platform below, a tall man stepped out from the excited crowd and winked, bowing gallantly before the boy's father. "Would you allow me the honor of one dance with my sister?"

His uncle! His uncle looked so strong—the boy had forgotten his uncle ever looked so youthful. There was no cancer sickness in him, no sorrow, and as he took the boy's mother in his arms they swirled together.

"You did well," the mother commended her brother.

His uncle responded with a knowing smile, "As promised."

His mother's laughter filled the air. "What took you so long!"

The boy wanted to join them—countless cousins, long-unseen aunts and uncles, familiar kind neighbors. The old mama and her son, the headhunter who brought him to America, the elderly couple in the kibbutz, friends from his class—people who the boy thought died years ago!

He wanted to remain there, to never have to leave.

"Dad? Dad, can you hear me?"

DARKNESS

An hour later the train slowed down. The border. The edge of Poland, leaving his home country, the country that no longer was home. The train slowed to a stop. The border police officers climbed on the train wagon, their footsteps thumping loudly, in rhythm with the young man's anxious heartbeat.

Will he be able to continue his journey?

LIGHT

A voice from above seemed to interrupt the idyllic party on the platform. "Dad?"

He felt his body move around. A needle pressed into a distant arm, miles away, telegraphing him of pain. Cold metal surfaces touching his chest. Liquid—no, gel—smeared on his belly, then a cold instrument rolling over it.

He wanted to return to the train platform.

He heard a voice coming from far away. "Dad, can you hear me?"

DARKNESS

"Passport!" the border police officer shouted at him.

The young man handed his Polish passport.

"Where to?"

"France," the young man choked out. "Paris."

He saw a flicker of jealousy on the officer's face. The officer examined his passport.

The young man's heart pounded.

LIGHT

The old scientist wanted to remain on this train platform forever, to descend and land among them—his kin—his family, to be enveloped in a never-ending hug by his mother and father.

"Dad? Dad, can you hear me?"

Pain in his chest.

"Dad, I'm right here. We're all here, the entire family is here, praying for you. Dad, please wake up!"

His daughter's sobs pierced his heart.

Why was she crying?

Could she not see the perfection of the celebration? Could she not behold the dancing, the eager crowd of happy people, the violins?

He heard his wife. "Sweetheart? Please wake up. Everyone is praying for you. Even in Poland, the children of the maid… they're all praying for you. Please return to us. I beg you."

His wife. He owed it to her.

But how does one return?

He tried to open his eyes but could not.

With a mighty effort, he struggled to stir, summoning every ounce of willpower, he strained to move.

He struggled again to pry open his heavy eyelids, as if they were weighted down by stones, imprisoning him in darkness. Could he ever lift the floorboards to see the light of day?

Light stung his eyes.

He heard his wife exclaiming. "He's waking up, he's waking up! Call the doctor!"

DARKNESS

The young man looked at the Polish border officer. After a long moment, the officer handed the passport back and walked to another passenger car.

Relieved, the young man let out a sigh. The train began moving forward, carrying him into Czechoslovakia. Mountains shone in the darkness, a grand lake spreading below. The shimmering waters of the lake mirrored the moon above.

LIGHT

"He's back!" his wife called.

Blurry, bright light stung his eyes. Through the mist of pulsating brightness he saw a beautiful face. An angel smiling at him. *His wife.*

"You're back!" she whispered, shaking her head with gratitude. "I knew you would come back."

A distant memory gnawed at his heart: a train platform full of an expecting party. *Was it a memory? A dream?* It felt so real—more real than life itself.

He had seen them—his parents—so clearly! How happy they were! He *had* to tell his wife.

His mouth was unyielding to his command. He tried moving his lips, but they did not respond.

His wife leaned closer to his mouth. "Are you trying to speak?" She tilted her ear to his mouth. "I am listening, sweetheart!"

His voice would not give. He tried to shout, scream it out. Finally, he murmured. "I…"

"Yes?…"

"I saw…" he inhaled, sharp knives piercing his chest. "I saw them."

"You saw *who*?" she looked at him, confused.

"My parents… They—seemed—so—happy."

His wife's eyes welled up with tears. She nodded, her lips quivering.

Darkness

The young man was relieved when the train arrived in Switzerland four hours later. One last country before France. Border control officers again asked for his papers. He showed his passport, his breath steady this time, amazed at the ease of travel from place to place without needing to hide, without searching for a hidden pit to bury himself in.

As the train sped through Switzerland, the young man, face glued to the window, wondered what it would be like *there*. In Paris.

Paris—a distant dream soon to be within reach. The train journey had carried him farther than he had ever ventured. He had never traveled so far away from home.

Paris, with its iconic Eiffel Tower, beckoned to him like a lighthouse.

Light

An authoritative voice. "Ma'am, can I have a word with you alone?"

"What is it, doctor?"

"Your husband—his organs…I'm terribly sorry."

"What, Doctor?"

"His organs are rapidly failing him." A long pause followed. "I'm really sorry."

The old scientist heard crying, sobbing around him. "Doctor! Isn't there anything you can do?"

"His condition has taken a severe turn. He is experiencing multiple organ failure. His lungs and liver, kidneys… They are all failing, I'm afraid we have exhausted all available medical interventions."

"How long, Doctor?"

"Given the extent of organ failure and the… complexity of his situation, I believe he has only a few hours left with us. I am sorry."

Why was everyone so sad?

Did they not see the celebration?

Could they not hear the violins?

Could they not see his entire family—all of them—at long last?

DARKNESS

When the train crossed into France in the early morning, he showed the border officer not only his new Polish passport, but also his visa. He hoped he would be allowed to enter.

The officer returned the documents to the young man. "Bienvenu en France."

Welcome. To. France.

LIGHT

Crying. Someone was telling a story.

His granddaughter's voice. "Do you remember when grandpa insisted on teaching me math? How did he help prepare me for that exam? The patience he had!"

Beeping of monitors, squeak of gurney wheels, clatter of medical equipment.

His daughter's voice.

"We were in the desert somewhere, and he decided he must find his parents' friends from Poland. They immigrated to some God-forsaken kibbutz. There was no chance of us ever finding them. And then, lo and behold…"

Hiss of oxygen tanks, sliding of privacy curtains, clang of metal trays.

His son's voice—"Then he suddenly pulled out this yarmulka, and all these Germans looked at him stunned, and he began praying in front of everyone—can you believe it?"

He heard laughter, he heard sniffling tears.

His wife's voice. "He came to pick me up at the library, and we went to the beach. He was such a gentleman…"

How long has he been lying there? He lost track of time.

Then warmth near his ear. It was his wife's lips. "Sweetheart, can you hear me? I have something important to tell you."

DARKNESS

The young man recited those three words as if they were a prayer. In two hours, he would arrive in Paris.

The train sped up. He recited the words again: "Bienvenue en France." Though the language was foreign to his ears, he vowed to make it his own.

The young man sat by the window, his face pressed against the cool glass, eyes wide with wonder. He looked at the bright sky. Back home, the light was soft, almost timid—peeking shyly through the clouds, casting muted shadows on the worn cobblestone streets. It was a light that never fully revealed itself, always retreating behind a veil of mist.

But here, as the train sped further, everything seemed to change. The light in the sky grew bolder. The sun, no longer hesitant, poured down with a warmth he had never felt before, flooding the fields in golden hues. The light was dazzling, almost overwhelming, as if the sky itself had opened wide to welcome him into a new world.

He was leaving behind a world of shadows, stepping into a realm where the light embraced him. An adventure, a new beginning.

LIGHT

His wife's voice. "I want you to know… I want you to know that it's okay," she whispered. Tears fell from her eyes. "If you must leave, you can… I will be alright. I promise."

Really?

He managed to open his eyes.

Their eyes met.

His vision became blurry, overwhelmed by his wife's love. A thick lake filled his eyes. He wished he could speak. His lips were numb.

She looked at him, melting into his eyes, like in their wedding in Jerusalem thousands of years earlier, when he allowed himself to love again.

"It's okay," she repeated. "If you *must*—you can go. If you have to, I will understand. I'll be okay. I promise."

She kissed him, a long, gentle kiss.

Leave.

She promised.

She will be okay.

He tried to move his heavy head, and to his surprise, he felt he could do it with great ease. He suddenly felt much lighter, nimble, free. It was the brightest light he had ever seen.

The train sped through France. He was almost in Paris. He pronounced the name as the French did. *Pari. Pari! Pari.* He savored the word on his tongue, rolling it like a fine wine. *Pari—* the city of dreams.

The rhythmic hum of the train wagon gradually diminished as it eased into the bustling station. The young man glanced eagerly out of the window. He saw many people on the platform excitedly waiting to greet their loved one—waiting for him.

AUTHOR'S NOTE

Over a decade ago, my father pressed me to watch a documentary by journalist Haim Hecht, *The Final Victory: The Story of Felix Zandman* (2005). The film was 58 minutes, tracing the life of Felix Zandman through research and personalized interviews—of his 17 months of hiding, and down the path that led him to become a world renowned scientist. It was inspiring, just like every perspective wrung from the Holocaust's victims, but there was something more to Zandman. For me, the connections between our own heritage and religious migration were mind-blowing. How could a man as mortal as myself survive something of such lengths? This ultimately put me on a journey of my own, as I began research into Felix Zandman's legacy.

I've read and reread an exhaustive series of articles and books on Zandman, let alone the events of the war. There are so many great reads surrounding everything—all of which capture different elements of the same outcome which I would soon hope to capture. Great sources for those interested include *Never the Last Journey* by Felix Zandman himself, both in Hebrew and English, and *We Were Just People* by Bill Tammeus. My research led me to what his life was about outside of the holocaust, like his work and inventions—neatly compiled into Zandman's own publications such as *Resistor Theory and Technology: Revised Printing,* and *Photoelastic coatings (SESA monograph ; no. 3).* Though complex, they were invaluable to my own research and understanding of Zandman's accomplishments, of which the journal, "Business America," accomplished elaborating on in its tenth volume. There is so much on Felix Zandman, on his company Vishay, in his insights as the founder of an Inter technology global high-tech manufacturer, in his life in general, it becomes hard to not share relevant titles: Bertram Korn's "Survivor Triumphant: Felix Zandman's life story is a saga of success" in the *Jewish Exponent*; Peter Clarke's "Felix Zandman, Founder of Vishay, Dead at 83" within *Electronic Engineering Times*, Mordecai Paldiel's *Saving the Jews*, and Zandman's own "2008 Speech to March of the Living."

While independent studies were fantastic and informative, the lack of primary sources regarding Zandman were disheartening. I knew that if I were really committed, I could find a way to accrue real accounts and accurately retell Zandman's story—so I contacted the Zandman family directly. I spoke to Ruta, Zandman's late and wonderful wife, first. How fortunate I was not not only to have gotten the chance once, but what would turn into several times! She was the embodiment of joie de vivre, dedicated to her husband's work and history, keeping him alive through memory and practice alike. Ruta had personally played such a pivotal role in both their business and personal lives, revealing a lens to the Zandman family that I hadn't even known existed. Throughout our talks, Ruta told me of so many things reflected within this novel. Rather notably included the influences in her husband's life, and the importance of figures like his grandmother Tema, who taught him that "the only measure of wealth is what you give away." I was—and remain—enamored by Zandman's tale, in which I was thereby required to impress my own rendition of upon. But, there were many challenges which I faced.

I took many liberties in the writing of the novel itself. In order to successfully recreate Zandman's story in a way that not only preserved his legacy, but creatively informed about the fictions of trauma. For one, I tried to avoid using names, which led me to several complications and the need to simplify merging characters. The seamstress required further research into her personal past, as she was originally just defined by her place as a wife. Knowing well by now the true impact women seldom are acknowledged for, I made sure to expand upon her depth. I gave her life through her history in seamstress work which had guided her up until that point. In addition, though some might find it odd, I kept the boy's unbridled fascination with her beneath the floorboards—as she played a large role in his developing life away from the world. In similar taste, there was a fifth woman that had lived in the pit I did not mention, where I was forced to pick and choose, therefore combining her among other characters to free other aspects of the book.

And it wasn't just the characters' roles I struggled with. I also changed the timelines, limited by the freedoms which written narrative could offer. For example, the temporality of the court case. I moved it two decades back in time for not only the intrigue and suspense, but to shepherd the family's major events within a reasonable timeline to be produced in a novel. In a similar manner, there were also moments with setting and mood I needed to reengineer, like in France where Zandman had landed. The reality of things was so unbearably dismal in other authors' words. But instead of being guided by their poetic sorrow, I picked at the flecks of hope that had been hidden by the loom of tragedy. As a result, life was given to characters like the moneychanger and the old mama. Close to my heart, the old mana is based on personal recollections of my own, from matriarchal figures in my family that guided me in ways reminiscent between her and the boy. I knew that if I were to write this novel, my whole heart would be smeared in between the pages to give it life.

In the end, I created my own nod to the Zandman legacy. A gesture of respect and acknowledgement to what should remain an undying tale of warning and life, a book that represents tears I have shed in my journey of discovery, and ultimately reflects the terror of war within a generation still alive. A novel that ultimately exists because one day what had started as a recommendation, grew to be a fascination and role model in its own right. A story that puts hope within fear.

John Kiss

SHORT BIOGRAPHY OF FELIX ZANDMAN

Felix Zandman, May 7, 1928 — June 4, 2011

Felix Zandman was the founder and CEO of Vishay Intertechnology — one of the world's largest manufacturers of electronic components.

Felix was born in Grodno in the Second Polish Republic (now Belarus) and lived in Kresy until the Nazi-Soviet invasion of Poland.[1] Following Germany's Operation Barbarossa in October 1941, he arrived at the age of 14 at the Grodno Ghetto (liquidated by the Nazis at the end of 1942) with his family. He survived the

Holocaust thanks to a righteous Polish family, Jan and Anna Puchalski, who hid him and three other jewish refugees for 17 months.

One of them, his uncle Sender Freydowicz, taught him trigonometry and advanced mathematics in the long hours of darkness.[2] The advancing Soviet Army liberated them in July 1944. He stayed with other survivors in Poland until he was able to immigrate legally to France in the summer of 1946.

From 1946 to 1949 he studied physics and engineering at the *University of Nancy* in France. In parallel, he was enrolled in the Grande École of Engineering, *ENSEM* (École Nationale Supérieure D'électricité et de Mécanique). He received his PhD in physics at the *Sorbonne*, on the subject of photoelasticity.

After finishing his studies, Zandman worked initially for two years as a lecturer at the École de l'Air, the French Academy of Aeronautics.[3] He then worked as an engineer in his specialty field of voltage measurement for a publicly owned company that manufactured aircraft engines.

In 1956, Zandman presented his methods and self-developed instruments for the first time in the United States. He was eventually employed by Tatnall Measuring Systems in Philadelphia as director of basic research. Initially, he concentrated on measuring the development of his case, voltages of optical coatings.

In 1962 Felix was awarded the Edward Longstreth Medal from the Franklin Institute.[4] That same year he started his path as an entrepreneur. Initially, he developed a temperature-resistant electrical resistor. His employer, however, had no interest in the marketing of this invention, which led Zandman to found Vishay Intertechnology.

A relative of his, Alfred P. Slaner, provided financial support for the initial funding. Among its first customers were the US Army and NASA. Zandman helped develop shunt resistors for NASA's first satellites.[5]

The company developed into a Fortune 500 company with many subsidiaries and over 22,000 employees worldwide. Today Vishay Intertechnology is a publicly traded company with a market capitalization of over a billion dollars. It trades on the New York

Stock Exchange under the initials VSH.[6]

In April 2008, Felix Zandman attended the March of the Living, where he shared the story of how he was rescued by the Catholic Polish Righteous Among the Nations, Jan and Anna Puchalski. Felix told his story to thousands of young students from around the world who had gathered in Auschwitz-Birkenau to observe Holocaust Remembrance Day.[7]

In 2009 Felix was awarded the Lifetime Achievement Award from the National Electronic Distributors Association (NEDA). NEDA has presented its Lifetime Achievement Award only five other times in the 70-plus-year history of the association. Zandman received the award in recognition of his successful career as a scientist, inventor, entrepreneur, and corporate leader in the electronics industry.

In the ceremony, it was cited that "Dr. Felix Zandman's breakthroughs have transformed the electronics industry."[8]

Felix's second wife, Ruta Zandman, played a pivotal role in getting him to speak about his experiences during the Holocaust. She said in an interview, "We passed days and nights [of him recounting his memories to me], that were extremely difficult…with a lot of crying and pain…"[9]

"Over time I told him it was impossible that his own children won't know everything that you've been through. I suggest that in our many travels, you will speak, and I will record or type, and we'll put together some booklet to describe your experiences." [10]

Later, with the support of his wife, Felix joined hands with the talented writer David Chanoff. Together they wrote an autobiography titled "Never the Last Journey," published in 1995. The book has been translated into eight languages. [11]

In an interview, Felix said, "I never dreamed of money, I never dreamed of becoming a big boss… All I dreamed about was to be a good engineer, and to invent something that could help others."[12] Apart from the awards cited above, he was awarded the Best Strategic Investor Award from the Israel Manufacturers Association (awarded by the President of Israel); the Order of Merit for Research and Invention (France), and the Legion of Honor, France (awarded by the President of the Republic of France).[13]

THE MAID AND HER HUSBAND:
ANNA AND JAN PUCHALSKI

Anna and Jan Puchalski were the Polish husband and wife who lived in the village of Lososna in north-eastern Poland on the outskirts of Grodno (now 20 km into Belarus) during the Nazi German occupation of Poland. Together, they rescued Polish Jews from the Holocaust, including escapees from the ghetto in Grodno before its brutal liquidation.[14]

At the onset of World War II, Jan Puchalski worked at a tobacco company, where he earned a small salary. The Puchalskis resided as innkeepers in a summer cottage, in the Lososna forest. The cottage was owned by an entrepreneurial Zandman family who leased similar cottages to city tourists before the war, with Grodno's reputation as a retreat, confirmed by its century-old summer palace of the Polish kings. The Puchalskis were very poor, having to support five children: 15, 16, and 17-year-old daughters and two toddlers, aged one and two years old.

On the evening of the Nazi German murderous raid on Grodno Ghetto, which took place on February 13, 1943, six Jews who escaped showed up at Puchalskis' door. Among them were much-loved Felix Zandman of the Zandman family (age 15) who used to play with their children before the war, Sender Freydowicz (his uncle) who lost his wife and two children to the Nazis, Mottel Bass, a lawyer who knew Sender, and his wife Goldie, and two more Jewish fugitives.[15] The latter two soon left, and the four remained in hiding with the Puchalskis for 17 months. Meanwhile, the ghetto in Grodno was razed by the Germans with all of its 29,000 Jews deported in Holocaust trains, and exterminated in the gas chambers of Auschwitz and Treblinka.

At first, the four hid outside the house in a cellar, which was not safe enough, with the Nazi threat of the death penalty looming over everyone, including the Puchalski children.[16] Subsequently, with the help of the family, a dugout was built under one of their two bedrooms. The dugout was very small. The entrance was through a narrow opening beneath the bed, and covered with wooden floorboards. An air duct was made leading out to the garden with an opening covered under the bushes. For added security, Jan Puchalski moved the dog kennel to that place.

Mottel Bass, a lawyer by profession, had some money, which helped the Puchalskis with their new expenses.

In July 1944, a mighty battle raged around the River Niemen, north of Grodno. The Red Army eventually took over the river's southern bank, pushing some 100,000 Wehrmacht troops towards central Poland. The four Jews were still hidden in the pit underneath the Puchalskis' house. The retreating troops ordered the Poles to evacuate the house, leaving their hidden guests without food. They had no choice but to forage at night for food, with Germans all around them. After walking a few yards, they got caught. They told the Germans that they were escaping the Bolsheviks on foot, and that they had been marching from the forest. The Germans were convinced and let them go.[17]

When the war ended, Felix Zandman was a broken man, both physically and mentally. He went back to Janowa Puchalski, who treated him like a mother would, feeding him and helping him regain his strength.[18]

After the Liberation, Felix Zandman and Sender Freydowicz emigrated to France. They kept in touch with the Puchalskis, and according to Felix, "We were like one family." In 1986 Zandman submitted his testimony to Israel's Holocaust Museum Yad Vashem with other survivors. As a result, in June 1986 the Puchalskis were posthumously awarded the title of Righteous Among the Nations. A year later, on June 14, 1987, their surviving children visited Jerusalem and planted a tree in the Garden of the Righteous at Yad Vashem. In the ceremony Felix remarked: "The Puchalskis never lost courage, never. We lost courage. They built our morale up." [19] Felix concluded: "In our Bible it says that man is made in the image of God. For me the Puchalskis are such people."[20] One of the Puchalskis' grandsons works today in Vishay USA as a successful engineer.

Testimony by Felix Zandman

From the archives of the Yad Vashem Holocaust Museum, Israel:

"...So we were four. And we were like that for quite a time. There were problems of 'how to live in a civilized society of four people, completely enclosed, without light, without killing each other...

"My uncle, of blessed memory, was a very intelligent man; he immediately installed a system of law and order. He said: 'We are here to survive. We may be here for months and months, God knows for how long. We have to make sure we live like civilized people, so we are not ashamed of each other when we leave, and we don't tear up each other alive.

"'So, number one: no sex.' So there was nothing.

"'Number two: continuously change the place where you lie down.' This was to make sure that nobody got a better place to rest than others. So every two hours there was a rotation.

"'Number three: a wise division of food…'

"[and so as] not to get crazy in the hole, my uncle taught me math….

"She [Anna Puchalski] did something that was absolutely out of the ordinary. You speak about heroism, heroism in a battle — somebody gets wounded, you jump, in two-three minutes you pull him out from the fire, big deal, and you get a medal for that. Big hero, right? Here, they risk not only their lives, or her life, but the lives of the children! And it's not for five minutes, it was for 17 months! 24 hours a day! Terrible. And they did it."

Acknowledgements

This book was a labor of love. It took nearly a decade to complete, and, as I keep incorporating reader's suggestions, it is still a work in progress.

People often say that writing is a lonely profession, and it's true, but it can also be a brilliant party filled with interesting, amazing guests who speak in a shorthand that only a few understand. To my tribe of proofreaders, editors and co-authors who are always willing to give my manuscripts a quick read. I couldn't have done it without you—and more important, I wouldn't have wanted to.

I would also like to thank Ruta Zandman and the family of the late Dr. Felix Zandman, whose generosity was an unexpected gift in the writing of this novel. Ruta took time out of her busy schedule to help me make the novel as accurate as possible. I am forever and profoundly grateful. Of course, any and all mistakes (and creative licenses) are my responsibility alone.

It literally takes a village of dedicated people to make a single book live up to its potential. I have been fortunate to work with some truly incredible individuals. Ky, Alex, Nadun, Shwetha, Alayna, Sydney, Ilana, Nermina, Genevieve, Theo, Minnah, Josh, Una, Sam, and Ray. Thanks to all of you for your precious edits. A special shout-out to Kimberly French, who changed the course of my career and helped me find my voice.

To the folks at *YourBookTeam*. Your support and enthusiasm has had a profound impact on my career and my writing. Thanks to Birhane, Kim, Jill, for your tireless enthusiasm and your enduring friendship. For the Graphic Design team: Arfin, Moaray, Sarim, Hanardy, Haejin

David Tsoury of Small Heroes, Motti Abramovitz, Adi Lev, Ron Rivlin, Joe Woolf, John Zarobell, Daniel Edward, Craig Elliot, Yariv Egozi, Iris Elhanani, Benno Kalev, and Lance Carter, Florian Weigensamer, David Wolf and Ann Bardacke, Henri and Sally Alster, Yair Medina, Jeremy Siegman, Shauna Aminath, Roger Gastman, Peter Berkowitz, Marcio Lempert.

My heart champions Barbara Yamada, Cathy Coltrin, Rochelle Kramer, Audrey Ades, Carol Kline, Edna Ziv Av, Susan Leibtag, Marie-Noelle Belanger-Levesque, Samantha Silverman and Cyndi Silverman, Geoffrey and Lilian Tindyebwa for your magical red pen; Alison Gardner for continuing Peter's legacy; Louise Guenther, Itai Froumin, Rachel Abramovitch, Rina Baruch, Cynthia Mackenzie, Daniela Kraemer; Sherry Crowther, Gita Baikovitz, Jack Canfield, Ilan Hasson, Avi Ben-Simhon, David Gerstein and Mikhal Yahalomi, Ahuva Pundak, Deb Sandella, Khursheed Sethna, Holly King, Alissa Bickar, Bryan Mannion, Gloria Belendez Ramirez, Lotte Vesterli. My mentors, Elizabeth Gilbert, Lizzie Velasquez, Nick Vujicic, Tyler Oakley, Neil Strauss, Whitney Thore.

My peace warriors Jean and Dr. Reed Holmes, Andrea Kross; Sarah Stooß, Riman Barakat, Cara Bereck, Michelle Gordon, Atheer Elobadi, Karym Barhum, Tom and Hind, Max Budovitch, Micah Hendler, Eliyahu Mcclean, Amer Merza, Tarek Kandakji, Adi Yekutieli, Adaya Utnik, Alisa Rubin, Peter Berkowitz, Chaya Pomeranz, Oded Rose, Anat Marnin, Omer Golan, Vardi Kahana, Rakefet Enoch, Avi Deul, Yosef Avi Yair Engel, Noa Karmon. Latif Nasser, Carly Mensch, Liz Flahive, Edna Zamir, June Moore, Michelle Tessaro, Ileana Bejarano, Mike Cameron, Jennifer Zorrilla, Judith Beiner, Bobbi and Yaki Vendriger, Gaby and Yaki Reiss, Abigail and Dan Chill, Carmen Braden, Gadi BenMark, Chen Arad, Natan Voitenkov, Niki Kotsenko, Tal Wilson, Daniel Shteiner. To my Pearson and UWC family; my Esperanto tribe, your constant encouragement is water to my inner garden. Thank you!

Last, but certainly not least, to my family: Jasmine, Hallel, Steve, Romi, Moria, Elinoy, Yoav, Shani, Dor, Yanush, Alyona, Jaiden, Kylee, Shella, Misha, Ilana, Shlomo, Karin, Boaz, Yaron and Yafim. And to Irina Kiseleva for holding my hand and constantly supporting me.I love you guys. Above all, to my parents, Betty and Isaac, for your love and constant encouragement. This book is a tribute to you.

Book Club Topics

1. Lack of names: According to the author, "I wanted to attempt writing a novel with no names at all, in a sense offering the reader to inject themselves into the nameless characters." How did the lack of names affect your connection to the characters? Did it make them more relatable or more distant? Some readers think this element of lack of names is a weakness of the novel and harmful to the narrative—what is your view?

2. Influencing the boy: How did the secondary characters—such as the old mama or the boy's uncle—impact or influence the main character's choices?

3. Tooth removal scene: While hiding in a pit beneath the maid's bed with three others, the uncle's tooth becomes abscessed. It was too dangerous for the maid to search for a dentist to remove it, for if the dentist told the Nazis, the Jews hiding in the pit and those hiding them would be killed. However, the maid's husband was able to find a dentist's kit. The boy used this kit to pull out his uncle's tooth and save the man's life. How did you feel when the uncle was in agony in the pit getting his tooth pulled out? What other scenes stood out to you?

4. Guilt and Revenge: Survivor's guilt is defined as "a condition of persistent mental and emotional stress experienced by someone who has survived an incident in which others died." The young man struggles with the guilt of leaving his family behind for his own survival, at one point thinking; "He was haunted by self-hatred. A true brother would have stood by his sister; a dutiful son would have remained by his parents; a proud grandson would have protected his elderly grandparents."

5. Later, the young man buys a gun with the intent to enact violence on those who took his family from him. On his way to his destination, "With every hour of journey he thought of the trains taking his family, and the trains returning empty." Clearly, the young man is filled with rage towards those who killed his family, but he also appears to blame himself for not being able to save them. How does the young man attempt to use revenge as a salve for his grief and rage? Were the young man's desire for revenge and his survivor's guilt in any way connected?

6. Trauma: Trauma is the result of or a reaction to extremely upsetting, frightening, or stressful situations that are either beyond our control or too tough for us to handle. It could be a single incident or a series of related ones that take place over time. Following the incident, shock and denial are common reactions. Unpredictable feelings, flashbacks, strained relationships, and even physical symptoms like headaches or nausea are examples of longer-term effects. In what ways did the scientist's trauma affect his relationships with his family and others?

7. Honoring the dead: What choice of the young man/scientist do you think most honored those he lost?

8. Belonging: The boy goes through a rough time as he transitions into adulthood. From being in Poland which feels like a graveyard, he goes to France which is a completely foreign place to him with people whose language he does not understand. Just as he begins a family there after learning the language and adapting to the culture, he goes to America, where again he has to settle in and learn another language.

9. His struggle can be seen when he tries to connect with his children after he and his wife get a divorce. They were brought up in America and he had to learn the lingo and try to understand them better and bond with them. When he comes to Israel as well, he constantly compares himself to the Jews he sees around himself and how they are comfortable in their own skin.

10. Why do you think the scientist did not feel like he belonged in Israel, or anywhere else? How does this novel deal with

the feeling of detachment and search for identity?

11. Art: Art became something that emotionally moved the young man after the war. When he visited the Louvre, he was not impressed with the Mona Lisa, and instead spent a long time admiring a painting of a lacemaker. The next day he visited a museum of impressionism. When he saw these paintings, tears welled in his eyes and he felt as though he were flying. What is the difference between art that touches the young man's heart and art that does not?

12. Music: The image and sound of the violin appear several times throughout the narrative, e.g.: "Before the war the boy played the violin. That is, until a couple of soldiers came to their cabin, and one of them slammed the violin against the wall and broke it, hitting it several times, breaking its neck and body."

13. The next time the violin is mentioned is at the party the maid threw to cast off suspicion. The boy notes; "The violin was lively and energetic. A set of a dozen dances inspired by traditional folk tunes. The boy recognized each tune. These were the sounds of his childhood, of living, of celebrating lives…He wanted to pull the floorboards away, to get out and yell, "Here I am! Shoot me if you want! Call the soldiers if you'd like! But, for now, just give me that violin, and let me play! Just one song! One dance!""

14. The last time he hears the violin is in his joyful vision of heaven, at the end of his life. Stuck in a coma, the vision begins "He was floating, somewhere. Violins were playing." What does the violin mean for the scientist throughout his life? What does it symbolize?

15. Relevance: Compare this period of history with today. In our current era, we hold deep empathy for the Jewish community that suffered during WWII. Why do you think people in that historical period did not share this same perspective? What factors led them to embrace such a harmful ideology? Consider the historical context, including widespread propaganda, social and economic pressures, and the psychological mechanisms of conformity and obedience. How did these influences shape their beliefs and actions?

16. Heroism: There are many characters in the novel who could be perceived as heroic: the maid, her husband and their children; for hiding 4 people in a pit from the Nazis, the moneychanger and his old mama; for supporting and accepting the young man into their family after he had lost so much of his own family during the war, the librarian; for supporting the scientist through his trauma and encouraging him to testify at the butcher's trial, and the scientist; for his testimony, for achieving his revenge through scientific success and connecting with his family.

17. Some people define a hero only as someone who saves another's life, some define it as someone who has a great positive impact on others, and for some it is defined by bravery in the face of adversity. What defines a hero to you and which of the characters in the novel would you consider a hero?

18. Perspective and trauma: Post WW2, the young man found his perspective on seemingly innocuous things had changed, such as his nervousness around authority figures, trains or his relationship with food. How have significant life events altered your perspective on everyday occurrences?

19. Testimonial: When the scientist gets a call regarding the trial of the butcher, he does not want to see him in any way, shape or form. He did not want to testify against him, because that would mean appearing in the court in front of him. The butcher is responsible for many of his nightmares and his trauma associated with the war since he saw his cousin and others get killed by him.

20. However, with the support of his family, he is able to go to court and testify against the butcher. The scientist's testimony helped in the sentencing of the butcher.

For more topics for discussion, please visit:

www.underthefloorboards.org/bookclub

End Notes

1.   Korn Jr., Bertram. "Survivor Triumphant: Felix Zandman's life story is a saga of success." *Jewish Exponent,* October 20, 1995.

2.   Paldiel, Mordecai. "Sheltering and Hiding." Chapter in *Saving the Jews.* Rockville, MD: Schreiber, 2000. pp. 82-83.

3.   Dr. Felix Zandman Receives Lifetime Achievement Award from the National Electronic Distributors Association. *Power Electronics,* powerelectronics.com. December 21, 2009.

4.   Franklin Leate Database - Edward Longstreth Medal 1962 Laureates. Franklin Institute. Retrieved November 16, 2011.

5.   Hernik, Yuval. "The Invention and Evolution of The World's Most Precise Resistor, The Legacy of Dr. Felix Zandman." In "50 Years at a Glance: Vishay Foil Resistors." *FACTS* #050, vishaypg.com, 2012.

6.   Korn Jr., op. cit.

7.   Zandman, Felix. 2008 Speech to March of the Living. https://www.youtube.com/watch?v=ptGvGvNRsDs

8.   Dr. Felix Zandman Receives Lifetime Achievement Award, op. cit.

9.   Arava TV, Felix Zandman's family visiting Ein Yahav, 2012. Video available online, AravaTV on YouTube (Hebrew).

10.   Ibid.

11.   *Missing Felix.* Video on Eli Goddard's YouTube Channel.

12.   Dr. Felix Zandman Receives Lifetime Achievement Award, op. cit.

13.   Poray, Anna. *Polish Righteous, Those Who Risked Their Lives: Jan and Anna Puchalski.* 2007.

14.   Paldiel, Mordecai, op. cit.

15.   Poray, Anna, op. cit.

16.   Ashkenazi, Dana. "From Darkness to Photoelasticity. Felix Zandman: Scientist, Inventor and Industrialist," Galileo 105 (2007).

17.   Poray, Anna, op. Cit.

18.   *Those Who Risked Their Lives.* http://www.savingjews.org/righteous/pv.htm

Further Reading

American Society for Testing Materials. Symposium on Shear and Torsion Testing. Publication number 289. ASTM sixty-third annual meeting, June 28, 1960.

Ashkenazi, Dana. "From Darkness to Photoelasticity. Felix Zandman: Scientist, Inventor and Industrialist," Galileo 105 (2007).

Hernik, Yuval. "The Invention and Evolution of The World's Most Precise Resistor, The Legacy of Dr. Felix Zandman." In "50 Years at a Glance: Vishay Foil Resistors." FACTS #050, vishaypg.com, 2012.

Paldiel, Mordecai. "Sheltering and Hiding." Chapter in Saving the Jews. Rockville, MD: Schreiber, 2000. pp. 82-83.

Paldiel, Mordecai. The Righteous Among the Nations. Jerusalem: Yad Vashem, 2007.

Rogers, Wayne. Make Your Own Rules: A Renegade Guide to Unconventional Success. New York: AMACOM, 2011.

Rubenstein, Eli (March of the Living). Witness: Passing the Torch of Holocaust Memory to New Generations. Toronto: Second Story Press, 2015.

Tammeus, Bill & Cukierkorn, Rabbi Jacques. They Were Just People: Stories of Rescue in Poland During the Holocaust. Columbia, MO: University of Missouri Press, 2009.

Zandman, Felix & Chanoff, David. Never the Last Journey. New York: Schocken, 1995.

Zandman, Felix: Redner, Salomon & Dally, James W. Photoelastic Coatings. Iowa City: Iowa State University Press, 1977.

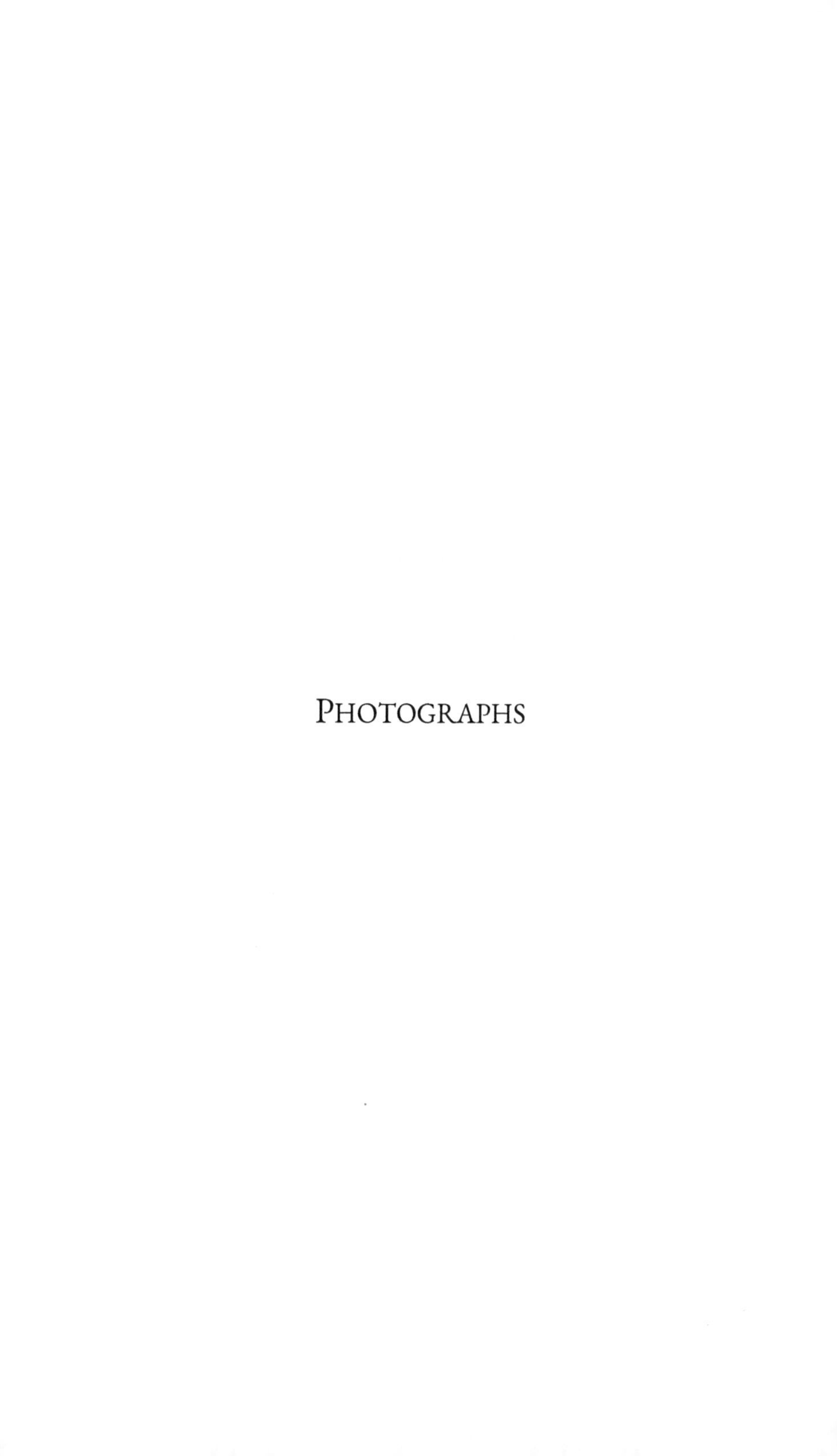

PHOTOGRAPHS

Felix and his uncle Sander ice skating, circa 1935

Felix and Anna Puchalski ("The maid") shortly after the war, 1945

Felix, Ruta and the grandchildren

Felix and Ruta visiting Ein Yahav, Israel

About the Author

John Kiss is a prize-winning author, artist, and peace activist. John began writing at an early age. Born Jonathan Kis-Lev, at age 21, John won the Bamahane Prize for Short Story.

Known for thought-provoking art, John's work often carries messages of social justice. Notable projects such as "The Peace Kids" and the "27 Club Graffiti" have garnered international attention and acclaim. John was recognized as a force for change by the late president of Israel, Shimon Peres.

A descendant of grandparents who survived the Holocaust, John has a passion for telling inspiring true stories. The debut novel "Under The Floorboards" reflects a deep commitment to exploring complex human experiences. With a background rich in visual storytelling, John's writing offers a fresh perspective on the human experience, blending an artistic vision with a powerful narrative voice.

John lives in Los Angeles.

"Scan the QR code at the end to leave your Amazon review!"

www.ingramcontent.com/pod-product-compliance
Lightning Source LLC
Chambersburg PA
CBHW051244150726
48001CB00017B/4